Commemorating Hell

Commemorating Hell

The Public Memory
of Mittelbau-Dora

GRETCHEN SCHAFFT
AND GERHARD ZEIDLER

University of Illinois Press
URBANA, CHICAGO, AND SPRINGFIELD

Library of Congress Cataloging-in-Publication Data
Schafft, Gretchen Engle.
Commemorating hell : the public memory of Mittelbau-Dora /
Gretchen Schafft and Gerhard Zeidler.
  p.   cm.
Includes bibliographical references and index.
ISBN 978-0-252-03593-7 (cloth : alk. paper) —
ISBN 978-0-252-07788-3 (paper : alk. paper)
1. Dora (Concentration camp)
2. War memorials—Germany—Nordhausen (Thuringia)
3. World War, 1939–1945—Monuments—Germany—
Nordhausen (Thuringia)
4. Memory—Social aspects—Germany—Nordhausen (Thuringia)
5. Collective memory—Germany—Nordhausen (Thuringia)
6. Concentration camp inmates—Germany—Nordhausen
(Thuringia)—Biography.
7. Nordhausen (Thuringia, Germany)—Biography.
8. Nordhausen (Thuringia, Germany)—History—
20th century—Sources.
9. World War, 1939–1945—Social aspects—Germany—
Nordhausen (Thuringia)
10. Concentration camps—Social aspects—Germany—
Nordhausen (Thuringia)
I. Zeidler, Gerhard. II. Title.
D805.5.D6S33   2010
940.53'1853224—dc22   2010020851

*No single lesson is to be garnered from the
memorial at the concentration camp site of
Mittelbau-Dora in Nordhausen, Germany, but
no visitor leaves there untouched. In the midst
of differing ideologies and political realities,
directors of the memorial have made their
respect and sympathy for those imprisoned at the
camp paramount. Each has communicated this
effectively, and, thus, this book is dedicated to them.*

Contents

Introduction

Gedenkstätte: a place of remembrance, a memorial.

The importance of the concentration camp memorial, or
Gedenkstätte, is that it helps its community of stake-holders,
those who care about what happened there, to build and
transform knowledge, understanding, values, and memory.
Changes in the exhibits' themes, characters, media presentations,
and structure occur over time, but these changes are less important
than the stability of the site itself. Events that the Gedenkstätte
commemorates are interpreted in large measure through the place
where they occurred and individual interactions with it.

This book is about the Nazi concentration camp "Mittelbau-Dora," which
controlled the lives of up to sixty thousand slave laborers from twenty countries for about nineteen months from August 1943 until April 1945. Although
Mittelbau-Dora was not a death camp in which planned extermination was
carried out through gas chambers, in the short time that Mittelbau-Dora
existed, approximately twenty thousand of the sixty thousand prisoners in
the main and subcamps died. However, *died* is the wrong word to use, for
the prisoners were given little chance to live, and, indeed, their survival was
of no concern to their captors. Toward the end of the camp's existence, at
the end of the war, there was a plan to exterminate those remaining in the
camps through a Nazi policy called "Death through Work" (*Vernichtung
durch Arbeit*), in which the goal was to eliminate each prisoner within a few
months of their coming to the camp.

The prisoners were engaged in the final stage of World War II as slave
laborers in the complex public-private enterprise of the "Mittelwerk," an
underground rocket-assembly plant in the middle of Germany. Encyclopedic
works have been written in German and English about the establishment
of the camp and the rocket development over a period of decades. Linda
Hunt bravely explored the postwar importation of Nazi rocket scientists and
hundreds of their technical people to the United States, where their pasts
were ignored or hidden and their contributions exalted as an irreplaceable

contribution to the U.S. space and weapons programs. It was Hunt's dogged efforts through the Freedom of Information Act that released much of the previously unknown documentation about the link between Mittelbau-Dora and U.S. space exploration and won her the respect and admiration of survivors of Dora. Jens-Christian Wagner, as a young doctoral student, conducted extensive research that led to the most complete German documentation of the camp. On the other side of the ocean, seasoned rocket historian Michael Neufeld, working within the structure of the Smithsonian Institution's Air and Space Museum, culled archival research and literature to document the development of German rockets and the life of Wernher von Braun. All three are still involved in the story.

Not wishing to repeat these contributions by trying to rewrite the well-covered history, the current authors looked in a different direction, that of exploring the meaning of the camp and its public memory primarily through the eyes of witnesses of events in three wartime and postwar periods. These witnesses included the survivors of Mittelbau-Dora and the outer camps with whom the authors had worked and been associated for many years, the townspeople of Nordhausen who had integrated the events of the 1940s in various ways in their writing and recorded memories, and the local historical record to the extent it existed in archival form. Interviews, review of prisoner testimony and memoirs, and public records of commemorative events offered differing views of Mittelbau-Dora and the memorial that was established decades later.

The authors also found that the war itself played a crucial role in the relationships of the citizens of Nordhausen to the camp itself and its memory. Strategic bombing raids by the British and Americans devastated the city's infrastructure and killed thousands of the city's inhabitants only days before the camp was liberated, leaving an ambiguity about how to assign blame and guilt, perpetrator as well as victim status.

This book is unmistakably an anthropological work. The disciplines of history and anthropology differ, even when the anthropologist is looking at events in the historical past and even though the historian sometimes uses anthropological theory and methods. The historian views events and assembles evidence that took place in a certain sequence and in a certain context. The anthropologist looks at how people find meaning in events, how that meaning is produced, and how and by what means it changes over time.[1] This book uses subaltern theory to reanalyze the story of Mittelbau-Dora in the Nordhausen region. It uses official records as the documentation of events, but emphasizes what Pandey calls the "fragments" of documentation, memory, and reflection that exist in the form of poems, mementos, memoirs, and oral histories. These fragments are unofficial, unsanctioned by government or bureaucracy, and stand alone without pedigree. They stand in contrast to the documents that come from the time and place and are saved in libraries and archives. Those official documents have the aura of authenticity because they are associated with the authorities of the time. Yet they too may be selective, self-censored, reflective of a particular point of view, or written to defend, protect, or protest one's innocence. Both kinds of documentation, thus, are surprisingly open to bias and must be viewed with care.

The emphasis on one or the other documentation, either the traditional or the subaltern, also places authors in very different positions regarding their interest in social class, political capital, and the status of the people about whom they write. Their resulting work carries a different kind of weight in traditional views of empirical evidence. In describing a range of events "from the bottom up," however, subaltern studies have been successful and stand alongside other documentation as valuable contributions to understanding social events and particularly social conflict.

The Mittelbau-Dora concentration camp existed at one time and in one place. Its memory, however, has been maintained by people living and working in many countries and under a variety of political regimes. The camp itself came into being under the Nazis. Not even two years later, it was liberated by Allied forces. For several weeks, the U.S. Army and the Joint Chiefs of Staff tried to bring order to the mass of camp refugees, the refugees streaming in from other parts of Germany and Europe, and the bombed-out residents of Nordhausen. Because of the Potsdam Treaty among the Allied forces that determined the division of territory once the war ended, Nordhausen was under Soviet control by July 1945. After several years, this occupation ended, and the new country of the German Democratic Republic (GDR) began its forty-year history. Germany was reunified in 1990, and that brought another government and new values to Nordhausen.

Each of these shorter or longer eras had its own set of values, perspectives, imperatives, initiatives, and positively and negatively sanctioned positions regarding the appropriate way to look at the Mittelbau-Dora concentration camp. After the war, the United States, Soviet Union, and Federal Republic of Germany (FRG) each had its own way of positively or negatively sanctioning aspects of memory. Although no individual memory can be wiped out by fiat, each governing body discovered how to put its stamp of approval or disapproval on public displays of memory that in themselves reinforced individuals' approaches to the local history of the war and the camp and influenced the way in which individuals could recall what they had seen, heard, or known.

In this book, we look at events and public history. We use the subaltern approach to present the reader with a range of information and documentation, and we especially give valence to the words and events that are often set aside: the beliefs, values, perceptions, and stories of the "outsider" to those official views. The people who are considered "outsiders" and the prestige or disdain they experience under a particular government change as a new system replaces the old. Thus, an "insider" of one system not only can be but likely is the "outsider" of another. Looking at Nordhausen's public history over a half century illuminates this process.

The limitations of using the subaltern approach and relying on the nontraditional and noninstitutional resources that are available are well known. Personal memoirs are not always written immediately following events and, thus, lack the accuracy of recall without intervening events and perspectives. They also reflect only that "slice of life" that is observed and lived by the individual, not the broad experience of the camp itself. There may be personal agendas that are not transparent or available for analysis in assessing the accuracy of the document. The writer may have an audience in mind and a motivation to steer the recollections in a particular direction. And, we are reminded, only those who survived could tell their stories; those who were killed before liberation left their stories only to onlookers.[2]

The authors themselves recognize the value of each of the politically influenced representation of the events that took place under the Nazis. Although we agree that some accounts of the camp are more "accurate" than others, our most salient point of view is that an analysis of how a town's trauma is experienced is possible only through the intentional lifting of the time-constructed partisan lens. This is a worthwhile endeavor in itself that allows the reader to take a deep look into the variable meaning of extreme violence, the uses and misuses of its memory, its transformation into trajectories of shame and pride, and ultimately its use of public space and time. We see this book as an anthropology of the use of memory, that memory being of exclusion, horror, terror, and sorrow, but also of triumph, hope, and goodwill. We hope it will be read in that vein, as a reflection on what can be learned from voices, mnemonic devices, museum discourse, and manipulation of people's lived experience in crisis and trauma.

We would like to thank those who helped us during the writing and production of this book. At the University of Illinois Press, director Willis G. Regier, editor Joan Catapano, and copy editor Annette Wenda polished it until it reached its final stage. Harry Schafft was very helpful in preparing various drafts of the manuscript for submission. He worked tirelessly with the authors in the final stages of editing, and his spirit led us to the "finish line." Carol Godley and Jorge Martinez also assisted in organizing the materials for submission.

We had the knowledgeable assistance in finding resources and adding their own experience to ours provided by Kurt Pelny (deceased), Cornelia Klose, Peter Kuhlbrodt, and Jens-Christian Wagner, at various times directors of the Mittelbau-Dora memorial site in Nordhausen. The staff of the memorial were very helpful, including Angela Fiederman, Torsten Hess, Manfred Feyer, and especially Regina Heubaum, the librarian and archivist. Of great assistance over the years were Wolfgang and Christa Köhler (deceased), Fritz Kowalski (deceased), Elfrieda Kowalski (deceased), Kurt Hermann, Reinhard Gündel, Ilse Hagen, Hans Hagen (deceased), Manfred Schröter, Pfarrar Peter Kube, and Pfarrar Johann Eisele. In addition, Hans-Jürgen Grönke of the Nordhausen Stadtarchiv was both helpful and kind.

We are grateful for the people who provided us with hospitality and friendship in Nordhausen, such as Otto and Heidi Hilpert, Wolfgang and Gundrun Leiss, and Irmgard Pelny, as well as Leo and Leopoldine Kuntz of Zernsdorf and Iris Pelny and Wolfgang Nossen of Erfurt.

Linda Hunt, Michael Neufeld, and Eli Rosenbaum made materials available to us that were valuable and useful. Their long experience with the people and events at Mittelbau-Dora was irreplaceable. Michael Neufeld, in particular, read the manuscript carefully and patiently provided corrections to our interpretations of the rocket history. Christiane Grieb also provided careful commentary on the GDR and Nordhausen, her hometown. Terry Katz clarified details of her father's life in the excerpt about Martin Adler.

Finally, for the many survivors who were willing to tell us their stories and some who became close friends, we leave our biggest debt of gratitude. You deserve to be remembered as heroes, no matter what the political winds bring. You are heroes for having survived, for going on with life when memories were overwhelming, for living among those who could never understand no matter how hard they tried. Without your own awareness of the gift you gave to others, you often exuded hope to the rest of us who knew you. If you could survive that horror, then we certainly must find meaning in our current lives and solve our own dilemmas. You left a bigger legacy than you ever imagined. We have before us memories of the dignity of Jean Mialet, the gentleness of Albert von Hoey, the sparkle of Yves Béon, the friendship of Martin Adler, the sweetness of Otakar Litimisky, and the stalwartness of Herbert Ricky Adler. We have tried to be true to the words attributed to Julius Fucik, a victim of the Third Reich:

One thing I ask of you.
You who survive this time;
don't forget.
Don't forget the good
and not the bad.
Patiently gather all the evidence
about the fallen.
One day, this today will be the past.
People will speak of that terrible time
and will speak of the nameless heroes,
the history they made.
They were men, who had names, faces, longings and hopes.
Therefore, the pain of the least of them was not smaller
        than the pain of the greatest of them whose name
        has been remembered.
I want you always to keep them near,
like acquaintances, like relatives,
like yourself.[3]

Commemorating Hell

1. Conceptualizing Horror

KZ-Gedenkstätte. KZ- Mahn- und Gedenkstätte. For speakers of English, these German words are without meaning. However, for a few, whose numbers are dwindling, these are *key* words. Key in the sense of being among the most meaningful in one's vocabulary. Key in the sense of *unlocking* for an individual the most deeply needed information and emotional truths.

Take Leo Kuntz, for example. The concentration camp Mittelbau-Dora is for him a center within his cognitive space, a phrase that is vivid in mental pictures and constructions that are inseparable from his personal history and his current concerns. The camp, once a widely held secret, now is a site of public history, open to interpretation and reinterpretation, and it impacts Leo's own conceptions, adding to or detracting from his own sense of self in the most fundamental ways.

What had been the grounds of a notorious concentration camp, where V-missiles were assembled under murderous conditions by slave laborers, has been commemorated since the 1960s in the same geographic space where the actual events occurred as a memorial site, a "Gedenkstätte." Germans refer to this concept as commemoration in "Ort des Geschehens," or on the site where the events took place. For many, this combines two functions: providing a reference to historical events within the concentration camp and also commemorating the resting place of its victims. How these functions are carried out is important to survivors, their families and friends, people with political agendas that include or depend on this history, and people of strong moral or righteous convictions that the past must not be repeated. Leo falls into several of these categories.

Mittelbau-Dora was founded in the last years of the Third Reich, which projected a thousand-year reign of the National Socialist Workers Party (Nationalsozialistische Deutsche Arbeiterpartei, or NSDAP) that lasted twelve years. First an outer camp of Buchenwald populated at the end of August 1943, Mittelbau-Dora became independent of this larger camp in October 1944 and operated until April 1945. The purpose of this particular camp was to provide the workforce to assemble "wonder weapons" for the Third Reich, the last hope for victory in an already failed war. The abandoned mines of the Kohnstein Mountains (hardly more than hills) were to be enlarged to make the largest-ever underground factory. The camp, which expanded to include forty subcamps, held approximately sixty thousand prisoners in this period, of whom about twenty thousand did not survive.[1]

Leo's father, Albert Kuntz, was one of those prisoners who did not return from Mittelbau-Dora. In the last months of the camp, he was seized and taken to the "bunker" on the camp grounds where he was tortured and beaten to death in order to discover the roots of a resistance cell operating in the camp. Or perhaps he was taken to the Gestapo (Nazi secret police) headquarters in nearby Ilfeld. Most of the records were destroyed, and much is left to speculation. Perhaps he was seized not because of the illegal resistance committee he was thought to have formed and fostered throughout his tenure in several camps but for some other reason. Perhaps the SS believed he had to be killed before the camp was captured by the Allies because he knew too much and had experienced too many years in the confines of SS prisons and camps.

The significance of Mittelbau-Dora to Leo is that it is the place where the answers to these riddles reside, either within its collected documentation or in the minds and hearts of survivors he may meet there or come to know through the records and networks of those intimately connected with the history. The documents that are available to him, the people he might come to learn of, the connections he might make will lead him to answers, or so he hopes.

On the other hand, the way in which Albert Kuntz is remembered also defines that for which he stood, those ideologies that took him from his family, his loving wife, his larger group of relatives, his little son, Leo. Those ideologies have to be recognized as legitimate and humane in order to make the sacrifice that Leo made as not only a fatherless child but the progeny of "an enemy of the state" bearable and even meaningful. Elie Wiesel has said it best: "'Memory' is the key word. To remember is to create links between the past and present, between past and future. To remember is to affirm man's faith in humanity and to convey meaning on our fleeting endeavors. The aim of memory is to restore its dignity to justice."[2]

Thus, the existence of the Gedenkstätte is critical to Leo's identity, and the content of its historical record is a significant determinant of his mental and physical health. Now in his eighties, Leo has experienced changes in the presentation of this public history and the history of the German state(s) with trauma and has emerged strong, watchful, critical, and empowered in his own right, while very aware of his limits in controlling the presentation of the historical record.

In many ways, Leo's journey is mirrored not only in the lives of other survivors but in that of the Gedenkstätte itself. It too has both evolved and been dismantled and regrouped under the critical direction of many different individual, governmental, and corporate forces and lobbies. It does not now exist, and never has, outside of the political realities of its times, for the Nazi concentration camps were political institutions set up within a political context. How the camps are remembered by subsequent politically based regimes defines their own relationship to this original political ideology and, thus, defines their values and predicts their behaviors. The commemorations have deep-seated consequences for the perceived legitimacy of states, or lack of it, by the citizens.[3] Most people will not be very concerned about the commemorations, but for some, the interpretation of the past will be intensely watched and critically assessed.

The Concept of the Nazi Concentration Camp

Hitler came to power January 30, 1933, with the plan to restructure the German state into a totalitarian, modern, rational, and terror-driven country that would expand its borders in all directions. His assumption of power was quick, although in the first election, he won no majority of the people's votes.[4] The Nazi Party's personally directed paramilitary forces, the "Sturmabteilung" (SA) and the "Schutzstaffel" (SS), were ready to move. They immediately arrested and put into "protective custody" in "wild concentration camps" those who might produce resistance to the state. These were temporary places of internment: factories, warehouses, local jails and prisons, unused buildings of any kind that offered secure enclosures.

The term *concentration camp* was first used by the British in the Boer War of 1899–1902 in which they "concentrated" Boer families in large enclosed areas. Hitler began to use this existing concept early in his speeches and writing. In 1927, at a party meeting, Hitler had declared that his opponents "must get a taste of what it is like to live in a concentration camp."[5] Other forms of imprisonment were also used, but it was clear from the beginning that the state would be holding such large numbers of people that camps would be the most efficient. They also could then be the sites of labor for the state, medical experimentation, "reeducation" through torture, and elimination of unwanted societal elements.

As he often did, Hitler combined in his threats the Jews and the Communists as "Jewish Bolsheviks." The burning of the Reichstag, or parliament building, in Berlin on February 27, 1933, provided the first excuse for massive roundups of Communist and other political opponents amid the overwhelming support of the German population.[6] "The Emergency Decree for the Protection of the Nation and State," signed on that very day, provided the legal basis for eliminating many basic civil liberties, such as freedom of the press, freedom of assembly, and freedom of speech.[7] Political opponents or potential opponents of Hitler were the first to be taken into these concentration camps. Jews, certainly a major target of the regime, were not arrested early in Hitler's regime unless they had a political connection that placed them in this initial category of opponents. Regulations, however, began to affect their ability to access and maintain employment, to move freely, to maintain their standard of living, even to be considered full citizens.

The three major political opposing forces to Hitler were the Communist Party, the Socialist Party, and the labor unions. From March to October 1933, twenty thousand Communists were imprisoned and between five and seven hundred people murdered.[8] Women active in the Communist Party of Germany and other active female opponents were not exempt from internment. They were taken in the fall of 1933 to "women's protective custody camps" first in Moringen and later to the ancient prison in Lichtenburg in 1937. Other camps held women as well, but Ravensbrück was the most famous of all the women's camps, established in 1938–39.[9] Both women and men came under the same administration unit, the Inspectorate of Concentration Camps, and in addition to the hard labor they endured, they were also subjected to punishments such as withdrawal of food, physical force, solitary confinement, and imprisonment in punishment cells. Men and women were often in the same camps in different sections or outer camps.

The original "wild concentration camps" quickly evolved into permanent camps that grew in number and geographic range. The temporary holding places were closed, and the first actual concentration camp built by the SS was Dachau in April 1933. The system became more permanent, although new improvised camps sprang up as needed to service particular manufacturing or processing needs of the state or even private enterprise. Columbia-House in Berlin, Dachau near Munich, Esterwegen in northwestern Germany, Lichtenburg in the Southeast, and Oranienburg/Sachsenhausen north of Berlin provided coverage for much of the country within the first years of Hitler's tenure.

The reason given for imprisonment was usually the necessity for "protective custody." This was defined as "to protect against all persons who through their manner or acts endanger the security of the people or the state."[10] There was no further definition, nor any way to effectively protect oneself against the charges.

A variety of types of camps existed, and each independent concentration camp had a large number of subsidiary camps and *Aussenkommandos,* or work details, outside of the main camp that often had hundreds of prisoners. The various types of camps included work/education camps, transit camps, prisons, ghettos, internment camps, prisoner-of-war camps, punishment camps, impressed-labor camps, and death camps.[11] Thus, it is difficult to give a definitive number of concentration camps existing on German soil and in occupied countries, but if one were to consider all the variations, most likely they numbered in the thousands.[12] Mittelbau-Dora itself was "host" to more than forty *Aussenkommandos,* and could be considered to incorporate the characteristics of a work camp, a transit camp, a prison, a prisoner-of-war camp, a punishment camp, and an impressed-labor camp. Because it lacked a gas chamber, it could not be considered a death camp, although to a third of its prisoners, that distinction had no meaning.

The post–World War I period had been traumatic for Germany: in addition to losing the First World War, there was uncontrollable inflation, reparation payments under the Versailles Treaty, as well as a major cultural shift. Modernization brought unfettered behavior, especially in Berlin, and changes in lifestyles overall. It also brought rapid innovations in industry and new roles for university faculty in industry. Political life took to the streets in violent demonstrations, and people no longer felt safe. Increased security under the Nazis was temporary and came with a price tag. Civil liberties for everyone were severely reduced. Although many were worried and at least privately were against the Nazis, the majority of Germans threw their support and enthusiasm to the new regime in overwhelming numbers in the mid-1930s. The cost to the "others," those increasingly well-defined outsiders, remained of secondary importance to the large majority of citizens. With the outlawing of first the Communist Party and then the Social Democratic Party, as well as the imprisonment of their leaders, there was no serious opposition to the increasing takeover and *Gleichschaltung* (regimentation and homogeneity) of the German people and their institutions. For those with thoughts of opposition, the concentration camps and those who returned from them served as powerful deterrents.

The concentration camps imprisoned increasingly those considered "aso-cial," including those without work, unwed mothers, prostitutes, petty crimi-nals, homosexuals, and Jews or Gentiles who violated the Nuremberg laws. These laws, among other things, defined who was "a Jew" according to Nazi precepts, and deprived those so defined of their German citizenship. By the summer of 1937, mainstream German society became defined by its very lack of diversity and its willing compliance with directions and orders from those in charge of almost every aspect of life (the Führer Prinzip).

Administration of Concentration Camps

> It is easy for the outsider to get the wrong conception of camp life; a conception mingled with sentiment and pity. Little does he know of the hard fight for existence, which raged among the prisoners. This was an unrelenting struggle for daily bread and for life itself, for one's own sake or for that of a good friend.
>
> —Viktor E. Frankl, *Man's Search for Meaning*

The words above were written by psychiatrist Viktor Frankl, some years after his release from Auschwitz. They stand in counterpoint to the Nazi rationality of the planning of the camps and their careful administration and show the subjective space between the hegemony of the system and the lives of prisoners.

Hermann Göring stood next to Adolf Hitler as the named successor and head of the Air Force (Luftwaffe). More important to the concentration camp history was another central force behind Nazi power: Heinrich Himmler, the national leader of the SS (Reichsführer SS) and also police commissioner/president of Munich.[13] Hitler gave almost unlimited power to Himmler to coerce the German people into a single force, eliminating all opposition. The "wild concentration camps" were under the jurisdiction of local authorities, state agencies, party groups, and political police.[14] A few months after Dachau was built, however, Himmler and the SS had complete charge of it, the first long-standing concentration camp, designed to hold all those in protective custody in Bavaria. Hermann Göring, the Prussian state minister, was given authority over several other camps for a time, but all of the camps reverted to Himmler's control when he became head of the political police in Prussia on April 20, 1934.

Himmler placed Theodor Eicke, who had been the first commandant in Dachau beginning in the summer of 1933, in charge of expanding the con-centration camp system.[15] Eicke was head of the Totenkopf (death head) units of the SS, as well as a member of the secret police, or Gestapo. In the post of inspector of the concentration camps, Eicke developed under Himmler's guidance the basic plan and model for the use and "training" (punishments) of prisoners. The system was in place for the permanent detention of anyone who posed a threat to the regime.

Whitehead has pointed out that the nature of systematic violence is always rule governed and has meaning to both the perpetrator and the victim.[16] Part of that meaning comes from the culturally shared symbolism of the rules and punishments. However, in the case of the Nazi concentration camps, rules came from a small group of men who had no understanding of the multinational prison population they were about to see in their camps. There was no single national or religious culture to be shared. Instead, the shared understandings came from a deeper source: the terror itself that created a single urge among prisoners to survive and, for some, to retain some vestige of personal agency.

One of the insidious methods of camp administration was the use of prisoners as "trustees" or, as they were called, *Kapos*. These functionaries actually carried out the day-to-day routines and discipline. They often beat the prisoners, sometimes to death. They were under the supervision of the SS, but had permission and encouragement to use their authority over their charges in the most brutal ways.

> The Kapos, the senior camp prisoners, the block chiefs and room chiefs, the rapport clerks and block clerks were integrated into a network of social relations. First, prisoner-functionaries were obliged to maintain absolute obedience, and were dependent on the *protekcja* of the SS. Second, they had to defend their position against the attacks and intrigues of their rivals. Third, they had to keep their subordinates under supervision and make sure order was maintained. Fourth, they were surrounded by dependent clients, beneficiaries, and cliques. The prisoner-functionary elite stood between guard personnel and inmates; it fought for privileges and sought accessories for support.[17]

In some camps, the *Kapos* were selected by the SS from among the hardened criminals who were also in the camps. In some camps, the German Communists were able to get into these positions due to their understanding of the language and their cultural premises shared with members of the SS. Some may have even known one another prior to Hitler's assumption of power. Whether prisoners assuming functionary positions in the camps were able to keep a set of values different from those of their overseers is in question. Bettelheim claimed that a few were able to intervene when prisoners were being mistreated by the SS, but this was such a dangerous position to take that few rose to the challenge.[18]

For the *Kapos,* the position was often one of self-selection. It was often possible to volunteer to be a foreman or a group leader. Eventually, in some camps, some of the political prisoners organized among themselves to decide who might serve best in these capacities. For the prisoner deciding whether to be a functionary, the decision had to be made in the knowledge that along with increased privileges, there were considerable risks. These fell into two major categories: on the one hand, the prisoner would lose social solidarity with his comrades, and, on the other, he would lose his invisibility in the crowd. Ultimately, he would be held accountable by the SS for the behavior of his prisoner group and, thus, had a great motivation to see to it that they followed orders to the letter.

The psychological regression that is widely reported to have occurred among the prisoners was also true for the *Kapos* who were drawn from the total group.[19] Part of that regression was an identification with the SS and with the German hierarchy as father figures. To the extent that this occurred, the *Kapos* would have been very willing to carry out the disciplinary measures that the SS required of them.[20]

In Ravensbrück as in Buchenwald, the political prisoners gained control of the appointments to functionary positions and were able in some cases to curb brutality. However, those who could most often helped members of their own group first, and others may not have experienced any particular benefit of their leadership.[21] In Ravensbrück in its later phases, the older functionaries did not help the newer non-political prisoners, according to at least one report.[22]

The Concept of "Education"

Prisoners experienced terror from the time of arrest, and even during the transit to the concentration camp. It was designed to break the new "recruits" completely. As Bettelheim described his own experience:

> If the distance was short, the transport was often slowed down to allow enough time to break the prisoners. During their initial transport to the camp, prisoners were exposed to nearly constant torture. The nature of the abuse depended on the fantasy of the particular SS man in charge of a group of prisoners. Still, they all had a definite pattern. Physical punishment consisted of whipping, frequent kicking (abdomen or groin), slaps in the face, shooting or wounding with the bayonet. These alternated with attempts to produce extreme exhaustion. For instance, prisoners were forced to stare for hours into glaring lights, to kneel for hours, and so on.

From time to time a prisoner got killed, but prisoners were not allowed to care for his or another's wounds.[23] The guards also forced prisoners to hit one another and to defile what the SS considered the prisoners' most cherished values.

They were forced to curse their God, to accuse themselves and one another of vile actions, and their wives of adultery and prostitution. I never met a prisoner who had escaped this kind of initiation, which lasted at least twelve hours and often much longer. Until it was over, any failure to obey an order, such as slapping another prisoner, or any help given a tortured prisoner was viewed as mutiny and swiftly punished with death.[24]

The SS made efforts to engender the idea that the camps had an "educational function." The word *Erziehung* was used, a word usually associated with education in the sense of "bringing up" a child, not in the sense of cognitive learning of information or skills. This Erziehung would be accomplished through work under the direction of those in charge. It would provide discipline of a particular kind. Many of the early prisoners were assigned nonsense tasks that brought them to the end of their strength, such as moving boulders, digging ditches and filling them again, or pulling carts filled with heavy loads as if they were pack animals.

Whereas the concept of this kind of *Erziehung* would not have had as quick a response in other countries perhaps, in Germany, the authoritarian family and school or apprenticeship structure of that era was such that it was a continuation rather than a disjunction of cultural norms. The paterfamilias in the German household of the early twentieth century held rein over wife and children, rules were clear and unassailable in most households, and punishments were swift and corporal. The antiauthoritarian and liberal strain found in urban Germany in the 1920s was a cause for great concern and anxiety among more provincial Germans, who readily agreed to harsh measures to bring nonconformists into line. In the context of "behaving," a child would be referred to as *unerzogen,* or untrained, if he were not behaving well, and, thus, the need for prisoners to be *erzogen,* or trained to behave correctly, made a certain kind of sense to many Germans.

At the door of almost every larger camp was engraved in wrought iron "Arbeit Macht Frei" (Work Frees). This was meant to awaken the hope of eventual release if tasks were carried out according to orders, but that possibility became continually dimmer as the concentration camps turned to serious labor assemblages. The political prisoners, who were often older men, broke quickly under the strain of intense physical labor and, if released, as happened more frequently in the early years of the camps, came back to their homes and communities physical and often mental wrecks.

All aspects of the camp led to infantalization of the prisoners. Starting with the trauma of the transport itself, which usually exposed the prisoner to extreme thirst and hunger as well as a sense of physical restriction, the individual lost agency. Arriving at the camp, he was subjected to more torture and an introduction to his future experience as an inmate.[25] Thereafter, no action could be taken absolutely independently, although the prisoner functionaries were often the direct supervisors and directors of activity. Eventually, many prisoners learned ways in which to bypass some of the orders by a variety of manipulations, any one of which could put them at risk for severe punishments or death.

Ordinary physical needs of toileting and washing as well as hours of waking and sleeping were established through the order of the guards and could be manipulated to increase the agony of the prisoners.[26] How long had it been since any of them had had to ask permission to urinate or defecate? When had they ever had to perform these biological functions in front of others? Who had last told them to lie still in their beds or kept them up "past their bedtimes" when they had a great desire to sleep? These orders were reversals to a childish state but under the enormous stress of terror.

Referring to the childhood experience of *Erziehung* completed the infantalization of the prisoners. Along with losing their adult agency, they also had to cope with the constant reminder that they were *unerzogen,* or poorly brought up, something each had most likely heard repeatedly in childhood. Robbing prisoners of their will to resist was both the goal and the result of these actions.[27]

Loss of Orientation and Identity

Much has been written in recent years on the "subjectivity" of those experiencing violence.[28] Under conditions of violence, the individual loses critical signposts of identity. The interactional daily events that give place, meaning, and verification of who one is can be removed. In their place, often in the midst of physical pain, there arises uncertainty about facts, time, relationships, moral certainties, memories, and even geographical location. What is left is the subjective reality of feelings and needs.

Our cultural orientations and experiences provide us with a "way of being" in the world. Yet the trauma of the seizure and transport to the concentration camp and the violence with which the prisoners were greeted were beyond their previous experience. There was no context for the new environment, behaviors, and expectations.[29] Perhaps being reduced to a childlike state is a psychologically vital condition for survival in a totally alien field of action and being.

Prisoners were assigned numbers upon entering a concentration camp. Numbers were not tattooed on prisoners' arms in camps located in Germany, however. The prisoner's name was kept in records, but not used in the reference to him within the camp. Few of the prisoners knew each other's names unless they had been acquainted earlier. In most instances, all body hair was brutally shaved off in the first hours, and often another round of torture followed with showers that were often freezing cold or boiling hot. One survivor of Mittelbau-Dora told the authors that one of the most difficult tortures he had to endure was the enforced shower in which the guards alternately turned the temperature from boiling hot to freezing cold and then drove the naked prisoners, who had arrived from Auschwitz in unenclosed cattle cars, into the open plaza (*Appellplatz*) to stand at attention until many died.

The loss of identity, through the physical change in appearance and the loss of name, was accelerated by the loss of personal documents and belongings. Few prisoners had their own package of clothing and items they brought with them returned after the showers. They were issued the clothing at hand, usually sanitized in a delousing procedure and not likely to fit. Wooden clogs were issued in some camps, guaranteed to cause open sores on the feet and great pain and infection that could be a precursor of death. The ill-fitting clothing also informed the prisoner that he as an individual did not exist for the state, that his personal characteristics and needs were of no interest.

The prisoner also felt the loss of a personal "archive" or record of who he had been, what role he had played, and to whom he had belonged—in other words, his history. Most had been wrenched from their homes, leaving loved ones with little information about where they were going to be held. Prisoners not held in secret confinement were allowed to write home twice a month under very restricted circumstances and under strict censorship. Thus, Albert Kuntz was able to inform his family of his whereabouts in various prisons and camps for almost a decade before he was sent to Mittelbau-Dora.[30] In this sense, the concentration camps were public and known to the citizenry.

> Dearest Ellen, my dear ones!
> Finally, I can shorten your painful waiting. I sit in the Kassel Police Prison in protective custody and wait for the further transport to Lichtenburg, which will probably be tomorrow.[31]

For many middle-class Germans, the prisoners were dangerous people whom one would not like to see on the loose. And for members of prisoners' families at home, the danger of being labeled "asocial" or a threat to society was greater for them than for their neighbors and a powerful motivation to live in conformity with community standards. This often meant separating oneself and one's family from the very support groups and members of resistance organizations that might have offered aid and comfort.

The combination of not knowing one's location and not having reference to one's previous identity caused mental disorientation and a desire to follow external orders in many prisoners.[32] The depersonalization process was also met with a psychological splitting of reality, so for many the brutality of prison or camp life seemed alternately to be something one observed, whereas the pain and suffering were something one felt.[33] This was only a part of the fragmentation that afflicted the prisoners. Along with the fragmentation of personality, the fragmentation of one's usable past was immediate. Social or political capital that one might have had in previous life was meaningless in the camp, where the new identity was found only in erasure of the individual and melting into the unidentifiable mass.[34]

The Evolving Nature of the Population in Concentration Camps

Prisoners were identified in several ways. Triangles were sewn onto uniforms in colors that defined the prisoner category: red for political, green for criminal, pink for homosexual, and so on. If one were a Jew, a second triangle in yellow was sewn over the other triangle to make a two-colored star. "Then you approached a hallway facing a sliding glass door, where they asked you if by chance you had any gold teeth. Then a compatriot of yours with hair, who had lived here longer, wrote your name down in a large book and handed you a yellow triangle, a thick stripe, and a ribbon, all made of canvas. In the center of the triangle, which signified that you were Hungarian, was a large letter U, and on the stripe you could read a printed number."[35]

A few of the functionaries were able to keep their hair, or grow it back, as the case may be. They also selected various articles of clothing or traded them for favors from the rank-and-file prisoners. National groups tended to have sympathy for one another within their ranks, but the number of people with whom one could have any kind of reciprocal relationship was limited among the average prisoners to a very few.

Privileged prisoners were those who had a function within the barracks as a block leader (*Blockältester*) or room leader (*Stubenältester*). Other functions revolved around the sick bay (*Revier*) as doctor or medical assistant, or on the work details or around camp as *Kapos*. People in these positions were responsible for the orderly running of the camp, and besides staying indoors for much of the time, they had the possibility of supplying themselves with food and clothing that were not available to others. They had many more opportunities for communication, often within a larger area of the camp.

Prisoners who identified a skill upon entering camp and registering were more valued and were sometimes able to get work assignments that could prolong life and health. Building skills were needed in the beginning of each camp. Mechanical or electrical expertise was also valued. Experience in production and assembly work was needed at Mittelbau-Dora, as well as in many other camps as they were being established. For those who could identify no particular skill, a construction job or camp maintenance was assigned. Work that had no function but to exercise sadistic control over others was common. Construction was heavy, dirty work that often was led by those who were under pressure themselves to achieve unrealistic goals from their work slaves, who were most often in no condition to do manual labor. It was thus not only difficult but dangerous as well.

The composition of the prisoner population changed over time. After the first wave of political prisoners entered the system, the regime still hesitated to arrest other categories of people they considered outsiders. This was partly because of the 1936 Olympic Games being held in Berlin. The world press was watching, and exposing the true nature of the government's intentions would have been counterproductive. By the time the games were played, how-ever, the country was crisscrossed with significant camps, the administrative arm was established, and by January 1937 eight thousand prisoners were in "protective custody." A year later, those labeled "asocial," homosexuals, and Jehovah's Witnesses were targeted, and women's camps were increased.[36]

Hitler annexed the Sudetenland and forced Slovakia to release all claims to it in the fall of 1938 and in March 1939 took over the rest of the country, calling it the Protectorate of Böhmen and Mähren, and Slovakia, which was nominally independent. Britain did not intervene. In September 1939, how-ever, Germany invaded Poland, and Britain and France declared war. The Polish Army could not withstand the superior forces of the Germans and quickly fell, marking the beginning of World War II.

Also in 1938, Germany moved quickly against its own Jewish population. Pushing seventeen thousand Jewish residents with Polish citizenship over the border into Poland without notice or prior arrangements caused great panic and displacement. A young man in France, having heard that his parents were among those removed, assassinated a German diplomat. This was the excuse for a coordinated attack on Jewish businesses, synagogues, and homes (called the Night of Broken Glass, or *Kristallnacht*) and the arrest of more than thirty thousand Jews, who were then sent to Sachsenhausen, Dachau, and Buchenwald, doubling the size of the concentration camp population almost overnight.[37] For the next three and a half years, the majority of concentration camp prisoners were Jewish. As the Nazi leadership set its goal of making Germany *Judenfrei,* or free of Jews, the Jewish population was deported to the East until, in 1942, few Jews were left in the concentration camps on the original German soil (*Altreich*).

Beginning in October 1941, Jews had been sent notices to appear at collection places for "evacuation." Where they were headed was unknown to them. Ghettos in Poland and the occupied areas of the Soviet Union filled with Jews from Germany, Austria, and other occupied countries.[38] The pre-1939 boundaries of Germany were becoming the demarcations of a fictive "Aryan nation." The Wannsee Conference of January 1942 sealed the fate of those identified as Jews. From ghettos to extermination was a short step, but arguments remained within the various administrative units of the regime that their labor should not be wasted and that the appropriate action would be to work them to death.

At the same time, with the war in progress, opponents, who were often nationalists in the occupied countries, were increasingly sent to the camps. Others were targeted for impressed labor, but could be transferred to a more rigorous "disciplinary" setting if they were believed to be "difficult" or were targeted for infractions of rules. And no longer were all the camps located in pre-1938 Germany. Stutthof opened in September 1939 near Gdansk (Danzig) and Mauthausen in Austria in the same year. The populations of the camps became international in character.

Making Use of Prisoners

The concentration camps were the sites of slave labor that engendered a high mortality among the prisoners. At first, the misuse of prison labor was a result of the efforts at *Erziehung* or just willful abuse by those for whom no restraint was required, but later became a goal in itself referred to as *Vernichtung durch Arbeit.*[39] Men and women were used as "workhorses," saving mechanized vehicles and tools for more important uses.

The use of the phrase *slave labor* has been questioned in relation to concentration camps, with some objecting to its use, while others embrace it. One objection is that slaves were maintained for their ability not only to work but also to reproduce their own kind, whereas the laborers under the Nazis were almost always expendable.[40] For others, there is no other term than *slave labor,* as the concentration camp prisoners could not excuse themselves to go home, and only rarely did they receive leniency or were they able to express their own will.

The first six years of the Hitler reign, prisoners in the concentration camps were used for hard labor, including quarrying stones for building projects, road construction, and building additional camps, such as Flossenbürg, Ravensbrück, and Mauthausen. Hitler put people back to work after years of unemployment and economic crisis. Several schemes provided his regime with the money needed for federal projects. He started massive savings programs for the common person (the money from which he then used for his own purposes), he "fined" the Jewish community or required "contributions" from them in ever-higher amounts year by year, and he added the money from corporate contributors to his program in return for which they enjoyed the exclusion of unions from their midst and increased spending of the government on projects that increased their own profit margins. In conjunction with the "Four Year Plan" designed to put Germany on a wartime footing with an economy that could sustain it, the decision was made in 1939 to use concentration camp prison labor as a rational adjunct to the workforce available in the civilian population.

The occupied countries provided Germany with an inexhaustible source of labor that could be impressed into service according to need. These laborers were not coming to Germany of their free will, yet they were not all concentration camp prisoners. In the first years of the Third Reich, many were allowed to go back to their homes periodically and were paid wages, although low. Between 1939 and 1945, twelve million such foreign workers were in Germany, taking a third of all of Germany's jobs.[41] No longer did foreign laborers have rights of return to their homes, as trains were filled with military servicemen.[42]

The SS Economic Administrative Main Office (Wirtschafts-Verwaltungshauptamt) was responsible for ordering labor and assigning it. They found it profitable to rent out the slave labor to private industry and even to private persons according to various wage scales, all of which reverted to the SS. In 1938, the currency conversion rate was 2.50 Reichmarks per dollar.[43] Skilled workers could be "rented" for about 6.00 RMs per prisoner a day and an unskilled worker for about 4.00 RM. At the same time, the costs of keeping the prisoner were kept to about 1.22 RM a day for women and 1.34 for men.[44]

With work orders rising, requests were sent to local work offices in the occupied countries for certain numbers of people to be sent to specific places. Roundups were used to achieve these "recruitment" goals. In the process of such sweeps, many younger children were taken along with adults. Once in the camps, it was to the youngster's advantage to list his or her age as older than it actually was in order to be assigned to a work detail instead of being assigned a much worse fate, which might mean becoming the subject of medical experimentation or being sent to a death camp.

The use of prison labor for all kinds of companies led to the construction of outer camps, or commandos, in the area of the workplace or even in the workplace. Thus, outer camps sprang up all over Germany, and companies began either to build their factories and assembly plants at the site of the concentration camps or to build a camp at the site of the factory.[45]

The change from the "educational" function to the economic exploitation of workers caused concern among some of the SS, not for the prisoners but for the image and public relations with the German public. Himmler wrote in 1942 to the head of the SS Economic Administrative Main Office: "The question of the incarceration oversight as well as the training (Erziehung) purpose of the concentration camp is unchanged. It could be (if we are not careful) that it will be thought that we arrest people, or keep people who have been arrested, in order to have workers. I remain of the opinion that even with 100% of the prisoners at work, the job of the camp commander is Erziehung or instruction."[46]

The SS had its own industries almost from the beginning of its existence. Starting with a publications house for propaganda, it moved to a building-supply company and a porcelain factory soon thereafter. As Jewish-owned businesses were taken over by the state, many fell into the hands of the SS. By the end of the war, more than 150 SS industries existed.[47] Money for SS enterprises and for its industry-laden camp system was readily available through the Dresdener Bank, which cooperated so thoroughly with this arm of the regime that is was referred to as "the SS bank."[48] Some of the concentration camp labor went into the profit centers of the SS, such as the work in stone quarries that was a prominent part of many concentration camps. These rocks were used as the foundations for autobahns and for massive public venues planned and constructed by Albert Speer, Hitler's public works architect.

For imprisoned workers from France and the Low Countries, the work created by Organization Todt was central. This was a cooperative venture between private firms and the state construction administration of the Third Reich. It began in 1933 with the construction of the militarily important highways and developed into the construction arm of the "Atlantic Wall," a structure meant to hinder a sea invasion of Germany, and the West Wall, sometimes called the "Siegfried line," to protect German-occupied western Europe from invasion. Envisioned as encompassing three thousand kilometers, the effort required massive infusions of labor, for which not only the French and Belgians were used, but so were Soviet prisoners of war, Jews, and African prisoners. Speer was directly responsible to Hitler for this organization, and, at the same time, he served as Reich minister for weapons and munitions. Within six months, six hundred Soviet prisoners of war had died from the terrible work conditions on these projects.[49]

In the beginning of the 1940s, there was little difference between the categories of prisons and concentration camps in Germany. Those from the eastern occupied countries or the Soviet Union were given an armband marked "Ost" for East or "P" for Poles. These laborers were meant mostly for farm labor, but increasingly were selected for munitions work. The laborers from the western countries were more likely sent directly to the munitions plants to work on skilled or semiskilled tasks.

From the Excitement of Victory to the Fear of Defeat

Six months after the invasion of the Soviet Union in June 1941, the situation with the war reversed itself for the German Wehrmacht (armed forces). The conquests through "Blitzkrieg" and "Blitzsiege" (lightning war and lightning victory) were over and replaced with the winter weather and mud on the small roads. This blocked German troop movements, destroyed bridges and rail lines, and increased the resistance of the inhabitants. In December 1941, the United States entered the war against Germany.

The last vestiges of forced labor were over; virtually all foreign workers were held against their will, even if there had been an element of volition in the earlier stages of the war. The Germans no longer raised questions or had reservations about the foreign workers, as they were needed to clear the bombed-out factories, homes, and shops in more and more German cities. Those in concentration camps were put to work in munitions plants, and many foreign workers who had possibly had a modicum of freedom in impressed labor were transferred to concentration camps where security could be maintained and they could be more reliable for secret work.[50] The prisoners were now surrounded by barbed wire, and the only way out was "up the chimney." Most camps had their own crematoria as the mortality rates rose. It was in this atmosphere of an established concentration camp system and "total war" that the camp Mittelbau-Dora came into existence.

Conclusion

The social and political context of the Nazi concentration camps was couched in language that was disingenuous and created an environment for the prisoners that was totally divorced from the life they had known previously. Robbed of their identities, their histories, and their sense of adulthood made them less and less able to act in their own behalf. The system of terror made the consequences of asserting one's identity fatal.

For those who did not experience it themselves, trying to understand the concentration camp system requires that someone else's experience must be learned secondhand. The use of self-excusing or protective language by the Nazi hegemony, as seen in the term *Erziehungslager* (education camp), provides an ongoing basis for de-emphasizing the terror apparatus of the camps. The various terms used to describe the unwilling labor of those collected in occupied countries against their will can be used in the same way. Although many such laborers, men and women, were allowed home visits during the first year or two of the war, they were all "in the system." At any time, if their behavior or mannerisms displeased their overseers, they could be sent to a harder, more restrictive form of imprisonment. Thus, in this book, unless specifically speaking of those who were in protected work settings, the authors will use the term *slave labor* to describe foreign labor in Germany during the Second World War.

Much as in the experience of American slavery, the Nazi concentrations camps were made up of prisoners from many different countries, using no single common language or sharing any single culture. The prisoners were stripped of common identity symbols, from their names to their personal histories. What they learned as culture was terror and strategies to survive.

This book presents the history of the Gedenkstätte Mittelbau-Dora in the social and political context of Nazi concentration camps, but also concentrates on the subjective reality of the people who were impacted by the camp in so many different ways. The background of concentration camps as they were used by the Hitler government helps to explain their character and impact on survivors, their families and communities, and the town of Nordhausen itself. The nature of the "total institution," the limited strategies for survival that often pitted one prisoner against another, led to difficulty in both memory and remembrance. "Survival guilt" was palpable for many and influenced discourse. For the prisoners and their offspring or those with whom they associated after the war, the bare truth did not match realities in the "real world." Changing the stories from within the camp to meet the listeners' ability to understand, or simply not to speak of them again, became part of the postcamp coping strategy. Reestablishing an identity was work for many survivors and their offspring. As we shall see, the political environment greatly influenced the strategies of this reidentification for the individual survivor of the camp. This individual adaptation, massed into common belief patterns regarding what camp life had been like, influenced the ways in which remembrance in the form of memorials and public functions came to be structured.

2. The Camp Mittelbau-Dora

Today, in the twenty-first century, more than sixty years after the end of the Second World War in Europe and the end of the Nazi Reich, the whole world recognizes that the Hitler regime was synonymous with a reign of terror, a major part of which was the gigantic network of concentration camps. Mittelbau-Dora, one of the approximately twenty thousand camps established by the Third Reich, was the site of the largest underground factory in the world where the V-1 and V-2 missiles were assembled.

Nordhausen, a city in the northern region of the German state Thuringia (Thüringen), almost in the middle of Germany, now has a population of more than forty-three thousand. It lies on the southern border of the Harz Mountains and has no direct connection to major train lines or roads. Today a highway skirts the town, but it is still awkward to connect to middle Germany. There are good roads north through the Harz Mountains and south through Thuringia, but until most recently, there were no major highways.

The central location of this region in Germany, and its being somewhat removed from important transport connections, must have entered into the thinking of those who planned the development of Mittelwerk, for the rocket assembly and end-production plant would be hard to find from the air and safe from damage by Allied bombing. Within the Kohnstein, a very small mountain outside of Nordhausen, a small mining operation for anhydrite and gypsum had begun in the 1920s by the I. G. Farben Company. It was taken over by the Economic Research Company (Wirtschaftliche Forschungsgesellschaft or Wifo) in the mid-1930s, as early preparations for rearmament began. A plan for enlarging the tunnel system in the future and storage space for large fuel tanks envisioned the coming aggression of the German state.[1]

The location was also well suited for constructing such an underground facility because of the geological features of the region near Nordhausen. The area of northern Thuringia has many hills and outcroppings of anhydrite, a relatively common sedimentary mineral that forms massive rock layers, caverns, and caves as a result of dehydration. The resulting contraction leaves deposits of anhydrite, a rock that is so hard that it does not need shoring up to support internal open spaces. Thus, it was relatively easy to enlarge the tunnels' already naturally occurring caverns. Seven years before the establishment of the camp, in 1936, engineers had enlarged some of these spaces in a small ninety-seven-meter "mountain" called the "Kohnstein," just two and a half miles north of Nordhausen. This was originally done to store reserves of oil and other strategic fuels as part of the prewar secret rearmament plans of the Nazi government.

This underground facility needed housing and at least minimal infrastructure for its workers, and in the summer of 1943 that concentration camp became known as "Dora." Germany's able-bodied men were at war, and, therefore, the use of slave labor had become not only the solution to the labor shortage in weapons plants throughout the country but also a given

The Kohnstein "Mountain" in which the Mittelbau-Dora tunnels were dug and the factory, Mittelwerk, where rockets were assembled for the German war effort. (Gretchen Schafft, photographer, Nordhausen Collection)

by the populace at large. Dora had a terrifying reputation among the prisoners in other camps, who had heard of it through rumors that spread rapidly throughout the camps.

In the winter of 1942–43, it appeared clear that the Nazi army had met its match at Stalingrad, and the end of the Hitler regime was in sight.[2] The only hope was to develop "wonder weapons"—specifically, the missile weapons that had been under development for a decade. A variety of rockets and "flying bombs" were already close to being successfully launched in Peenemünde on the Baltic Sea.[3]

Peenemünde

The German government signed the Versailles Treaty at the close of World War I. This set in place decisions made by the Constitutional Assembly that had met in Weimar in January 1919, establishing the Weimar Republic and forbidding a military rebirth in Germany. By 1935, however, Germany abandoned the treaty, began conscription for the armed forces, announced its new air force (the Luftwaffe), and openly rearmed.[4] The treaty had forbidden not only a standing army but also the building up of paramilitary forces or starting rearmament in other territories outside of Germany. The treaty had not mentioned specifically the development of rockets for aggressive use.

Rocket research had begun during the late Weimar Republic and continued under the Nazi regime. In 1932, a small army rocket research group was formed to develop the technology for liquid-fueled rockets (ballistic missiles). The group established a program to design and evaluate such rockets and was put into operation at the army firing range in Kummersdorf, some tens of kilometers south of Berlin.

Beginning in 1936, the town of Peenemünde at the northern tip of Usedom, an island on the Baltic Sea, became the experimental site of the German Army's Ordnance Offices' (Heereswaffenamt or HWA) division for rocketry.[5] During the 1930s, the research and engineering group pursued, initially at Kummersdorf and then at Peenemünde, the development of rockets codenamed *Aggregat* (aggregate or assembly) with designations A-1 to at least A-10. During these years, propulsion, guidance, and control systems were in a constant state of redesign in the A-rockets. Work continued on the shape of the rockets' fins and the inner and outer structures. A fruitful learning process came out of this work, which was aided at Peenemünde with a very large infusion of government money, administrative competence, a single experimental and manufacturing center, and the added expertise of university and civilian engineers.

The Peenemünde site was large enough to offer many advantages over the previous location for rocket development, Kummersdorf. A new modern facility was built with room for engineers and a large technical staff, and it was possible to carry out research on more than one rocket system at a time. The launchpad was not far from the development center. In addition to the army, the Luftwaffe also collaborated in rocket development and shared the Peenemünde facility, developing rocket engines and missiles for use with aircraft.[6]

Wernher von Braun, Walter Dornberger, and Arthur Rudolph were key players in the race for rockets in the Third Reich. Von Braun and Rudolph were located in Peenemünde, while Dornberger was in Berlin except for a few months in 1943, when he joined them in Peenemünde. Von Braun, a man still in his twenties when he created the German Army rocket team, was clearly the genius of the program. He worked closely with Rudolph, a young engineer of great promise who was chief engineer of the Peenemünde factory, and Dornberger, an artillery officer and rocket enthusiast with political savvy to push the rocket program through when others, including Hitler, were in doubt about its efficacy. The three were linked for many years in Germany and, after the war, in U.S. military and civilian rocket endeavors.

Peenemünde was not only about engineering, however, for there was also a need for labor. At first, small numbers of foreign forced laborers were used for construction and housed in a small concentration camp on the island of Usedom. By August 1942, the "halls were filled with prisoners so that now, in the current month, the last hall is being converted to prison-labor operations."[7]

During 1942, Germany was on a total war footing. After the defeat at Stalingrad in February 1943, the country required virtually all able-bodied German men to report for military service, leaving a critical labor shortage in the expanding German Reich. The numbers of slave laborers increased throughout Germany, and in Peenemünde, secrecy was difficult to maintain.[8] Slave laborers from many countries, but particularly Poland and the Soviet Union, were used for many different jobs in rocket manufacture throughout the war industry.[9]

It is important to understand how the labor force for Peenemünde was put together. Of course, the civilian force could be recruited in normal ways. The prisoners, however, were taken from various camps and prisons. Some attempt was made to find candidates with engineering or technical experience, but in reality, most prisoners would claim any skill to better their positions among the terrorizing conditions they found in their incarceration. Working in a production capacity had always offered more chance for survival than did construction or hard labor.[10]

At first, prisoners were transported only from nearby Buchenwald concentration camp or from Peenemünde, but later they came from camps in the East and endured deadly transits. It was common practice to transfer prisoners from one camp to another, and many of the prisoners had already been transported and processed through several camps. In each, they had to endure a wretched initiation rite.[11] The transport itself was often unbearable, and the previous incarceration had often weakened the prisoners. Later in the war, many prisoners arrived at their destination dead.

After the early German victories, starting with the invasion of Poland in 1939, the winds of the war changed for the German Army in the winter of 1942–43 with their defeat at Stalingrad. With this turn of events, the German Army and Hitler's staff sought to accelerate progress in their rocket program for the development of liquid-fueled rockets. The A-4 rocket was selected for production. In response to the first effective night air raids on civilian centers by the British Royal Air Force (RAF), beginning with the city of Lübeck in March 1942, Hitler wanted to have "vengeance weapons" with which to retaliate. As a result and with the efforts of the German Propaganda Ministry, the A-4 ballistic missile later came to be known as the V-2, where *V* stood for *Vengeance*. The V-2 rocket was a ballistic missile with a warhead weight of twenty-two hundred pounds. The other Vengeance weapon, the V-1, was originally designated as the Fi 103 and was the product of a competing project of the German Air Force. The V-1 was the predecessor of the sophisticated cruise missiles developed later in the century. The V-1 was propelled by a pulse-jet engine, had a warhead weight of almost two thousand pounds, and was much less expensive to build than was the V-2. The problems of the early 1930s were addressed through a large infusion of funds, the single-center experimental and manufacturing hub, the added expertise of university and civilian engineers and scientists, and administrative competence.[12]

The production plant at Peenemünde, which was to assemble operational missiles, was given the go-ahead in 1939, but met with many delays because of steel shortages, manpower shortages, and the indecisiveness of Hitler himself regarding the value of putting the enormous resources needed for the venture into an unproven rocket program. Slave laborers from Poland, Italy, and France were added to the thousands of civilian workers, but their numbers remained in the hundreds, and they were regulated and managed by the Peenemünde administration and not the SS. It wasn't until 1942 that using the A-4 as a terror weapon against Britain drew total support from Hitler for the rocket team in Peenemünde.[13] By that time, the need for labor was much greater, and the camp of Karlshagen was made ready for several thousand prisoners.[14]

In October 1942, the first successful launch sent a V-2 (A-4/V-4) rocket downrange about 130 miles, while reaching an altitude of some 50 miles.[15] This success was not followed immediately by others, but it did encourage the rocket engineers' optimism. The development of the A-4 continued over the winter of 1942–43, as the engineers struggled to make the complex technology work.

Dornberger and von Braun met personally with Hitler on July 7, 1943, and confirmed his enthusiasm for rocket development and production. Hitler wanted immediate and unrealistic production goals to be put into effect, but up to that time, not a single working rocket had been produced at Peenemünde for use in the war![16] Now, four plants would attempt to meet high production quotas with a workforce of twenty-five hundred concentration camp prisoners. This would not happen, however, at least not in Peenemünde. In the summer of 1943, the Royal Air Force, acting on intelligence about Peenemünde, prepared an attack.

The Attack on Peenemünde and the Death of Concentration Camp Prisoners

On August 18, 1943, the British bombed Peenemünde in the most highly targeted attack of the war. Based on reports from Polish slave laborers and Swedish intelligence, the British devoted almost their entire bomb squadron to the Peenemünde attack. This decision indicates the importance that Britain assigned to protecting its country from rocket attacks. In all, 596 planes, 4,241 men, and 1,924 tons of explosives were used; Britain lost 40 bombers. The experimental station and other buildings were hit, including the housing of technicians and scientists, killing several hundred.[17] The bombs also fell on the camp where thousands of prisoners were housed, and hundreds of them died. This camp, Trassenheide, three kilometers from Peenemünde, was surrounded by barbed wire without a way to get out.[18] The facilities for experimental research and production were somewhat damaged, and the staff painted the roofs to make them appear even more destroyed than they were. Von Braun and most of the technical staff continued to work in Peenemünde on improvements to the weapons. The air raid, however, had demonstrated the vulnerability of the complex at Peenemünde.

A decision was made to secure the further development of the rockets and their assembly by moving the operation into the Harz mountain region and doing what no group had done before: continue the work of rocket assembly totally underground. The tunnels of the Kohnstein near Nordhausen were chosen for the site. The Nazis had already developed the site in 1936 for the secret storage of oil and fuel and connected the rail line to Niedersachswerfen, the little town closest to what came to be called Mittelwerk.

Moving Underground

At this time, there were two main tunnels within the Kohnstein Mountain, each about a mile long with forty-six cross-tunnels between them. They belonged to the Economic Research Company, a state-owned firm.[19] More like large hills than mountains, the Kohnstein tunnels had been created by miners before the war. After adding a fueling facility, the underground facility constituted 125,000 square meters.[20] There were connections of railway tracks in the tunnels to the outside world through a branch system of small-gauge tracks. It was thus both accessible and could be totally secret.

The concentration camp Buchenwald, located about 50 miles southeast of Nordhausen, was the nearest large source of slave labor. On August 28, 1943, the first transfer of 106 prisoners from Buchenwald was sent to the new camp, Dora, an area consisting of the tunnels and the surrounding acreage.[21] They were housed at first in tents outside the main entrance to the tunnels. Very soon, however, they were moved into the tunnels themselves and saw the light of day only at their weekly roll calls on the "roll call square" (*Appellplatz*). These prisoners enlarged the capacity of the underground facility, Mittelwerk, through difficult and horrific circumstances. For the first fifteen months, Dora was an administrative subsidiary of Buchenwald. Records were kept in the larger camp, and trucks carried dead prisoners, killed through the careless construction of the tunnel, murder, starvation, or illness, to be cremated in Buchenwald, which had the capacity to burn bodies.[22]

Other concentration camps bore the names of the towns they were near, such as Dachau, Flossenbürg, or Sachsenhausen. Buchenwald bore the name of the landscape in which it was located: the birch forest. The SS had chosen the name Dora out of the alphabetical code words that were commonly used, in order to hide its location. Even the mail was sent to another town, Sangerhausen, some distance away, to avoid disclosing just where the camp and the factory were located.

In the last months of 1943, the assembly line and the machinery that would be necessary to assemble the rockets arrived in Mittelwerk from Peenemünde.[23] A larger workforce of about 600 men from Peenemünde and other camps arrived with the apparatus. The plan was to begin the rocket assembly in the Kohnstein tunnels at the end of 1943. The SS arranged for transports of prisoners from other concentration camps according to the work needs of the new factory and the need to replace prisoners who had been killed through physical violence or the conditions of the camp. While waiting for the new installation, prisoners had the hideous job of blasting new tunnel space into the mountain, without any kind of protection or ventilation, virtually twenty-four hours a day.

The management of the underground factory was cobbled together from managers and engineers who had been vetted by the Armaments Ministry or were already known through their work in Peenemünde, where they were experienced with rocket development. They were under the control of Albert Speer's Armaments Ministry. The SS was in charge of the security of the operation and the management of the camp and its labor. There was often tension between these two controlling entities.

Thus, besides those with technical expertise, there were members of the SS including SS-Sturmbannführer Otto Förschner, as the so-called security representative (*Abwehrbeauftragter*). An advisory group had the say in the direction of the work and consisted of some members of the Armaments Ministry, Karl Maria Hettlage and Gerhard Degenkolb; from the military weapons department General Dornberger; and finally SS commander Hans Kammler, who was Himmler's personal representative responsible for V-weapon production. Only Kammler was actually on-site in Mittelbau-Dora.

The head of the SS, Heinrich Himmler (Reichsführer SS), and Minister for Armaments and War Production Albert Speer visited the tunnels to assure themselves of the progress of the work. Certainly with an eye to his own situation as a postwar prisoner, Speer wrote from his prison cell in his memoirs:

> In a lonely valley in the Harz Mountains a widely ramified system of caves had been established before the war for the storage of vital military chemicals. Here on December 19, 1943, I inspected the extensive underground installations where the V-2 was to be produced. In enormous long halls prisoners were busy setting up machinery and shifting plumbing. Expressionlessly, they looked right through me, mechanically removing their prisoners' caps of blue twill until our group had passed them.
>
> The conditions of these prisoners were in fact barbarous, and a sense of profound involvement and personal guilt seizes me whenever I think of them. As I learned from the overseers after the inspection was over, the sanitary conditions were inadequate, disease rampant, the prisoners were quartered right there in the damp caves, and as a result the mortality among them was extraordinarily high.

In a footnote, Speer added: "The shocking effect the camp had on us is indicated in the deliberately veiled phraseology of the *Office Journal* entry for December

10, 1943, 'On the morning of December 10, the minister went to inspect a new plant in the Harz Mountains. Carrying out this tremendous mission drew on the leaders' last reserves of strength. Some of the men were so affected that they had to be forcibly sent off on vacations to restore their nerves.'"[24]

In September 1943, the facility within the Kohnstein Mountain was officially declared "Mittelwerk," or central factory, which was developed through a combination of government and private financing. Concentration camp prisoners in Dora, originally funneled through Buchenwald even if they came from distant camps, numbered almost ten thousand men by December 1943.[25]

Building and Enlarging the Tunnels

The slave laborers were taken from the trains transporting them directly into the tunnels, where they were housed in four cross-tunnels. Their first task was to enlarge the tunnel system. The prisoners were assigned places in four-tiered bunk beds that ran the length of the space between the two main tunnels. They were lit with only minimum electricity and had no ventilation system or sanitary facilities. The temperature remained at about fifty degrees, and a severe shortage of water made it virtually impossible to wash themselves. Prisoners relieved themselves in large barrels cut in half to serve as latrines. This environment became known among prisoners as the "Hell of Dora."[26] In terms of danger, size, and the physically and psychologically damaging atmosphere, it was unmatched. As one shift went to work, the other came to the sleeping area and took over the same bunks that had just been vacated. Noise of the explosions as the tunnels were excavated was ear shattering and mind destroying. One Czech prisoner, Otakar Litomisky, remembered it in this way:

Our trip (from Buchenwald) lasted three hours and ended at the foot of a small mountain. We jumped out of the truck and fell in for the usual counting. High above us a predatory bird circled—a buzzard. A hundred meters from where we were standing a small-gauge railroad ran into the mountain through what appeared to be a tunnel. The question we asked ourselves, however, was: "Where was the camp?" There were no barracks to be seen, but only a few tents in which the SS were living. It was not long before we were driven at a run over sticks and stones directly through a pile of rocks onto the railroad tracks. In this way we came to the tunnel entrance. At the entrance, there were two green houses, one for the watchmen and one for the SS guards. Again, we had a count of the prisoners that seemed to last forever.

After a long time, we were led into the tunnel, where a cold, wet breeze blew. The change from the light of day to the darkness of the tunnel was so sudden that we fell over the stones and bumps in the ground. Light in the tunnel was provisional, about every 100 meters a strong lamp burned high in the ceiling. In the distance, about 300 meters ahead, the tunnel entered into a huge stone gallery. Here our first surprise was waiting. On the right side was a gigantic factory hall at least 30 meters high and about 300 meters long. Over the floor, lit by the red lights of carbide lamps, people were working like ants. Everywhere, from the tunnel ceiling to the walls, cold water was dripping, and it collected in huge puddles on the floor where it had no possibility of being drained away. The SS watchmen showed no empathy for our astonishment and drove us further into the mountain.

After about 50 meters, we found ourselves in a wide hall cut in a dome about 15 meters wide and 300 meters long. There were more and more halls cut into the walls at regularly spaced intervals. At first glance it looked interesting, but it was still not clear to us where we were going to sleep after work. The answer waited for us in a further tunnel, where in the middle there was a pile of straw mattresses and a few blankets made of thin synthetic material. The SS watched these "valuables" and after awhile divided them among us. Each one got an armful of wet straw, and every two prisoners a damp blanket. We Czechs held together, and so I shared a blanket with Eman Krejci. We spread the straw on the hard stone, lay as close together as we could, and after a time, like two cats, we went to sleep. I do not know how long we slept, for we needed it so badly. All of a sudden, in the middle of the night, there was an ear-shattering explosion that left us in a cloud of dust and seconds later a shower of stones fell on us. We thought an accident had happened, and we sprang from our straw. In our sleepiness and in the darkness, we bumped into one another helplessly. When the repetitious explosions finally came to an end, swearing broke out on all sides. The next moment the SS were there with their dogs, screaming at us that we should shut up and go back to sleep. We had to obey, but we could not sleep anymore. We were terrified of the next explosion, and the possible consequences it could have. . . .

The next morning, a cry went out: "Get up! Fast, fast!" We got up quickly and wanted to wash off the dust, but there were not even a few drops of clean water to be found, only dirty puddles that we did not dare touch. So we went to work unwashed. During the first day, it did not particularly bother us, but after two weeks, we were so terribly dirty, that it was almost impossible to stand it. The whole body itched terribly. We helped with the food, so that we would get an extra portion of "coffee" which was worthless anyway, with which we tried to wash ourselves. Our work commando was called "cable laying" and involved laying cable from the power source in the first of the tunnels in broad lines. It was a very tiring job and dirty, carried out in two shifts of 12 hours each.[27]

Otakar Litomisky was a survivor of Auschwitz, as well as of Buchenwald. He had been in the Reserve Officers' School in Czechoslovakia in March

1939, when the Germans invaded and disbanded the Czech troops. Otakar managed to steal the records of his regiment and helped to form an illegal organization of resistance. Being a radio specialist, Otakar put into operation a radio sender in Prague. He continued to work in the underground until his arrest in 1942.

It began with "impressed" labor in a factory. With the war at full tilt, the Germans were taking Czech civilians and placing them wherever they could be most helpful to the effort. From the factory, Litomisky was taken to prison, for someone had informed on his resistance activities. Many harsh interrogations and much hard labor followed in a string of prisons in Czechoslovakia and Germany, until he was "selected" to proceed to Auschwitz.

After many months of backbreaking labor in Auschwitz, Litomisky was able to register as a "political prisoner" and was removed to Buchenwald.[28] There, he reported himself to be an electrician, a profession needed in the tunnels of Dora. Thus, his further transfer and his initiation into hell.

Otakar Litomisky lived through his experience and after the war returned to Prague as a survivor. He remembered his years of suffering by meeting for decades with a group of comrades in that city. For years, they had to meet under various guises other than as a survivor group, as the state did not sanction their independence in forming and reinforcing their own memories and perhaps feared these meetings would lead to other kinds of independence from the state. Nonetheless, these survivors made frequent trips to Nordhausen for commemorations at the camp.

Litomisky was unfailingly polite and kind to everyone he met at those meetings and managed to write his memoir, insisting to those who responded to his friendship that they translate it for him. Thus, his memoir became available in Flemish as well as English and German, and Czech, although it had no real distribution.[29] It sits in archives in various countries waiting for someone to pick it up and marvel at the story it holds.

Because of the conditions, deaths in the tunnels between November 1943 and March 1944 numbered almost three thousand. Beyond this toll, there were also another three thousand "muslims" (*Muselmänner*), prisoners unable to work because of grave illness, injury, or psychological shock. These men were sent on to Bergen-Belsen or Maidanek with little chance of survival.[30]

The Assembly of Weapons in the Tunnels

The weapons had entered production before they were perfected in design and manufacture. Many had not worked on the test stand. Errors in their assembly led to a large percentage of them being unworkable, largely because the workers were unskilled, sick, and resistant. The technical staff recognized that there were many technical problems, but also suspected sabotage by the prisoners themselves. The extent of the sabotage and the contribution it made to the rockets' failures have remained points of controversy throughout the years. Whatever the cause or multiple causes, the goal of 900 rockets a month set in winter 1943 was not reached. That goal could never be reached, for the production line had to be changed according to test results from Peenemünde and from occupied Poland. Instead, in March 1944, 170 rockets were completed; in May 1944, 437; and in July 1944, 86.[31]

In order to get on with the rocket production, the enlargement of the tunnels was halted. For the prisoners, this meant a certain relief. In April 1944, 250 rockets were completed, most of the production line was finished, and the assembly line (*Taktstrasse*) in one of the long tunnels was completed.[32] Thus, prisoners from twenty countries began to work on the completion of rockets that might even be aimed at their own loved ones in countries still fighting the Germans in open warfare.[33] Finally, seven months after the tunnels were filled with prisoners, barracks were begun outside the tunnels for the use of the slave laborers.

The expected success of the "wonder weapons" was not immediately realized. Nevertheless, a week after the Normandy invasion, June 6, 1944, the first few and soon hundreds of V-1 cruise missiles were sent on their way to London every week. Three months later, the V-2 rockets were being manufactured at a rate of 600–700 a month in Mittelwerk and were ready to be fired.[34] They did not do enough damage to change the course of the war, but did create the terror for which they were designed.

The completion of the barracks with washrooms in the spring and early summer of 1944 and other accommodations, including a sick bay staffed by medical personnel, while not adequate, was a large improvement over the murderous conditions of the tunnels. The number of deaths fluctuated drastically, lowering when the conditions improved and rising when new transports of prisoners arrived from the East.[35]

The landing in Normandy marked the beginning of the Western European invasion. It also marked the Germans' more intensive use of the V-2 rockets. Of the more than 5,000 V-2 rockets assembled in Kohnstein by the prisoners of Mittelbau-Dora, 1,500 of them landed in London and Southeast England, killing more than 2,000 people. Another 1,500 V-1 and V-2 weapons were aimed at Antwerp, Belgium, killing almost 7,000.[36] It would appear that more prisoners died in the concentration camp serving Mittelwerk and further development of the "wonder weapons" than did helpless civilians in Germany's enemy countries.

During this period of high production, thousands of slave laborers were sent to Mittelwerk from all over Germany and neighboring countries. Approximately 5,000 of these men were prisoners selected for their "expertise" in specialties needed for the montage of the rockets. As reported in October 1944, 3,000 workers were German civilians, most of whom were used as managers or skilled workers placed in supervisory positions over the prisoners.[37] Members of the SS did not supervise the production lines, but instead were responsible for the discipline and punishment of those who did not meet the absolute standard of obedient behavior.

Because prisoners were engaged in different kinds of work, it became apparent to them which jobs offered the best chance of survival. Working inside on a technical job was superior to working outside on construction of roads, rail lines, or further tunnels. Some prisoners were "rented" by firms in Nordhausen as a commando or work group and taken in and out of the city in formation. In some cases, they were housed at the site. Depending on the type of work required and the nature of the supervision, there were some chances for a little extra food or news of the war, or just a better chance to see the next day. The unlucky ones could just as well end up in a "trip to heaven commando" (*Himmelfahrtskommando*).[38]

In seeking to get into a better work situation, prisoners often claimed they had experience in an area about which they actually knew nothing. This may have influenced the quality of the output of weapons at least as much as any act of sabotage. Sabotage and organizing among prisoners were always hopes among political prisoners, and many reports of prisoners gathered by those interested in survivors relate such acts. There is also evidence that an international ring of prisoners in active resistance to the SS was operative until at least November 1944.[39]

In Mittelbau-Dora, as opposed to Buchenwald, for example, the degree of organization was very limited, most likely. It is known that one resistance group existed in the infirmary led by Jan Čespiva, a Czechoslovakian doctor. That Albert Kuntz was active in such organization is the deeply held belief of many who held him in high esteem, and the strongest documentation is the fact that he was arrested in the final days of the camp for organizing sabotage, tortured, and murdered. Some survivors have mentioned him in their memoirs and in their discussions with his son, Leo.[40] Another point of view is that there was little possibility of organizing an international committee for several reasons: the camp was late to come into existence, it was tightly controlled because of the high production standards and output goals, and the discretionary time that prisoners had to themselves was even less in Dora than in other camps.

Prisoners grouped themselves by nationality or, perhaps more important, language. They often helped one another in groups of twos or threes as best they could, but also fell victim to the overriding hunger and exhaustion and looked only to their own survival. Stories of both narcissisms and altruism abound in the concentration camp literature and in memoirs. Some prisoners who had either contact with others through the sick bay or through oversight of construction, such as Albert Kuntz, had the possibility of some organizing. Language was not always a barrier across national boundaries, for many prisoners were fluent in several languages.

The camp structure generally allowed for a hierarchy to develop among prisoners and even fostered it. The head of a barracks was referred to as the *Blockältester,* and he often had assistants known as the *Stubendienst.* In the work details, the leader of a work group was the *Kapo,* a person who gained favor with the SS when he was brutal and drove his prisoners to the breaking point. The *Kapos* at Mittelbau-Dora were usually those wearing a green triangle, meaning criminals. Many were career criminals, although some had gained this distinction by infractions of rules of the Third Reich. In general, they were a feared and hated group in Dora.

Heinrich Himmler, head of the SS and chief of the German Police, said in a speech to the German Army on June 21, 1944:

> You see then these 40,000 political and professional criminals—please don't laugh—they are my junior officers for this whole company. We have here—and it is only a part of what Obergruppenführer Eicke has put together—this obedient Subservience of underdogs, managed by so-called Kapos. So, one is the responsible overseer, I want to say prisoner trustee of thirty, forty, a hundred other prisoners. During the time he is Kapo, he doesn't sleep with the others. He is responsible that the work quotas are fulfilled, that no sabotage takes place, that they are clean and make their beds properly. The [German] soldiers would have a time of it, for most of [the prisoners] can't speak a word of German. A recruit would never be able to keep order in the [prisoner] barracks. Therefore, the Kapo is responsible. He must beat his men. The minute we are not satisfied with him, he is not a Kapo anymore and he sleeps with his men again. He knows, they will beat him to death the first night.[41]

This indirect method of administration pitted one national group against another. Prisoner accounts often refer to other nationalities as venal. There were great resentment and hatred against those who stole another prisoner's rations or meager supplies, which was often expressed in stereotyping a national group. Later, in speaking of reunions of the survivors, we will see how even now the relationships are within groups, not necessarily among them.

The SS held responsibility for the overall command of the camp and every function within it. All of the assignments given to prisoners were at the behest of the SS, and prisoners had to cooperate with them or face serious consequences. This often put the prisoner in the position of almost collaborating with the SS, even when it was not at all his intent. Many people filling these functionary posts intended to do well by their fellow prisoners, but this was hard to achieve because of the ultimate authority housed in the SS guard.

With the increasing bombing of German cities and armaments factories, especially the scarcity of parts for the V-rockets often brought the production to a halt. Therefore, more and more of the parts were manufactured in the neighborhood around Mittelwerk itself.[42] Mittelwerk gained in importance as a source of the wonder weapons and was totally at its limits of production.

The year 1944 was characterized not only by the increased production in the Kohnstein, but also through the increasing use of areas of the southern and western Harz region for enlarging the underground space for production. Along with this expansion came plans for new rail lines to transport the weapons around the camp to retain the secrecy of activities there. These lines were to go through the southern Harz region, but they were not completed.[43] The subcamp Mittelbau-Dora, now often referred to as simply Dora, developed its own outer camps of various sizes, more than forty in all, administered by the Dora personnel.[44] In the fall of 1944, Mittelbau-Dora was considered of such size and importance that it became a full-fledged, independent concentration camp. It was the last of the concentration camps labeled as such by the Nazi authorities before the end of the war.

Ellrich

The largest of Mittelbau-Dora's outer camps was in the little town of Ellrich, a few kilometers from the main camp. Built in the spring of 1944, Ellrich, or "Erich" as its pseudonym, housed up to nine thousand men working on various construction commandos.[45] It was one of the most deadly of all the camps, run under the auspices of the most vicious administrators. Even within Ellrich, there were two camps: Juliushütte, where most of the prisoners were held, and Ellrich-Bürgergarten.

Here there was no real sick bay, not enough clothing for all prisoners, nor dishes for eating or blankets. Prisoners sometimes had to take off their clothes and give them to the next shift in order to continue the work. Cannibalism was reported among the prisoners.[46] As the main camp was about to become an independent administrative body, a general inspection was made. In preparation, many of the sickest prisoners from Ellrich were sent to the infirmary in Mittelbau-Dora, where they either recovered quickly or were eliminated through murder or transport.

As we have described, the main camp Mittelbau-Dora had developed to the point in the spring of 1944 that the prisoners might be housed in barracks and report for work on the assembly line. The tunnels, still filled with noise, poor air, and no heat, were miserable, but the work was at least inside and for many became manageable. For those in the outer camps, in the construction brigades (*Baubrigade*), the food was absolutely not sufficient, the clothing was minimal and threadbare, and the work was conducted under all weather conditions. Perhaps even more important, the workers had no tools to do the work. In keeping with the goal of "discipline" within the concentration camp, workers were punished through the work itself. Making every task harder may not have sped the work, but, to the satisfaction of the SS, it did increase the suffering of the laborers. The fact that these conditions led to death for a large number of the slave laborers did not seem to bother their overseers, for there seemed to be an endless supply of these human machines. In his book, *Less than Slaves,* Benjamin Ferenz spoke of this philosophy by which human capital was so unacknowledged that there was little or only sporadic efforts to keep them alive.[47]

By 1945, prisoners of Ellrich and other outer commandos carried their comrades back to camp lifeless, but all prisoners were still required to "appear" for the count (*Appell*), dead or alive: "Every evening we came back with five to ten dead; bodies that just fell over. The number of sick who had to be carried was twice as many. Practically every shift, I was a 'corpse carrier,' for I was still able to hold my balance fairly well and I belonged to those who didn't look so bad. Four men carried a dead one. Two carried the legs on their shoulders, two others the arms. Through snow and mud this miserable procession made its way to the sickbay (Revier). There the rags would be stripped from the dead. With ink pen the prisoner's number would be written on his forehead."[48]

The End Stage of the War and the Camp

The camp now became a center for the prisoner evacuation transports coming from the East. As the Soviet forces advanced through Eastern Europe, the prisoners were sent on terrible transports and on foot to other more secure concentration camps. Mittelbau-Dora could use the labor, even if the wrecks of men lived only a few weeks. As the new prisoners arrived, others who had been "used up" in the mill of terror and slavery were sent on to camps that no longer supported life, such as Bergen-Belsen or even Boelcke-Kaserne in the city of Nordhausen. A prisoner's time was limited to the weeks that he could manage to stay on his feet and keep working. For those new to the camp, this was very difficult, for they knew none of the pitfalls or tricks of survival specific to this place and time.

Although Germany's policies had worked toward a time when the homeland would be free of Jews (*Judenfrei*) and had virtually achieved that goal by the end of 1942, a different perspective reigned in the winter of 1944. With the eastern camps being liberated by the Russians who were approaching from the East, the Nazi policy changed: Jews would be brought back into Germany to be worked to death. Thus, over the winter and spring of 1944–45, the camps of southern and middle Poland were evacuated, including Auschwitz, Birkenau, and Gross-Rosen. The trips were death sentences in themselves, and many prisoners did not survive them. Most of those who did arrive in Mittelbau-Dora were no longer put to work in the production of weapons, but rather labored in the enlargement of the tunnels and caves where weapons, weapon parts, fuel, and other materials could be stored. This was the most dangerous and life-consuming work, and the death rate of the prisoners soared. The emphasis was on getting all critical materials underground. Guards were transported with the prisoners, giving Mittelbau-Dora and particularly the outer camps an even more deadly aura.

The death rate followed the activities of the prisoners and the conditions under which they lived and worked. Building the tunnels, with the blasting, falling rock, and underground accommodations, took the greatest toll. Although the number of deaths declined when prisoners began to live in barracks and have some time in the open air and engaged in the assembly of the weapons, it again rose sharply as the transports with exhausted and traumatized prisoners arrived from the East. Over the entire life of the camp, about one in every three prisoners died while in Mittelbau-Dora.[49] In the spring of 1944, Mittelbau-Dora built its own crematorium to handle the cases, and no longer were corpses sent to Buchenwald for disposal.

The combination of the work tempo, the exhaustion of the prisoners, and the near certainty that the war would soon end made the incidents of SS punishment for sabotage greater in the end of 1944 and the beginning of 1945 than at any other time. Using torture and mass executions that prisoners had to witness, the "saboteurs" were punished and murdered. Even the civilian workers were subject to gruesome displays of hangings as they went into the tunnels to work.[50]

The SS based their decision to hang and execute prisoners on the incidents of sabotage they believed they had discovered. Certainly, there was a high degree of willingness to commit sabotage, but a much smaller possibility among the prisoners to do so. The fact was that the assembly of the rockets involved technical and complicated mechanical functions that many prisoners in their deteriorated state could not perform well. One survivor told the authors that the lights went out periodically, and in those moments, prisoners turned a screw or threw a piece of material under their workplace, hoping that the rocket would be damaged. At the end of 1944, it was determined that 20 percent of the A-4 (V-2) rockets were not suitable for launch.[51] However, the stages of rocket assembly were checked and double-checked by civilian workers and foremen whose lives and jobs were also in danger if they allowed damaged parts to slip past them. It must be assumed that both prisoner sabotage and unintentional errors led to the high number of failures of the rockets to reach their targets.

The terror engendered by the terrible measures the SS took against the prisoners was an end in itself. It could have also served as an outlet for the frustration of the Nazis in the end phases of the war as defeat was near. The will of the prisoners to survive, to not despair, to survive the fury of the environment and the personnel of the camp is repeated in conversations among survivors and in their memoirs. When possible, they encouraged one another to hold on to life, to make it to the end. This was a kind of sabotage in itself, an act against the will of the Nazis with their slogan, "Extermination through Work."

At the end of September 1944, the Volkswagen factories in Lotheringen, which had been producing weapons, stored the V-1 "flying bombers" in Mittelwerk. In addition to the machines, an additional three hundred Jewish prisoners, who had worked on the V-1 production, were brought to Mittelbau-Dora. The four tunnels that had been used for sleeping were then turned into further workspace where the entire V-1 guided missiles could be assembled. From January until March 1945, approximately six thousand of these devices were completed.[52]

As the complex of Mittelwerk grew, the need for extended infrastructure was greater. Civilian workers made up the majority of the workforce in the actual tunnels of Mittelwerk during the highest production time.[53] Prisoners were dispatched increasingly to smaller camps for the purpose of laying water and electrical lines, building filtration plants for sewage, and constructing roads and rail lines. Not only did the surrounding population see the prisoners, but they also increasingly saw their overseers. The guards and civilian workers frequented local bars and various "watering holes," where they were tempted to speak of the situation as they saw it despite the tight restrictions on spreading information. The Gestapo and secret agents were thick in the countryside to hamper the spreading of rumors or news of the rockets.

By the end of March 1945, the missile production in Mittelwerk was halted, as the war situation in Nazi Germany made their construction too dire to continue. Georg Rickhey, the general director of Mittelwerk, as well as the scientists and technical leaders, boarded trains and headed for southern Germany.[54] The Bavarian Alps served as a fortress for the survivors of the Nazi regime and was closer to the western countries than to the USSR; Wernher von Braun declared after the war that he had wanted to place his team in the hands of the Americans and not the Russians.[55]

The SS stayed behind and did their job: They burned files or stored them in what they considered safe places. Many of them led the "evacuation measures," leading prisoners by foot or in trains away from the camp and its outer subcamps and commandos. Many were driven to the southern part of Germany or Austria, where the prisoners, who were viewed as "carriers of secrets," were shot or put to work in other weapons production. Many others were sent to Bergen-Belsen to vegetate until death.[56] Still other prisoners were sent off to the Northeast, where the Nazis thought they would develop a front against the Soviet Army and could kill the prisoners with impunity. One such transport started on April 4 in Niedersachswerfen, near Nordhausen, and ended after a week with a death toll of more than a thousand prisoners in a barn in Gardelegen.[57] In the concentration camp Dora, a few hundred of the prisoners who were unable to march remained behind, close to death, and more than a thousand more were left in the Boelcke-Kaserne, in the city of Nordhausen, under unspeakable conditions.[58]

Wincenty Hein, who was a prisoner and worked in the infirmary, was able to save some of the documents about the concentration camp by hiding them, later helping the American liberators by giving them important original documents about the SS camp administration.[59] As the American troops of the 104th Infantry Division entered Nordhausen on April 11, they found a gruesome scene, which created an almost unmanageable outrage among them. They sorted through the dead and dying for those they could still save. The film crew with the army made motion pictures of the situation in the Boelcke-Kaserne that were widely released in the United States and serve today as documentation of Nazi horror.[60]

Conclusion

The very complex history of the missile and rocket development and assembly within the Third Reich requires an understanding of the economic, political, and technical environment during the 1920s, 1930s, and 1940s. This has been covered in the works of Michael Neufeld and a few others. That history is used here to give context to the lives and work of the concentration camp prisoners of Mittelbau-Dora and its outer camps. What is important to note is that the prisoners were expendable items within the large and competing bureaucracies of the system. Whereas their lives are now commemorated and not to be forgotten, they were numbers on tally sheets of matriculation and extinction within the camp's administration.

Not even the figures of those in the camp and the numbers of their deaths are accurate, for, naturally, the documents from Mittelbau-Dora, its outer camps, and Mittelwerk are not complete. However, the total count of sixty thousand prisoners is taken as the closest estimate of those going through the camp in the years of its operation. As we have noted, approximately twenty thousand of these prisoners died in Mittelbau-Dora and the outer camps. Questions remain about the accuracy of death counts. How were those who died on transports and after being sent to such end-of-the-road camps as Bergen-Belsen and Majdanek counted? Or were they?

The citizens of Nordhausen were not sheltered from the camp, although it was held in secrecy. Hundreds of them worked as civilians alongside the prisoners, and many more hundreds saw the prisoners being transported or walking from work site to work site. How they were to integrate memories of what they had seen and experienced into their postwar lives was in the domain of their psyches, their consciences, and their political leaders.

3. An End and a Beginning

The end of the war and events in Nordhausen in the battle's final days influence even today the way in which the Mittelbau-Dora memorial is integrated into the local community. While the memorial draws a national and international array of visitors, the townspeople of Nordhausen and the Thuringia area are those most likely to participate in the lectures, meetings, and events held at the site. This makes it critical for the memorial staff to place the events and gear the exhibit to the context of local memory and perceptions of what happened in those times. As we shall see in this chapter, the war left devastation in its wake for both the Nazis, who had started it, and the people of various nationalities, who were the victims. The degree to which the public history of the Gedenkstätte Mittelbau-Dora represented the reality of what townspeople knew and experienced during the last years of the war may well have depended upon a number of things. How well did it express horror, grief, guilt? How did it point to a way forward for victims and perpetrators, who were sometimes the same people?

Strategic Bombing in Germany

There were two different philosophies of strategic bombing held by allies the United States and Britain. The United States held the point of view that the air forces could bomb the resources on which the war depended, such as factories, ammunition dumps, and air fields, independent of forces on the ground.

> By 1939, a theory of employment had been derived. In brief, it may be described as follows: the most efficient way to defeat an enemy is to destroy, by means of

bombardment from the air, his war-making capacity, the means to this end is to identify by scientific analysis those particular elements of his war potential the elimination of which will cripple either his war machine or his will to continue the conflict; these elements having been identified, they should be attacked by large masses of bombardment aircraft flying in formation, at high altitude, in daylight, and equipped with precision bombsights that will make possible the positive identification and destruction of "pinpoint" targets; finally such bombing missions having been carried out, the enemy, regardless of his strength in armies and navies, will lack the means to support continued military action.[1]

As conceived by the British, in particular Viscount Hugh Trenchard, such bombing would "incinerate the civilian population and force the survivors to flee to an as yet unbombed city. The bombers would then devastate that city, creating a larger refugee population that, having made their way to the next city, would be blasted again."[2] Thus, the civilians would lose their will to fight and force their governments to sue for peace or surrender. This strategy has been defined as depending on the "logic of punishment."[3]

German bombs fell in World War II for the first time on Poland in September 1939 when 1,150 sorties terrorized the country, bringing a rapid end to effective resistance. The first German attack by bombing occurred on British soil in 1940 in the Orkney Islands during an attempt to mine the harbor there. The Royal Air Force retaliated immediately by bombing the island of Sylt in the North Sea. On May 14, 1940, the Germans marched into the Low Countries, and "on a strictly defined triangle north of the Maas bridges, the bombers unloaded ninety-seven tons of high explosives consisting of 158 bombs of 500 pounds and 1,150 of 100 pounds." From that time onward, each side escalated bombing raids and increasingly viewed civilian targets as an opportunity to attack the other's population and, in theory, break the morale of the enemy.[4] The year 1940 saw the German bombing of Rotterdam, Liege, and cities in England, whereby Coventry became the most notorious for its civilian casualties.

Bombing that destroyed great areas completely became known as area bombing. Among the advocates of area bombing were also those who were not only class conscious but dismissive of the working class. In order to endorse such a bombing campaign, it had to be preceded by determining the civilian targets as "others." The British had not lost their hatred of the German "Hun" since the battles of World War I. It was not difficult to paint the Germans as some kind of monsters, and as scholars have discovered, "mistreatment of civilians is more likely to occur in conflicts in which belligerents view each other as 'barbaric' or subhuman."[5] They wanted to save the mansions of industrialists but bomb to annihilation the neighborhoods of the industrial workers. The rationale was that the workers were the production force for war material. If they were disheartened by bearing the brunt of the bombing, their work would be disrupted and they would lose the will to continue to see their country in combat.

The bombing of London was the most severe to date when it commenced on September 7, 1940. The Germans dropped 13,000 tons of high explosives and 12,000 incendiary canisters.[6] Two months later, the German attack on Coventry took 554 civilian lives. Even with retaliation, the Germans were dropping three times as many bombs on Britain as the RAF on Germany.

British plans were on the books to bomb for the purpose of demoralizing civilian populations: "We never had the least doubts that sooner or later the gloves would come off, but our policy was to gain time—to improve our own defenses and to build up the great force of bombers."[7] As the bombing of cities continued, and the RAF eventually gained the upper hand, the United States entered the war. A new consideration of the bombing raids and how to conduct them was on the agenda. The U.S. military had entered the war with no intention of targeting civilian populations, and they made that clear to the British.

The Casablanca Conference that was held in Morocco on January 14–24, 1943, established the joint United States Army Air Force (USAAF)/RAF strategic bombing campaign and planned the approach to the war in Europe. Churchill, de Gaulle, and Roosevelt participated. For the first time, it established the possibility of American bombing of civilian populations as a strategy of war. Four "Lines of Action" were presented in the plan. In addition to bombing electric power systems, transportation systems, and oil and petroleum systems, the fourth was "undermining of German morale by air attack of civil concentrations."[8] It is interesting to note the use of language that obscures the fact that human lives are at stake in this decision. This obfuscation was even more apparent when the escalation of bombing while increasing targets of civilian populations totally eliminated rhetoric that would have described it as such, called instead "industrial area targets."

The United States by 1943 endorsed the British position of bombing civilian targets without reservation, a position they had resisted for several years, although the military hid that from the American public.[9] The RAF had found that night bombing was the way to avoid too many planes being shot down and suggested that plan to the United States, but the U.S. Air Force offered another plan: British planes could continue to fly at night, but American planes could fly during the day before and after the major bombing attacks with low-flying aircraft and carry incendiary bombs. Despite pressure from the British to fly at night, American bombers flew in tight formation during the day and hit what they called "industrial targets" that were, in fact, civilian centers.[10]

America's total involvement in the civilian bombing activities was demonstrated in the following way: "In 1943, the theoretical became reality when the Chemical Warfare Corps built mock German and Japanese working-class neighborhoods in the Utah desert. Exact replicas of the working-class 'rent barracks' of Berlin's densely populated 'Red' (socialist and communist) districts and the industrial towns of the Rhine were built. They were then bombed and studied in excruciating detail. Armed with the test results, including proof of the utility of the new anti-personnel M-69 napalm ammunition, the Allies bombed into rubble more 1920's socialist and modernist utopias than Nazi villas."[11]

The bombing of cities did not destroy Germans' will to fight. Nor could the Allies continue the bombing raids indefinitely. On June 13, 1944, a week after the Allies landed on the beaches of Normandy, a new element was introduced into the war: V-1 missiles. Civilian casualties increased, especially in London and other large cites, and the Allies took increasingly harder positions.

The culmination of the bombing raids occurred in July 1943 when Hamburg was bombed with a resulting fifty thousand people killed and the city destroyed. Dresden, more easily remembered, was bombed on February 13–14, 1945. The number of deaths reached thirty-five thousand in the firestorm that racked the city. There were as many as eighty-seven thousand casualties. Here the second wave of bombings was carried out by the RAF. However, as the news spread internationally and the public learned of the bombing of Dresden, opinion turned against both the Americans and the British.

Perhaps there was also concern about the possibility of being charged in postwar trials with crimes against humanity.[12] Tension was building, as some urged the continuation of the area bombing and others urged its cessation. Churchill, who had bragged to Roosevelt about the RAF's intention to produce nine hundred thousand civilian dead, one million seriously injured, and twenty-five million homeless, perhaps was becoming nervous. In a communiqué to his chiefs of staff on March 28, 1945, he wrote, "The destruction of Dresden remains a serious query against the conduct of Allied bombing." There is a need "for more precise concentration on military objectives . . . rather than on mere acts of terror and wanton destruction, however impressive." At the insistence of his staff, the communiqué was altered to a more self-serving statement: "We must see that our attacks do not do more harm to ourselves in the long run than they do to the enemy's immediate war effort."[13] After the war, it became a major theme in the Soviet bloc that the bombing of the eastern cities of Germany at the very end of the war had another purpose.

> As major points of attack were cities such as Berlin, Magdeburg, Leipzig, Chemnitz (Karl-Marx-Stadt), Dresden, Breslau (Wroclaw), Poznan, Halle, Erfurt, Weimar, Gotha and Eisenach. Officially the reason was given that it was to protect the advance of the Soviet troops. As Charles Portal, the head of the RAF, said, however, the heavy bombers were scarcely suited for these attacks and attacks on the hydroelectric plants would have been more useful, to which Churchill said, that their purpose was not to help in these troop movements but had to do with the destruction of East Germany. . . . Even Stalin would be impressed.[14]

According to Sebald, 131 towns and cities were attacked in the last years of the war, many completely destroyed. As many as six hundred thousand German civilians were killed or injured, and five hundred thousand homes were destroyed.[15] Nordhausen was one of these targets, the seventh in that list of severe bombing.[16]

The Bombing of Nordhausen

On the afternoon of April 3, 1945, the Royal Air Force of Britain began bombing Nordhausen, a thousand-year-old town or small city of forty thousand people near the center of Germany, known for its tobacco and liquor industries. These industries were often owned by members of the Jewish population, who in 1938 and 1939 were ruthlessly expelled. The first official mention of the Jewish population had appeared in 1290, when Kaiser Rudolf I wrote that this population was the most persistent population group in Nordhausen since its inception in around the year 1000. In 1933, there were 438 Jews living in Nordhausen according to the register, and they had a synagogue and a cemetery in the city.

The raid continued into April 4 and the following night. The target was the town itself, not the camp of Mittelbau-Dora except for the Boelcke-Kaserne. Almost all of the deaths were civilians, eighty-eight hundred, or 22 percent of the prewar population, and another nineteen thousand, almost 50 percent of the population were wounded.[17] City buildings, churches, parks, and monuments were destroyed in addition to private homes. Refugees who had gathered in or were passing through the town and slave laborers working there or being held in sick bays were among the dead and wounded; their shelter was even more insecure than that of the town's people.

Compared to the bombing of Coventry, which was still recognized as a terrible attack by the Germans on unarmed civilians, the Nordhausen bombing had killed almost sixteen times as many people! Even coming as it did after Dresden and Churchill's divided view of the usefulness of such a strategy, the raid was horrendous and can only be seen as a further attempt to break the will of the people. The targets that were soon in flames were most of the buildings in the city center, including the city's churches, administration buildings, and even the city hospital. According to an eyewitness account, "On the 3rd and 4th of April the hospital was completely destroyed. The chief of staff was killed and I, as the doctor in charge, had to take control of the organization."[18] Somehow the patients were transferred with farmers' carts and any transportation at hand to various safer places, at first a large guesthouse and then the tunnels in Dora. Infants were carried from the burning city two at a time in the arms of the nurses to a religious retreat house, Diakonissen Mutterhaus.

Following the standard Allied strategy, American bombers came in the days before and after the major British attacks to drop high-explosive bombs (*Sprengbomben*). Although the major bombing was done by the Royal Air Force, many people in Nordhausen to this day believe that the bombing of Nordhausen was an act of the USAAF.[19] Perhaps they confused the American troops who came to occupy the city in the first days after the bombing with those who had done the bombing, or perhaps they didn't differentiate among the various airplanes attacking the city. The Americans, flying by day, would have been more visible than the British flying at night.

During the days before the bombing, as the American infantry troops neared, the city administration of Nordhausen was busy. Civil staff destroyed personnel records and other documents that might have incriminated the city's leadership. Then these officials published in the Nordhausen paper on April 10: "Tattered white flags (Schandfetzen) are shameful rags." The order went out that any on display indicating the willingness to surrender had to be removed. With these orders in place, the city administrators fled, leaving only one of the city council members, Fritz Sturm, as interim mayor in charge of welcoming the invaders. As the Americans came into the city, the combination of the concentration camp horrors and the absence of white flags infuriated the soldiers: they were in a truly Nazi city.[20]

There was little resistance to the taking of Nordhausen. The troops assigned to defend the city were part of the German marines who had been trained in Denmark and had not seen battle on the ground. They were ill-prepared and disappeared as the Americans came into town. Stragglers or, perhaps, members of the Volkssturm fired on the approaching soldiers sporadically, but there was no need for door-to-door fighting in any part of the city or its surrounding hamlets. Although ten Volkssturm battalions had sworn allegiance to Hitler in November 1944 in the Nordhausen area, how many were still available in April 1945 is not known.[21]

The Boelcke-Kaserne was the one target that was assumed to be of military interest: it was hit repeatedly. It was located in the southeast corner of the town near the rail yards and housed French and Russian prisoners, who had been there as slave laborers for a machine production manufacturer, Mabag, since 1942. They lived and worked on-site. In 1944, however, six thousand new slave laborers arrived. They were sent to work on new tunnel construction on the other side of the Kohnstein from the Dora tunnels to build new armaments for the Junkers Werke, transported from the Boelcke-Kaserne on a small train on a spur of tracks designed for this particular destination.[22]

The Boelcke-Kaserne was divided by an electrified fence to separate the slave laborers' living quarters from those no longer able to work: the human refuse of the Mittelbau camp. Many of these inmates of Dora and the outer camps who were beyond any kind of useful war-related activity were sent to this holding area where they received provisions insufficient to sustain life and waited for their deaths among those already so dispatched. For this part of the complex, there was no organization or care for the prisoners who were left on heaps of filthy straw to die. The vision and threats of what further horror awaited them when they could no longer work were to serve as extra "motivation" to those laborers still being used to build tunnels or work in various enterprises around Nordhausen.[23]

The famous picture of the corpses lined up outside the Boelcke-Kaserne is often assumed to depict those killed by the Nazis, but it is a little more complicated. Many had been dead before the bombing raids, when many of their SS guards and some *Kapos* had run to save themselves, leaving the prisoners who were not able to move in the straw to molder. However, some others were killed by the raid itself, and although they had been left to die and would have succumbed shortly, their deaths were actually caused by the bombing. In total, 450 prisoners died in the first raid and about 1,000 more in the second.[24] Many of them were Jewish and had come to Mittelbau-Dora on transports from Auschwitz and Gross Rosen as the Russians approached from the East. Others were slave laborers from the occupied countries who had outlived their cost-effectiveness to the Nazi regime.

It is quite possible that some prisoners from the slave laborers' camp or its sick bay were also there at the time of the bombing. There were certainly babies and children on the side of the fence where the laborers lived. Among the slave laborers, having children was no anomaly. Some women were already pregnant when they were taken into Germany; others became pregnant through the careless and often violent relationships endemic to the camp. There was even some motivation to become pregnant, for as late as 1943, young women expecting children were sent home to have their babies. By the height of the war, this was no longer the case.[25] Testimony that comes from

Father Edward P. Doyle, who was with the 104th Infantry as they entered Nordhausen, mentions women and children: "I recall vividly . . . we took pieces of carpet and they became a litter, if you will, or a sheet or a door, any way by which we could carry these bodies and lay them out and find any living among them before we prepared for the mass grave. I saw men and women—some deny it—but I saw for myself women, and somewhere in my mind there is always a picture of a child, a bloated child, which has lived with me all these years."[26]

The bombing of Nordhausen left the city in ruins. Seventy-two percent of its buildings were totally destroyed. Landmarks and monuments no longer existed. Only a very few Germans living in the state of Thuringia still believed that the Führer, Hitler, would at this late date find his way to victory by use of the wonder weapons being produced in their own environs, and even those few were finally disillusioned as they saw the devastation. For the entire war, the town had suffered few direct attacks on its geographic space.[27] Of course, every family felt a cost of the war in some way: shortened rations, the loss of loved ones in the military or in cities that had been bombed, disrupted family lives. Now there was the total trauma of disorder, refugees roaming the streets and byways, the total disruption of food provision and water supplies. Most of all, along with loss of their habitat, virtually everyone had lost

Nordhausen a week after the bombing in April 1945. (Stadtarchiv Nordhausen, Kurt Hermann Collection, Kurt Hermann, photographer)

Nordhausen a week after the bombing in April 1945. (Stadtarchiv Nordhausen, Kurt Hermann Collection, Kurt Hermann, photographer)

family and friends in the bombing. The citizens of Nordhausen were bereft and in shock.

On the other hand, the bombing of Nordhausen brought a small window of opportunity to escape for a few of the slave laborers from the many occupied countries of Europe and the prisoners of war. Those in impressed labor on farms and in city enterprises looked for the right moment to slide into the milling masses of people in the city and find a way out. Some asked for help from the local people, but very few received it.

The Death March

At the time of the bombing of Nordhausen, preparations were already under way to evacuate the main camp of Dora and certain subcamps. One of these evacuations took place from April 4 to April 7, in which Dora prisoners, as well as those in subcamps in the region, were sent north and east on trains to other camps or on foot in the hopes that they would die of exhaustion in random places rather than be found by the invaders in the camps.

Death marches were under way throughout Germany. The problem facing the Nazi officials was what to do with the hundreds of thousands of prisoners who could testify against them in trials in case the war was truly lost. If they were found on the grounds of the concentration camps that now dotted the landscape, it would certainly lead to terrible revenge on the part of the Allies. On the other hand, if by some chance the war continued, it could be supplied only by the slave labor to which the German government had become addicted. A middle ground was to exhaust those prisoners still alive to the point of death and possibly find a use for those who against all odds would survive.

The number of guards needed to lead the death marches or transports was insufficient. Those employed in the camps were prone to saving themselves and leaving the prisoners to find their own way to anonymity and safety. Others were called into service, including *Kapos* from the camp, Hitler youth, and members of the Volkssturm.[28] There was little prior agreement about the routes various groups of prisoners should take on their death marches. It seemed to depend on the availability of transport, roads, and places to camp, on the one hand, and the availability of watchmen, on the other. Groups combined, separated, and recombined.

In one of the more horrific episodes of the death marches, trains from both the North and the South arrived on April 9, 1945, after many detours because of air attacks, at the station in Mieste, a town in the county of Gardelegen. There were cattle cars on the tracks in front of the station with prisoners from Niedersachswerfen carrying prisoners from the outer camps of Mittelbau-Dora. All together, there were more than two thousand prisoners from six-teen European nations from the outer camps of Mittelbau-Dora who had been herded together on the railroad cars.[29] During this transport, dozens of prisoners died from the terrible conditions and their total exhaustion and starvation, and they were thrown from the cars. In Mieste, the transports stood two to four days without regular food or care given to the prisoners who were imprisoned in them. The prisoners who tried to find something for themselves to eat were shot by the SS.

Some of the citizens of Mieste attempted to provide food for the prisoners, but could not find enough for the huge number that had suddenly descended on their railroad station. People from the Nazi Party in the town and even Luftwaffe (Air Force) soldiers were brought in from nearby airfields to guard the prisoners. On the evening of April 11, the SS put together a transport to bring the prisoners to Gardelegen. The American troops (the 102nd Infantry Division) were only a hundred kilometers away. Farmers were ordered to bring wagons to carry the sick and the weak. All those who could in any way walk were driven in three groups on foot or in wagons. On the way, those who could not continue were hit by the guards or shot. Many prisoners were able to escape during the forty-kilometer death march to Gardelegen.

On April 12, about twelve hundred surviving prisoners were brought to the horse stalls of the cavalry school in Gardelegen. The Nazi Party county leader, a man named Gerhard Thiele, ordered that the prisoners be killed, as directed by Himmler himself. He organized containers of gasoline and straw, placed the straw in the huge barn (*Feldscheune*) of Isenschnibbe, and ordered gasoline poured on the straw. As soon as the prisoners were inside, the straw was set afire. Each prisoner who managed to get to the door or crawl under the floor of the barn was shot. The soldiers threw hand grenades into the barn to finish the job. On the night of April 14, the SS and those who had perpetrated the act sneaked away from the terrible scene of death. The next day, the foreign slave laborers of the town of Gardelegen and the surrounding area were forced to drag the bodies out of the charred ruins and bury them in mass graves and get rid of all signs of the massacre. More than seven hundred corpses were already buried when the work was halted due to the capitulation of the town. The German military commander had been brought from the North to Gardelegen, but he realized the hopelessness of further defense of the town and had gone to the American Army in surrender.[30]

On the next day, April 15, American soldiers on a routine patrol near the site of the massacre discovered the *Feldscheune* and its hideous contents. More than three hundred half-burned bodies were still smoldering, and nearby was the evidence of quickly dug mass graves. Perhaps the capitulation of Gardelegen, which came suddenly as the Americans entered, left no time to hide the evidence, or perhaps there were other reasons. There was no sign of the SS or others who had committed this massacre. Investigations showed that the town's Nazi leader had taken part, but he was never found. His wife was taken into custody and put in the town jail, where she apparently hung herself. Other people who were implicated committed suicide, as well, including the officer who had ordered the deed and the men who had shot the prisoners as they tried to escape.[31]

In total, twenty-eight prisoners were able to survive the massacre: eleven Poles, eight Soviet prisoners, three Hungarians, five Frenchmen, and a German. Many prisoners had escaped before reaching the barn, and some found the American soldiers and told them what had happened. The Americans had the bodies exhumed from the shallow mass graves and found that more than one thousand prisoners of many nationalities burned alive. The commander of the American 102nd Infantry Division ordered that the entire male population of Gardelegen march together to witness the terrible scene. The mayors of all neighboring communities were also brought in under guard of the American troops to look at the half-burned victims of their Nazi regime. And they received an unmistakable order: they must tell their fellow citizens what they had seen. After that, the citizens of Gardelegen were brought to the area around the *Feldscheune* to prepare a cemetery.[32]

The soldiers of an American battalion rounded up able-bodied citizens at bayonet point to do the work at the site. The instructions were clear: all victims would have a worthy grave. The citizens of Gardelegen had to plot the individual graves, line up the bodies for burial, and place either a cross or a star of David on each one. There were many Jewish prisoners among those murdered, identified by the numbers on their arms, assumed to be placed there in extermination camps.[33] Many graves were not identified with name or number due to the condition of the bodies. Since that time, identification has been determined for the graves of a number of Polish prisoners, many Soviet, and some Hungarian, Roma, French, Belgian, Italian, Yugoslavian, Dutch, Spanish, Mexican, and German prisoners.

The order further directed that each family in the town was forever duty bound to care for a nameless grave. In the area around the cemetery there would be a white fence. After everything was completed, the Americans held a military ceremony of honor over the graves. The chief of staff of the division, Col. George P. Lynch, expressed the feelings and thoughts of all American soldiers as he said to the citizens of Gardelegen: "You have lost the respect of the civilized world."[34] The order of the division commander was to remain in force in perpetuity and was to be written into the town's charter. On the edge of the cemetery a large display was built that repeats these directions in English and German with the words: "These graves [will be] forever kept as green as the memories of these unfortunate souls will be kept in the hearts of freedom-loving men everywhere." (The bodies were mistakenly identified in this original display as Allied prisoners of war.)

Gardelegen is only one example of the terrible end of the war for many prisoners of the Nazi state. For the vast majority of the inmates of Mittelbau-Dora, the death march came to an end wherever they happened to be. It is not possible to say how many were murdered on the terrible and useless journeys throughout the countryside preceding the war's end. Each outer camp had its own route to take, and often the routes were determined while the march was already in progress. Some wandered back and forth, taking cattle cars when possible; other journeys came to an abrupt end when the SS abandoned the groups to their fate and ran away. Still other prisoners were massacred along the way either through shootings or, as in the case of Gardelegen, by a mass event.

The guards were threatened with being sent to the front, which was now around Berlin, if they did not do their duty in leading the prisoners to death. They were not to help or give aid in any way. Some guards "hired" prisoners to carry their heavy backpacks for them for a crust of bread, however. All the while, the prisoners and the guards were aware of the shooting of those who lagged behind.

> I saw how a prisoner stayed behind in order to take care of his diarrhea. He didn't have the strength to bend his knees and tried to do it while standing. He had let his pants fall so that I could see his spindly legs and he stood with his back to the ditch. Then I heard in the woods the bark of a dog and some SS people with machine pistols under their arms came out. It was the executioner of the prisoners' line of march. One of them saw the prisoner standing with his back turned and bellowed: "Look at that pig!" Lightning quick he had pistol ready and shot the prisoner down. I don't know how I made my way to the front of the line again, for I kept hearing the shot and seeing the prisoner fall.[35]

For some guards, the process might have been filled with fear and indecision. For the fanatics, it was an opportunity to follow orders to the bitter end.

The Occupation of Nordhausen by American Troops

Elements of the First Army, 104th Infantry Division, the "Timberwolves," working with and supported by the 3rd Armored Division, the "Spearhead Division," and troops from the 2nd Battalion of the 414th Regiment, were making their way from the West to Nordhausen in the early days of April 1945. Other troops were meeting resistance in the mountains of the nearby areas. Because U.S. supplies were short, Wehrmacht soldiers and supplies, including vehicles, were captured as the American troops advanced.[36] They were intent on moving fast, so the soldiers alternately rode and walked, requisitioning farm carts along the way: anything that would speed their way.[37]

> Actually, because of the nature of armored warfare, every man in the division saw something of action during the long drives. Supply trains were ambushed during their important trips back and forth over the roads of conquest; common post soldiers found themselves battling bypassed Nazi troops, and rear echelon maintenance men helped to round up prisoners of war.

Theoretically each of the spearheads was of the same basic composition. Due to a changing situation in action, this was not always the case, but deviation was the exception and not the rule.

Reconnaissance elements in light tanks and armored cars invariably rode the point of the attack until opposition was encountered. Tanks and infantry, always well supported by artillery, tank-destroyers, anti-aircraft units and engineers supplied the Sunday punch. Communications were maintained by signal men well to the front, and medical corps detachments also traveled with the probing spearheads in order to hasten evacuation of the wounded.

Driving immediately behind these forward elements was the command post, often within small arms range of the enemy; the heavy artillery, represented by attached 155mm self-propelled units, and the division reserve ready to go into action on call.

Division Trains were at the shaft of the spearhead. Here were the administrators, the supply, maintenance and medical headquarters which catered to frontline elements. In action, this entire phalanx of power was highly mobile and fluid of composition.[38]

The available troops were used as needed by their commanders and divided and subdivided as they entered the suburbs of Nordhausen where no previous U.S. troops had been. Prisoners of war were taken along the way, and the engineers repaired bomb craters and cleared roadblocks as they went along. Among the first reports of the discovery of the concentration camp Mittelbau-Dora is the following:

A huge camp capable of housing 30 to 40 thousand DP's [displaced persons] was found adjacent to the V-Bomb factory. Several hundred slave laborers, who were too weak to leave, remained in the camp, and several hundred refugees were found living in the factory itself where a large kitchen was set up and a hospital was in operation. Thousands of the slave laborers who were able to walk were marched off by the SS prior to arrival of U.S. troops. No workers had ever been allowed to leave the camp and when they became too weak to work were allowed to die and their bodies cremated at a crematorium within the grounds, and the ashes dumped into large holes. Reports indicate that approximately 150 bodies were cremated per day and there were about 30 corpses piled on the floor ready for the ovens. The bodies showed many signs of beatings, torture and starvation.

All camps were organized for the care and feeding of the inmates. Civil Officials were contacted and proclamations posted in the towns.[39]

The troops did not quite understand what they had found. They were concerned about the safety of the wonder weapons that they found at the site. A cable sent from the camp declared: "Night, guarded V1 and V2 plant and store in mountion [*sic*] cave vic. D-34633Q. At least 60 V-1s there intact as of last midnight."[40] At about the same time, the 3rd Armored Division troops were entering the city of Nordhausen, having encountered heavy fire outside of town but only light resistance in the town itself. Combat Command B under Brig. Gen. Truman E. Boudinot was the first to discover the Boelcke-Kaserne. "Hundreds of corpses lay sprawled over the acres of the big compound. More hundreds filled the great barracks. They lay in contorted heaps, half stripped, mouths gaping in the dirt and straw; or they were piled naked like cordwood, in the corners and under the stairways."[41]

The assumptions about who the prisoners were developed from the accounts that individuals could give them; there were no documents immediately at hand. The Third Army assumed that these beings whom they had found were "political prisoners of the Third Reich, German as well as other European nationals."[42] The records show a great deal of confusion about the various camps, which were sometimes described as the camp in Nordhausen, sometimes as the factory, sometimes as Mittelwerk. In reality, they had come upon the Boelcke-Kaserne in the city and Mittelbau-Dora about four miles away. Other troops were discovering the outer camps, most of which were devoid of their inmates, who were being massacred on death marches. No one was available who understood the entire concentration camp system or its manifestation in the Nordhausen region of the Harz Mountains. The townspeople knew of the slave laborers and the camps, but not in detail. Prisoners of war, SS officers, and others who were being picked up knew only the part of the system they had themselves experienced. No wonder the American soldiers and their commanders were producing contradictory descriptions of what they were discovering.

In some tunnels, the troops found the hidden treasures of German museums, archives, churches, and synagogues. For decades, most were not completely understood, and rumors circulated about their meaning and value.[43] Those with the most information about what had been hidden in Nordhausen seemed to be escaping into the chaos that was the war zone. They were not easy to find.

For the population itself, the reality of the slave labor that had supported their country and this regime could no longer be denied. As the bombing began, townspeople ran to shelter in caves and tunnels already occupied by the prisoners who were also hoping to escape their long and deadly servitude. When the bombing stopped, able-bodied workers either were forced to take part in the reclamation of the city or willingly volunteered.

For one such young girl, Ilse Kirchhoff, the war had been a nightmare. Never in favor of the Nazi regime, her father, who ran a very efficient little mill on a tributary of the Zorge River between the city and the camp, had been called upon to provide grain and flour for the camps and other Nazi requisitions. He made deliveries to Mittelbau-Dora and knew of the conditions there.

Ilse had an immediate concern. As refugees came into the city from the East, young girls and boys wanted to be confirmed. This was no longer done under the Nazis, but a local Protestant minister decided he would do it. There wasn't time to learn much catechism, but the children were prepared after a wartime fashion.

Ilse's grandmother had been confirmed. She went to church only to have the small glass of wine offered on communion day. She felt it was an abomination that the wealthy ladies and gentlemen of the town entered by a separate door and sat in pews separated from the riffraff. They also received their communion separately from the others. Grandma went to show that she could take part as well as any citizen of Nordhausen.

On the day of the confirmation, April 1, 1945, Ilse was in the church as bombing started. It was not the major bombing of Nordhausen, but a hint of what was to come. She and the others hid in the church, terrified, and emerged unharmed, but somehow that day became an important event in her life. Even today, although not a regular churchgoer, Ilse finds comfort in knowing that in church she is following a family tradition.

People started to build fortifications. It did not help. Between the third and the fourth of April, the British bombers, some flown by Canadian and Polish pilots, destroyed the city. They didn't reach as far as Krimderode, where the Kirchhoffs lived, but soon there were street fighting and tanks even in their neighborhood, on the edge of the city. The German home forces bombed bridges and roads to make it difficult for the Allies, but it only was a delay. They made their way beyond the city and found Mittelbau-Dora. The camp was liberated on April 11.

Ilse had reason to go to the Nordhausen hospital. Her sister was confined there with blood poisoning. She had to have a typhoid shot in her breastbone in order to qualify for food rations, which she still remembers as terribly painful. She too was well aware of the injuries and illnesses suffered by the survivors of the camps, the labor groups, and the citizens of Nordhausen. All of them were being treated at the hospital.

During this time, a boy walking down the street in front of their house in his "zebra" suit was looking for an open gate. The Kirchhoffs' was open. He came to the door and explained that he had survived the camp and had just gotten out of the hospital with typhus. He was still very sick, hungry, and weak. Ilse's mother took him in and put him to bed in an extra room. She asked Ilse to get a picture that was stored in the attic and clean it up to make the room more homey. She fed the young fellow diluted goat's milk and nursed him back to health.

As stated, Mr. Kirchhoff owned a flour mill, and in his deliveries to the camp, he had tried to do something for a few of the prisoners with whom he came in contact. Now he devoted himself to the boy in the back bedroom and talked to him about the war, Germany, and what had happened during the time behind barbed wire.

The boy's name was Sandor Strickberger, and he was a Hungarian Jew. From Auschwitz, like thousands of others, he had been sent to Germany to die in slave labor under the motto "Vernichtung durch Arbeit." In the last months of the war, the German authorities had decided that it made sense to kill the Jews by working them to death in the name of saving the Reich, so they had determined that a life span of three months would provide a cost-effective addition to the current labor force.

As Sandor recovered, Mr. Kirchhoff continued his long talks with him about the German people and Nazism. He wanted the boy to know that not every German was like the SS he had met in the camps. When Sandor recovered, he wanted to move on. He heard that Hungarians were meeting in Bergen-Belsen and would return together to Hungary. He decided to try that route and left the care of the Kirchhoffs. He promised to stay in touch and to write to them, but the Kirchhoffs never heard from him again. There was no way to find their "Bubi" in the aftermath of the war, but something had changed forever.

For Ilse, the camp was real. It became an icon. It was where she had to go to mourn the horror and idiocy of war. She began her pilgrimages with work crews that cleaned the camp and weeded the *Appellplatz*. She continued through the years of communism as the camp became a place of ceremony and function. She continues to this day as it becomes a place of historical significance. For her, it is a place of remembrance: of a time, an era, a friend, of things that should never have happened but did, and a lesson of how one behaves in the midst of overwhelming grief. Her friends do not share her commitment, but she finds her own way unapologetically, clear in her own purpose.

The exact numbers of those held in various degrees of slavery for the German state are not available for Nordhausen and the area surrounding it. Throughout Germany, there were more than seven million foreign laborers in 1944.[44] In Nordhausen by the end of the war, there were impressed farm laborers, factory workers, and manual laborers from a variety of countries. These impressed laborers were held in various degrees of servitude, but it can safely be said that virtually none was in Germany of his or her own free will.

The Labor Ministry of the Reich requisitioned needed workers who were then picked up in occupied countries through the prison systems quite specifically by giving the number of workers needed and the kinds of work they should be prepared to do. The men and sometimes women for these jobs were then assembled from the populations of detention camps, prisons, or through street *razzias,* or raids.[45]

The people of Nordhausen had been aware of the "foreign workers" and to some extent of the "zebras" of the camps, those wearing the striped uniforms made of heavy cotton in gray and blue stripes. The workers were often in the city as they were led to factories or plants, or as they walked under guard to the trains requisitioned to carry them to places in the mountainous region where they would blast new tunnels.

One gets the sense of the variety of groups in servitude to the Nazi state by reading various accounts. Not all accounts are complete, and some put a certain slant on the information that makes the practice of slave labor less odious. One such description that omits the thousands of prisoners of dozens of nationalities held in the concentration camp reports instead some of the more favored positions that slave laborers held as seen regularly by the townspeople: "A striking appearance in the city were the different groups of foreign prisoners. There were English prisoners of war. Some of these did light work in the tobacco industry. French prisoners of war were placed in small groups in small and handwork enterprises."[46] It took many years for the people of Nordhausen to "remember" that they had a more intimate knowledge of the prisoners, indeed had worked next to or even supervised them, observed them being transported in and about the city, had hired them from the SS for odd jobs in their own homes and gardens, and had seen them from their windows.[47] For those with no firsthand experience, there were enough stories and rumors going around the city for all to be aware of the imprisoned multitudes in their midst.[48]

Competition, as well as some cooperation, among the slave laborers and the townspeople became a postwar reality. During bombing raids, townspeople throughout the Harz Mountain areas sought refuge in the tunnels built by the concentration camp prisoners.[49] Various motivations determined the behavior among these groups. Some certainly felt fear of those who had been labeled criminals and a danger to society. They feared the violence associated with these creatures, their emaciated and hardened appearance, their desperation. They knew that rape and pillage were reactions of those who had been deprived for a long time and were the violent conditions of war in general. Others felt a sincere pity for those who had obviously suffered. They had empathy that came from their own losses, their own loved ones imprisoned under various circumstances, their religious or moral beliefs. Still others had no time for these reflections and were concerned for their own survival. Illness and disease were spreading throughout Nordhausen, and for the first time in the war years, food and water, household goods, and needs of daily living were in short supply.

The U.S. Army forces opened the city to the slave laborers for a kind of regulated looting. They were allowed to go into the stores and take clothing and bedding supplies. Soldiers with machine guns stood on the corners to be sure that this was kept within limits. The townspeople joined the refugees and former prisoners in the looting and to the extent possible were stopped by the American soldiers.[50]

The Burial of Dead Prisoners

The American troops reacted to the horror of the camps, particularly the Boelcke-Kaserne, with revulsion. They wanted the citizens of Nordhausen to take responsibility for what had happened and to acknowledge it in an intensely personal way. Therefore, the commander sent groups of soldiers with fixed bayonets into the city to requisition manpower. "Every able-bodied man in the town was warned if they're not at the camp to help they would be shot."[51] The men of Nordhausen were to bring with them their best sheet or tablecloth and to dress in their best clothing. According to the testimony of James Collins, a commander of the troops, "the 104th organized most of the males—or a goodly number of the males—left in Nordhausen to come out and dig trenches and carry the dead and bury the dead in these trenches."[52]

On April 13, the burial began and lasted several days; the men assigned to the job were not allowed to go home overnight. Only when the job was done were food transports allowed to enter the city and ration cards distributed.[53] There were many dead to be buried in Nordhausen, including the 1,278 victims of the Boelcke-Kaserne and thousands more from the city. The job lasted until April 16.[54]

Terry Allen, the commander of the Timberwolves, ordered his sanitation crew to stay behind until the dead could be collected and buried. "The Nordhauser, mostly old men, had to collect the corpses by hand and bury them in mass graves. The procession of the dead bodies will remain with the Nordhausers and the other observers their whole lives."[55] The irony of the situation was that the most involved Nazis were in hiding and some of the bearers of the dead were those who had been in opposition to the regime.[56] For all of the men of Nordhausen, forced at gunpoint if necessary to do this task, the danger of contracting disease was great. The corpses had been lying for days in rank conditions.

Conclusion

The juxtaposition of the two events, the bombing of Nordhausen and the liberation of the camp, came at almost the same time. Certainly, the people of Nordhausen felt unfairly victimized. This was a bombing raid targeted at civilians at the very end of the war, indeed when the end was in sight. It was seen as vengeance.

Although many of the townspeople knew of the camp, and hundreds had closer acquaintance through supplying it, working in it, or hiring prisoners, the citizens of Nordhausen had not decided directly to build the camp or to imprison the slave laborers. Even today, when the liberation of the camp is mentioned, it is not unusual to hear the negative reaction of townspeople. One man said to the authors with tears in his eyes, "Why don't you write about the bombing raids that killed all the people of Nordhausen?"

The dilemma of looking at the totality of experience in Nordhausen from 1943 to the summer of 1945 is found in the concepts of perpetrator and victim. Throughout the camp experience, especially by means of their indirect administration, those who suffered were in danger of becoming those who caused suffering. The bombing campaigns of World War II gradually escalated, first to include civilians, and then to terrorize civilians by targeting them. This occurred on both sides of the war, the Axis and the Allies. Less and less was the individual value of human life acknowledged, and more and more the objectives of war made human life expendable.

Denial of responsibility for the conditions that set this horror in motion is seen on all sides. The German people elected Hitler and supported his policies in overwhelming numbers until the consequences affected their own lives. They eventually felt powerless to change the circumstances in which their fellow humans were kept. It was easiest at the end of the war to remember their own unacknowledged losses or to compare them to the losses of others that they then diminished in magnitude. For the Allies, it was possible to manipulate discourse to avoid any responsibility for genocidal bombing missions that increasingly targeted populations of noncombatants. The impunity for crimes against humanity from air strikes was established and continues to play out in warfare to this day.

4. The Change of Command

Nordhausen was devastated by the April air raids just days before Allied troops arrived on April 11, 1945. Almost nine thousand people were killed: six thousand townspeople, fifteen hundred refugees, and thirteen hundred concentration camp prisoners.[1] That represented 14 percent of the prewar population, but Nordhausen's population had almost doubled by 1945 if one took into account those who had either been forcefully imprisoned in the camps and barracks or sought refuge from bombing elsewhere.[2] Tens of thousands were injured in the bombing raids on the city. Landmarks of the inner city were incinerated, including four churches and forty-six businesses and storefronts. Others were severely damaged.[3]

Many people were streaming in from Czechoslovakia and lands to the east and south. During the Hitler years, those with German ancestry were afforded privileges of German citizenship regardless of how long they had lived in Czechoslovakia. After the war, they were targets of revenge for the years of German occupation. Approximately eleven and a half million people defined as Germans were expelled from the eastern countries that had lived under German occupation, of whom two and a quarter million died in transit.[4]

The invading American Army had to push on after several days. They had used whatever equipment that they had to clear streets and fill in bomb craters. There were roadblocks to be removed and bridges to be repaired. Where this was not possible, bypasses were constructed to allow traffic to resume. As the Timberwolves went on to continue fighting in central Germany, they left only the 414th Infantry Regiment to continue the cleanup for the first few days.[5] This regiment was followed by the more permanent military government contingent determined to set up a civil structure that would endure. In Nordhausen, this temporary arrangement would have a short tenure, lasting only until the end of the war, for Nordhausen was to be under the control of the Soviet Union, within the Soviet Zone, as had been arranged under the Potsdam Accord before the war ended.

The Division of Germany and the Continued Bombing Campaign

The war ended in Nordhausen on April 11, 1945. President Roosevelt died the next day, leaving Harry Truman to take his place in the final days of the war. Truman had not been a confidant of Roosevelt and, in fact, was poorly briefed on the war. Roosevelt had said at one point, "I hardly know Truman."[6] It was up to Truman to carry on, and he did so by retaining the military personnel and following through on the treaties and agreements that were in place. Adolf Hitler killed himself on April 30, 1945, having appointed Grand Admiral Karl Dönitz as his successor and leaving General Field Marshall Alfred Jodl, operations chief of the German high command, to sign the surrender papers in Reims, France, a week later, on May 7. The Soviets had their own separate surrender ceremony on May 8 and celebrate the ninth as their victory day.

The Allies—the United States, Britain, France, and the Soviet Union—had been planning for the end of the war for several years and were in discussions about how the German land would be divided when and if victory was assured. There was a great deal of mutual distrust on the part of the Soviet Union toward the others and on the part of the United States, the British, and the French toward the Soviet Union.[7] Yet Roosevelt was more positively inclined toward Stalin than Churchill and led the Four Powers to agreements before his death.

The Yalta Conference held in February 1945 clarified the division between two spheres of influence in postwar German territory. The USSR would have the control of Poland and a good share of southeastern Europe, while the Western Powers would control three-quarters of prewar Germany. In the immediate postwar period, the Four Powers would share control of sectors of Berlin: the United States, Britain, and the USSR would each control about a third, with France a smaller part. A four-power Control Council shared the responsibility for governing occupied Germany, with various committees concerned with each country's specific interests. The USSR was insistent that all of its citizens would be repatriated despite their individual wishes.[8]

The Potsdam Conference was held in July and August 1945. France was excluded from the talks based on its ineffectual defense against the Germans and the collaboration of the Vichy government in the southern part of the country. Later Stalin, at the urging of the United States and Great Britain, reluctantly agreed to include France in the realm of the winners of the war. The division of territory led to a separation of Europe into two spheres that were seen, fairly or not, as "capitalist or socialist, West or East, free or unfree, democratic or folks-democratic. . . . [A] time of relaxation was followed by the Cold War. The remaining worthwhile goal was the peaceful coexistence of both halves of Europe."[9]

The war in Europe ended almost a month after Nordhausen was liberated, but the war in the Pacific raged on. Continuing the strategic bombing policy, American airpower focused on Tokyo, the first major target in February and early March, and under Truman's command continued in a campaign against all major Japanese cities. There were eighty-seven thousand dead in Tokyo alone on March 9–10 and a million homeless as a result of the incendiary bombing.[10] The atomic bomb, developed in competition to the Germans' own program of wonder weapons, was developed in secret, to the extent possible, and was deployed twice, in Hiroshima and Nagasaki, in August 1945. The war in Asia ended soon thereafter.

The American Occupation

By May 1945, tens of thousands of foreign slave laborers had been dispersed to their home countries from Dora and the outer camps.[11] Others were streaming into the city from areas where the fighting continued. The Mittelbau-Dora main camp was one of the logical places to put the refugees who had lived in the bombed-out town and those fleeing from the ongoing war. Other sites that were allocated to the displaced persons, the general term for all of those who happened to be in places that were not their hometowns or homelands, were the barracks of the recently freed slave laborers found in many different places around the city.

The eastern occupied countries that had suffered so terribly under Nazi rule and the ideology of the "master race" wanted Germans out of their lands as soon as possible. Several countries instituted expulsion policies and drove people they believed to be of German heritage, many so designated through the Nazis' Folks' List (*Volksliste*), from their borders.

> As a result of the shifting of Poland's frontiers agreed on at Potsdam, the expulsion of the *Volksdeutsche* from the Balkans, and the collective punishment visited upon the Sudeten Germans, some 15 million Germans were expelled in the postwar years, 2 million from Silesia, Pomerania, and East Prussia, 3 million from Czechoslovakia, nearly 2 million from Poland and the USSR; and a further

2.7 million from Yugoslavia, Romania, and Hungary. . . . [T]he majority ended up in Western Germany (especially Bavaria) where as late as 1960, some 28 percent of the federal government employees were *Vertriebene* (expellees).[12]

Nordhausen had little housing because of the bombing, and the decision was made to house people in usable empty barracks at the Dora main camp, where some enterprising people had spontaneously taken up residence. New barracks were planned to increase capacity for six thousand more people. Everyone had to help in the restructuring of the camp, its disinfection, and its cleaning. Before refugees could move in, they were isolated for fourteen days to be sure they had no contagious disease, as epidemics were rampant, including the scourge of typhus.

Many of the members of military governments throughout Germany were seasoned Allied soldiers who had grown old, battle-weary, or shell-shocked, or were wounded and not fit for active duty. Whether this was the case in Nordhausen is not known. It is known, however, that some of these men approached their jobs with feelings of anger and vengeance for their German populations. Despite their attitudes, they did their jobs.

The Western Allies' Supreme Headquarters Allied Expeditionary Forces (SHAEF) was responsible for the day-to-day management of the area in the period between the liberation of the town and the surrender of Germany. A military detachment, one of 130 such provisional units used in Germany to maintain civil services as the army pushed forward, remained in Nordhausen. William McElroy, captain of the military government, became the military governor and dismissed those remaining city leaders who had not fled. This detachment, the H2B9 Company B of the Ninth U.S. Army Military Government, had a great deal of work to do to manage the feeding and care of the townspeople and the many thousands of refugees passing through or remaining in Nordhausen. The barracks of Mittelbau-Dora were filled quickly with displaced persons. A large kitchen was available, and a hospital was in operation.

It may be hard for the non-German reader to grasp the difficulties of the situation in which no general surrender had been rendered or accepted yet hostilities had ended for the parts of Germany through which the Allied troops had marched. This necessitated a directive for the military government of Germany prior to defeat or surrender. Under the directive, all legislative, executive, and judicial rights belonged to the occupying power under the command of the supreme commander, Gen. Dwight David Eisenhower, and to others to whom he designated powers. These authorities were thus passed on to the military governor to exercise as he saw fit when no specific command was in place to match the circumstances on the ground. One of the objectives was to provide care, control, and repatriation for the DPs and "minimum care necessary to effect control of enemy refugees and displaced persons." At the same time, other objectives were to apprehend war criminals, eliminate Nazis through arrest and imprisonment, protect UN property, and control and conserve German foreign-exchange assets.[13]

Posters were placed throughout the area asking citizens to encourage German soldiers to surrender and to cooperate with the occupation forces.[14] The war in Europe was not over, nor were all parts of Germany pacified. The armed forces did not want trouble from snipers or those not ready to surrender. There was some fear that the various camps and subcamps of Mittelbau-Dora could be "booby-trapped," ready to explode if a truck or tank drove over an explosive.[15] However, there was perhaps more concern than actual danger.

Great need was experienced by the townspeople and the freed slave laborers. The difference between the two groups was still remarkable, however, for the slave laborers had been undernourished for months or years, while the Nordhausen residents had suffered relatively few severe shortages in their food supply until the bombing raid. Whereas some items were in short supply before the bombs fell, in the weeks thereafter, people stood for hours to get anything at all from the partially destroyed shops. The city services were demolished, as well as much of the water and electric power. Sewage was a great problem for most of the city and had to be rerouted into the Zorge River.[16] The city administrators had fled, and people in institutions were left to their own devices or to depend on the Americans. City records were hidden or destroyed by the departing Nazi regime. In short, chaos reigned. Men called to work in clearing rubble were given small rations, and real hunger set in.[17]

What were the townspeople supposed to make of their lives? After twelve years under the Nazis, the defeat, as it came to Nordhausen, led to confusion about how one was to go on with normal life. What was "normal"? What traditions would be reinstated from before the war, what ones would be retained from the Third Reich, and what new expectations of community involvement would be put forth by the occupying forces? What political groups would be favored, and to what extent would the old loyalists be punished? Having heard propaganda about the Allies for years, the townspeople wondered what positions they would take.

The military government was under orders not to provide economic rehabilitation except where it might be necessary for military objectives. No relief supplies were to be imported for or distributed to the German population or displaced enemy or ex-enemy nationals beyond that which was absolutely necessary.[18] In short, the DPs who were not German received the first measure of aid, and the German population, although also without many of the necessities of life, was taken care of as supplies and time allowed. Knowing that the town would be turned over to the Soviets in the summer, there was, most likely, even less motivation to rehabilitate it than in other more western German cities.[19] Having seen the concentration camp, and linking its creation and operation to the town's population, many American military personnel were not in any mood to befriend the Germans. Quite the contrary!

In the early months of the occupation, there were no free elections for determining city officials. Otto Flagmeyer was selected by the occupiers to be mayor primarily because of his prewar record of being a member of the Social Democratic Party in opposition to Hitler and a representative in city government. His anti-Nazi record had resulted in his arrest, and he had been taken to Buchenwald, in a general roundup of those known to be unsympathetic to the Führer, following the attempt on Hitler's life on July 20, 1944. He had had a construction business, which offered him both advantages and disadvantages. He certainly knew about construction and could be of significant help in the reconstruction. However, when the Americans turned the city over to the Soviets only eleven weeks later, he found that his identity as an entrepreneur created less consensus about his value to the city. There were rumors, probably unfair, that he had profited from the situation, and he was removed from office.

While the Americans had control of the city, Flagmeyer stood as the main interpreter of the American military command in Nordhausen. He was in charge of the distribution of directions and other delivery of the occupiers' news organ or gazette. He did put his name on the decrees, but they originated in the command office. He was in no way independent. Nordhausen had a town council, but it was only to help Flagmeyer administer the city, not to be coequal to the American occupation in making decisions or pronouncements.[20]

One of the first indications of the position of the American occupiers came with the decision of the military government to deny a May Day parade to the townspeople. These parades were a prewar tradition of at least the left-leaning part of the population, but one that had not been honored by Hitler's regime. Many hoped that the parade would be allowed to take place as a sign of victory over the Nazis. When Flagmeyer received the word that the U.S. military government would not allow any mass gathering of the people at this time, he accepted the order, as he had to do, and spread it further with a call for double work effort on this day in the spirit of rebuilding and "Nie Wieder Krieg!" (Never Again War!). Eventually, the Americans allowed a small demonstration led by Communists in the form of a march from the Boelcke-Kaserne to the cemetery. There a short speech was given, and the group dispersed.[21]

The Americans had much more sympathy for the slave laborers and the freed concentration camp victims than for the townspeople or Germans in general. Thus, a decree was made that those who had been slaves of the Nazi state would be allowed to plunder the city for a few days following the liberation, but this privilege was not granted to the townspeople, despite the fact that thousands had lost their homes and belongings. The random looting, however, became unmanageable, and on May 8, 1945, Flagmeyer, as mayor representing the occupying forces, had to issue another order, this one to be taken very seriously.[22] Any further plundering would be met with the death penalty. Looters could be shot on sight.

Flagmeyer issued another decree on May 10, 1945. All citizens of Nordhausen over the age of twelve would appear at the dedicated graveyard (Ehrenfriedhof) on the thirteen between 7:30 in the morning and 5:30 in the afternoon. They were assigned specific times to arrive alphabetically according to their last names. Flagmeyer stated:

> There are about 1500 corpses, prisoners in concentration camps, buried there. They were members of many nations and also Germans who stood against the Nazi regime. It is only a tiny part of the victims who died of starvation or through gruesome treatment in the concentration camps. So that each citizen can grasp the tragedy of this horror, each person will look at each grave before receiving papers and ration cards.
>
> I expect that each one [of you] will think about this and lay flowers on the graves. At the same time, we will through [this act] show that we have nothing in common with these reckless crimes.[23]

A knowledgeable Nordhausen citizen, in discussing this action, asserted that the townspeople were in such shock from their own losses that they hardly registered this additional horror, but a survivor of that time who was among those burying the dead had a different story. He claimed that his own father was still in a concentration camp or perhaps dead or liberated, the family had not yet been informed, and having to carry the disintegrating corpses from the Boelcke-Kaserne to the cemetery was one of the worst experiences of his life. No one could understand the double tragedy of being exposed to these wrecks of human life and imagining his father as one of them. Being assumed a perpetrator when he had been a victim for years as the son of a traitor was almost unbearable.[24]

Despite the general antagonism of the American troops toward the Nordhausen Germans, individuals did make contact with people they met in their daily routines. The military did not sanction fraternization, but there seemed to be an unspoken policy of not looking into it too closely. The nonfraternization policy was "the avoidance of mingling with Germans upon terms of friendliness familiarity or intimacy, whether individually or in groups, in official or unofficial dealings. However, non-fraternization does not demand rough undignified or aggressive conduct, nor the insolent over-bearance which has characterized Nazi leadership."[25] It was to be enforced through normal military disciplinary methods, but "issues of orders to the Germans or prosecutions of them for attempts to fraternize should be discontinued." Being kind to children was specifically exempted by Eisenhower, for to do otherwise would be going against human nature. Americans were seen around town with both German women and the freed foreign workers and possibly refugees. Fights broke out among various individuals and groups, and the townspeople feared that the former slave laborers had guns.[26] How many of the reports are accurate and how many reflect an exaggerated fear of revenge, however justified, are unclear.

Franz Kowalski was one of those survivors of Dora who might have been feared, but for no reason.[27] He was of small stature even in good times, a survivor of Auschwitz, who had come on the transports to Mittelbau-Dora in the winter of 1944–1945. Shortly before the death march started from Dora, he and a friend had escaped from the site where they were working and went undercover.

Kowalski had learned tailoring before the Holocaust and had survived in the camps at least in part by being useful to the SS as a skilled worker. Now he knew that with a sewing machine, he might be able to make his way. As the two wandered into a farmyard a few weeks after their escape, young Kowalski asked a woman of the house if there was a sewing machine that could be made available to him and his friend. With some persuasion, they immediately set up a small business, taking people's old clothes and making them presentable again. It was a good business.

Franz Kowalski was an easy person to like, and he spoke German. Quiet and unassuming, he was ready to work; he neither looked for trouble nor hid his own background. Within a year, one of the German helpers on the farm found Franz to be a fine match and agreed to marry him in a nonreligious ceremony. They moved to independent quarters in a village outside of Nordhausen and set up a small homestead and tailor shop that they maintained for decades. Franz Kowalski became a Communist. As a small Jewish community became established in Erfurt later in the Communist era, Kowalski was not embraced by the leadership. He and the head of the small Jewish community had both been in Mittelbau-Dora at the same time and, according to one informant, "knew too much" about each other to be postwar intimates.

Franz Kowalski knew the prayers in Hebrew, however, and was called on throughout southeastern Germany to officiate in ceremonies and especially to say kaddish at funerals. He became the secular leader of the Jewish community in Halle, about sixty miles from Nordhausen. Until his death, he had a divided identity within the Jewish community, both as one of them and as an outsider who was not trusted. A leader in the Protestant community called him "a convinced Communist and a convinced Jew."

Franz Kowalski died in 2005 and was cremated and buried in the community graveyard of his village without a Jewish ceremony. When the Jewish community leader in Erfurt telephoned Franz's children to ask if the Jewish ceremony was desired, he felt rebuffed by them. Franz's closest friend among the survivors was devastated at the news of the cremation and broke all ties with the family.

Many questions remain unanswered, such as how the decisions were made and how Franz had lived his life both as a Jew and as a Communist. His family never doubted his goodness, and his friends marveled at the life he built from ashes.

Franz Kowalski was not the only survivor in Nordhausen after the war ended. Shortly after the cessation of hostilities, the distance between the townspeople and the Mittelbau-Dora inmates decreased. After the bombing of Nordhausen, the American troops came into the camp, where there were only very sick prisoners who had been in no condition to travel on the death march. Some were found in the barracks or hiding under or around them. Others had been left in the sick bay with the expectation that they would be dead by the time the Americans arrived. Some of those who were able went into the tunnels to seek safety. Some of the townspeople of Nordhausen took shelter in the barracks that had been used by the slave laborers in the Nordhausen region after the bombing ceased, because their own houses had been lost. In these ways, new relationships and awareness of one another developed among refugees, former prisoners, and the townspeople. Each person or family group had to figure out for themselves where they could be safest and with whom they might forge an alliance.

As the occupation became established, more regulations went into effect through various military and nonmilitary organizations. The United Nations Refugee and Resettlement Administration (UNRRA) was active in supplying refugee assistance of all kinds, but had difficulty knowing with whom they were dealing much of the time. There was some confusion among the relief agencies. The United Nations had a refugee mission in Nordhausen that distributed food and aid to refugees. Would they also allow that food to be used for the citizens of the town who were bombed out of their homes? The U.S. Jewish Committee also provided food, but did not want it to be used for Germans. The U.S. military commander informed the committee that it was not possible to make this distinction under the circumstances.

Definitions were required. Some of the groups who were labeled DPs included:

- Germans who did not want to return to their homes in Soviet-occupied parts of Germany
- German citizens from areas still in the war zone who did not have resources in the Nordhausen area, but wanted a safe place to wait out the war
- Enemy (German) insurgents in the guise of refugees
- Former non-German prisoners of war, such as Italians
- Germans displaced by fighting in their own hometowns[28]

Among those who did not want to return to central Europe or areas under Soviet control were Jews who had experienced the anti-Semitism within their own countries before the war and during its first years. There were, indeed, many pogroms and lesser acts of violence against this group who had already suffered the ultimate: genocide. They feared for their lives if they returned. Even the train trips for the returnees were fraught with danger. New forms of group exclusion began again with the return of refugees.[29]

> Several reports have been received from Polish-Jews just returned from Poland to Germany. The general consensus of opinion is that the present Polish policy against the Jews is just as bad as the Nazis were. Jews are being murdered in cold blood and their goods taken away. Trains are stopped during the night and luggage of travelers and part of the clothes they are wearing are taken away from them. Their explanation for non-intervention by the Russian authorities is that Russia does not bother with internal Polish policy, and is concerned only with foreign policy. A member of the local UNRRA team relates that sometime during September, a shipment of Polish Jewish children was sent to Poland for repatriation and about half of the children returned to the UNRRA camp and related that the missing half had been killed by the Poles in Poland.[30]

Others who were reluctant to return home were Soviet non-Jewish prisoners of war who feared retaliation for their inability to rebel against the Nazis while in prison. Indeed, there was some suspicion of those who had spent the war years in the role of prisoner or refugee, and there was not a welcome for most of them upon return.[31] The Soviet command informed Eisenhower that they wanted Soviet prisoners of war to be separated from other refugees and to be held under Soviet administration. While the Americans might have been reluctant to send Soviets back against their will, the Soviets felt it a necessary right to repatriate all Soviet survivors. The thirty-five million people lost to them during the war years meant that every person who could return was very much needed to rebuild their country.[32]

Any Germans in Nordhausen who had been evacuated from occupied territory but were not prisoners of war were to be treated as enemy DPs and were the responsibility of the First Army, 12th Army Group command. German evacuees were interrogated and kept under watch until their status was cleared. The 12th Army Group command was also given the task of discerning enemy agents and war criminals from among the refugees and prohibiting them from leaving Germany and bringing them to justice or to detention centers.[33] Some were then sent to prison camps or were designated as being of special interest. Those were sent to special holding camps: "Ashcan" and "Dustbin." In this "Dustbin" category were at least two engineers discovered inside the Dora complex.[34]

In the interest of public safety and keeping order, the SHAEF command later in April 1945 ordered that no more refugees would be admitted into Nordhausen without bringing a thirty-day supply of food with them. How this was to be verified was not stated. However, within thirty days, refugees were expected to be able to find at least part-time work and rehabilitate damaged dwellings in which they could begin to make a place to live.[35]

A Congressional Visit to Mittelbau-Dora

There was tremendous interest in the concentration camps worldwide once they became headlines in the newspapers. Many people from all areas of the public sphere wanted to see for themselves just what had taken place. Representatives from various governments wanted to find out how many of their citizens had been in the camps and to find specific prisoners about whom they had information or suspected imprisonment. Even the Vatican wanted to send representatives.

The *New York Times* reported on April 21, 1945, that Eisenhower asked that twelve members of Congress and twelve newspaper editors visit Germany under the authority of the SHAEF auspices to "see for themselves." The *Times* opined that "it is a fair guess that General Eisenhower, at this climatic stage of the war, would not make the request unless he personally had been terribly shocked by what he has seen in Germany, and felt strongly that information about conditions in these German camps should be disseminated as widely as possible in America."

The reports to the American people had seemed so extreme that many had a difficult time believing they could be true. Edward R. Murrow of CBS visited Buchenwald a week before this report was issued and broadcast live from the camp. This convinced the vast majority that indeed the reports were not fiction.[36] On May 16, 1945, a delegation of congressmen and senators came to Nordhausen as part of the tour they were making of concentration camps. Everett M. Dirksen of Illinois and Cmdr. John S. Young are prominent, as the group was captured on film as they surveyed the grounds.[37]

Many were ready to come before the German surrender had been declared. It was finally necessary to control such visitors in the forward formations of combat.

> When concentration camps of political prisoners are first uncovered by the armies, experience is that conditions are extremely bad, and that first-aid treatment, nursing, dietetic and medical care is of vital necessity if lives are to be saved and identifications and evacuations made. The concern of the respective national authorities at such times, is for their nationals and the resulting desire to visit such points, are appreciated. However, it is felt that such visits, especially when made by distinguished persons, inevitably interrupt and delay the urgent first aid measure, and with limited personnel available in the early stages, add difficulties rather than ameliorate them. Visits which will in fact be helpful, such as visits of medical, dietetic and nursing experts, are always welcome. However, it is recommended that other visits, especially those of distinguished persons be discouraged, during the early days of liberation.[38]

The Spoils of Nordhausen

Intelligence units of the SHAEF command included in their responsibilities the identification and investigation of scientific personnel and laboratories, as well as their products. There were several purposes to this mission. On the one hand, the military had to be apprised of what it was facing in terms of weapons and new plans for weapons. It also wanted to keep these items in friendly hands and not let them fall back into either German or Soviet auspices. These intelligence units were traveling in the forward divisions and followed the troops or were called in when something of interest was uncovered.

It is not clear at what point the command decided to use scientific personnel for Allied purposes, but the compilation by Counter Intelligence Sub-Division, with the assistance of the Scientific Intelligence Advisory Section, had been under way at least since March 8, 1945. These specialized intelligence units were referred to as "T" groups and were set up by Supreme Commander Eisenhower after the invasion in each army group for the purpose of "seizing and freezing certain intelligence objectives." The objectives would then be assessed "for the purpose of exploiting these targets."[39]

Thus it was that on April 10, 1945, only one day before entering Nordhausen, the intelligence branch entered the town of Muhlhausen, about forty miles from Nordhausen. There, the intelligence branch investigated a part of the German Foreign Office to get the names of agencies and people active in the Nazi regime. They interrogated two officers whom they found and learned from them that the V-2 weapons were being assembled in Ilfeld, near Nordhausen. These informants said that there were about eighteen thousand workers there, most from concentration camps, and the entire staff from Peenemünde had been there until they evacuated to Bleicherode, a small town to the west of Nordhausen. Professor Wernher von Braun had been in an auto accident and was in the hospital in Bleicherode, according to the German bureaucrats.[40]

The T groups examined all aspects of a technological objective and interrogated relevant Germans, but they did not have the authority to remove raw material, machinery, tools, models, plans and drawings, or archival material. They first had to send a description to the Supreme Headquarters where decisions would be made before the specialists left the field. This effort, done in such a short time, is remarkable, as are the successful removal of vast amounts of material, both paper and other goods, from each area in which operations took place.

If the targets identified by the T group were of interest, the Combined Intelligence Objectives Subcommittee personnel would come in and report extensively and then arrange to remove the objects.[41] These forces, which included thousands of British and American enlisted men, came onto the European continent with the invasion of Normandy in 1944 and followed the push across the continent as the war moved westward.[42] Those arrested by the T groups were divided into priority lists and interrogated. Usually, the interrogations required moving the "targets" to a safe location, which required an escort.[43]

It was soon clear that Nordhausen had many tangible assets worthy of removal to Allied countries. The question was how much should be left for the Soviets and how much confiscated for the Americans, British, and French. The American troops began to pack up the finished rocket parts and about a hundred finished rockets in May. The machines and midlevel engineers were left for the Russians. Important documents were included in the cache and transported away.[44] A much larger storage space was discovered in a mine near Goslar, also in the Harz Mountains, and the Allies recovered fourteen tons of papers relevant to Mittelwerk.[45]

Hans Hagen, 1945 or 1946, on the grounds of Mittelbau-Dora with a rocket fragment. (Hans Hagen Collection, photographer unknown)

Disappearances and Removals

Werner von Braun was not captured in Bleicherode, having suffered major injuries in an automobile accident on March 12, 1945, after which he spent three weeks there in the hospital. Under orders from Hitler's newly appointed "plenipotentiary for jet fighter aircraft," Hans Kammler, 450 to 500 scientists associated with the V-2 were transferred in sleeping train cars to Bavaria. Wernher von Braun was, of course, with the group, but traveled in a motor vehicle because of his injuries. He remained in the vicinity of Oberammergau for a short time in a hospital and then recuperating in a private hotel until the time was right. With the help of his brother, Magnus, he turned himself in to the U.S. forces with his friend and colleague Walter Dornberger for interrogation and ultimate service to the United States.[46]

The Soviet Union was also interested in gaining access to the personal and technical assets in the tunnels of Nordhausen. While the Allies were divided about the degree to which they should treat the scientists differently from other "black targets," the Soviets were offering them good pay and the chance to move to the Soviet Union with their families. That was a sticking point for the Americans, and General Eisenhower himself was not pleased with the idea of importing many Germans to the United States, even if they were extraordinary scientists. He changed his mind, however, when it became clear that the Soviet Union might reap the benefits of their advanced technology. While the United States tried to clarify their position, many scientists were signing up to move to the East.

Before handing the Mittelwerk site and the concentration camp Mittelbau-Dora over to the Soviets, the Americans forced or enticed more than 1,000 scientific personnel from Thuringia to the American Zone.[47]

The Transfer of Power from the United States to the Soviet Union

In a few short weeks, the American occupation had brought some order to Nordhausen, but had faced great challenges due to the entrenched sociopolitical atmosphere and the physical damage due to the bombing. All records were burned, either purposively by the outgoing Nazi regime or in the firestorms of the bombing raids. Any system of welfare or caring for the sick and wounded had to be re-created.

The successes of the period of the American and early Soviet occupation from June 14 to July 20, 1945, however, were not small. They included reinstating many small businesses and some larger ones. The chewing tobacco company, the distillery, and the machine tool works were all in operation again. The Jewish businesspeople who had once been involved in their industries did not return to Nordhausen. Many were dead, and those who had survived the Holocaust emigrated in large numbers. The small-gauge rail system through the Harz Mountains (Harz Querbahn) was carrying needed supplies and foodstuffs. Although more than a hundred trucks had been removed to the West, the town had managed to find ninety others to take their place. They had buried thousands of dead and tried to keep a record of those individuals who had succumbed either in the concentration camps or in the bombing. They had started once again to manufacture roof tiles, but still could not find a glass supply for repairing homes.[48]

The relationship between the Soviet Union and the American occupying force was strained. Not only was the competition for the German assets a roadblock, but the growing distrust between the two sides marked the beginning of the cold war. The date for complete withdrawal of American forces was set for July 4, 1945, but, of course, it could not occur in a day. The plan was thus: on July 1 the Soviets would send reconnaissance troops into twelve towns, on July 2 they would send their reconnaissance troops to all the airfields, on July 3 the main body of their troops would be relocated, and on July 4 they would take over all responsibilities of occupation.[49] It appears

Reconstruction of Nordhausen along Töpfer Street, 1945. (Stadtarchiv Nordhausen)

that this timetable was not strictly adhered to, nor were the prisoners kept under guard. Indeed, on July 4, 1945, the Soviets found that the Americans had retreated to the American Zone, only a few miles away, and left the town to the new regime. There was no ceremony.

There were questions of security, for the Americans did not want to leave the military assets or the prisoners unguarded. The Soviets agreed to take over the prisoners, but did not want to take over the care of DPs who were not Soviet citizens. Voluntary welfare organizations under UNRRA had taken the responsibility for stateless people and would have to move them to other zones.

The Soviets found that the areas that were occupied by the Americans were in relatively good shape with functioning transportation and some supplies of food and consumer goods. On the other hand, they found that many "specialists" and those with businesses had left with the Allies. The American occupiers had set up an administrative system that seemed to be working well and could be kept in place for the most part.

The Japanese experienced the horror of strategic bombing and all-out warfare for a few more months and a final assault on civilians in Hiroshima on August 6 and Nagasaki on August 8, 1945, in which a half-million civilians were killed. World War II came to an official end on September 2, 1945.

Reconstruction of the Nordhausen center. (Stadtarchiv Nordhausen)

Conclusion

As the war drew to a close, the people of Nordhausen were in shock. They had experienced the incineration of much of their city; had lost much of a priceless, almost one thousand–year heritage; were in personal and civic ruin; and had already experienced two administrations by foreign conquerors. They had been brought face-to-face with the crimes of their landsmen and had seen with their own eyes the human waste that their country had created. They experienced in the last days of the war the full measure of the determination of the Allies to bring Germany to its knees. They were coerced into looking and seeing what had been done in their name.

The cruelty that they had experienced and had been a part of perpetrating led many to despair, but others to a sense of great purpose in getting their lives together once again. There was so much to do, much of it under the command of the occupation forces and much out of concern for their well-being and that of their families and neighbors.

The strangers, those who were DPs or expellees, as well as remaining former prisoners and slave laborers, finding themselves in this wasteland, had to decide how to continue their lives. Options were presented to them without their active participation. The few who found their own agency were the exceptions. Those very rare individuals, like Franz Kowalski, looked ahead at what was possible and headed straight for a life of pragmatism and purpose. Nordhausen was no longer a homogeneous small city, but a multinational hostel where almost everyone needed the basic necessities of life. It was self-preservation to care for one another, to create shelter and safe water, to prevent illness and cure the sick. In the immediate months after the end of the war, there were no longer throwaway people.

The hatred for the "other" was no longer supported. However, there were few signs of the once rich life of the Jewish community. The synagogue, the Jewish school, and virtually all the Jews were gone. Heterogeneity had a missing element, and Nordhausen had lost a major part of its human, as well as its material, heritage.

5. Shaping the New Land and Its Memories

There was such relief that the war was over, but there was also much anxiety as the new government of the Soviet occupation began in July 1945. The Mittelbau-Dora concentration camp and Mittelwerk assembly plant had been left in shambles by the retreating SS and looted by the Americans who took the missiles and the paperwork, leaving most of the machinery to the Soviets. The people milling around the ruins of the town of Nordhausen, looking for food and shelter, now had to deal with the new Soviet administration. No one had enough of anything: food, supplies, shelter, and clothing were all in short supply. The people of Nordhausen were scattered: many dead, many missing, many finding a home to the west or anywhere safer or more comfortable. Others had found the eastern part of Germany to be their final resting place and were buried there or were settling into this bombed-out Thuringian city that had once been very picturesque. "For millions of civilians on the move in 'treks'—at first refugees in the winter of 1944–45 and later expellees from lost eastern territories—the war's end was prolonged. Over three and a half million refugees were present in the Soviet zone in 1946, ranging from those who had been well-to-do landowners or members of the bourgeoisie in the areas now taken over by the Soviet Union and Poland (which had been effectively shifted westwards) to the very poor."[1]

Local Political Structure

The beginnings of political reawakening occurred very soon after the Soviet occupation began. At least four political parties were allowed to meet, but in April 1946, two of them, the Social Democratic Party and the Communist

Party, merged, not completely voluntarily, into the German Socialist Unity Party (Sozialistische Einheitspartei Deutschland, or SED).[2] Believing that the Socialists and Communists had not formed an effective front against the onslaught of Hitler and fascism, the parties, not withstanding great reservations on the side of the Socialists, now decided to come together to keep that from happening again.[3]

Those who opposed the merger in Nordhausen, as elsewhere, were dealt with harshly. By the end of the 1940s, at least five people in the city were arrested and sentenced to twenty-five years in prison for distributing literature against the SED and socialism and one to one hundred years of forced labor for spreading anti-Soviet propaganda. Of those sentenced, two appear to have died in custody.[4]

Opposition was effectively quelled, and the SED became the most powerful force in the German Democratic Republic (GDR), encompassing more than two million members by 1987 and sixty thousand affiliated organizations, making it the largest Communist Party in the world relative to its population base.[5] While other parties could be represented, and their representatives could discuss matters from their points of view, the SED, in all regards synonymous with the state apparatus, held the decisive power. This was understood to be in general alignment with Soviet policy, of course.

The city council, named the Antifascist (Antifa) Council, had much to do, including as early as October 1945, in deciding on how to approach land reform, how to turn individual businesses into state-owned operations, what to do about the refugees from the East, how to reform the legal and banking systems, how to rid the town of its Nazi element, and how to gather money for city coffers. *Antifa* is a broad term, a shortened form of *antifascist*. The term has a long history and is used by some to this day.

Land reform and confiscation of businesses caused a great deal of anger among those who owned property or enterprises. Choices were not allowed under the "dictatorship of the proletariat." Those who did not cooperate were summarily dealt with through harsh sentences or actions.

The council, which was composed in the early days of a broad coalition of representatives of all the parties, also wanted to produce a single antifascist statement of purpose and intent for the population as soon as possible.[6] Pressing issues included how to get in the harvest for this year, when so many men were missing and wounded and many were moving westward. Of course, the continuing reconstruction of the city was a great concern. It was decided that all four parties to the Potsdam Accord would have to be involved in reconstruction countrywide. Businesses that were run or heavily influenced by Nazis had to be taken over, but no one knew quite what to do at this early date. It was decided to wait for a broader mandate.

The number and severity of the problems that the new leaders of Nordhausen faced were impressive and daunting. Yet the town seemed to be brimming with goodwill and energy for the development of a new city. Above all, most people were relieved that the war was over and the bombing and killing had stopped.

Coping with Postwar Hardship

The Soviet occupation forces had to find building materials for housing the refugees and the workers of the small industries that were beginning to grow in Nordhausen. On August 7, 1946, just a little more than a year after liberation, the Soviet Military Administration granted permission to take apart the barracks at the Boelcke-Kaserne to build housing for the workers in small industry first and then housing for the incoming refugees.[7] This was a great help, because along with the barracks, other materials could be rescued, such as radio towers, waterworks, gas stations, and other vital materials.

The people of Nordhausen had to do most of the heavy work of clearing the rubble. In the summer of 1945, 72,000 hours of work were recorded, 70,000 square meters of rubble removed, 165 tons of debris hauled away, and 400,000 bricks and stone prepared for use from the destroyed buildings.[8] Old habits die hard, and soon the city leaders were suggesting that Polish workers and those from the East take over the outdoor work to the extent possible. "The workers from the east are health-wise and physically in another state than the Germans and can withstand the weather better than we. We would like to see the [public] work requirement rescinded [for Germans]." The council decided that the local prison camp, set up for higher-ranking Nazis and those not cooperating with the new regime, be used as a source of labor and for those who were "work-shy."[9]

As in all the bombed cities of Germany, women played a major role in clearing the rubble, as many men were missing due to war deaths and imprisonment in prisoner-of-war camps. In Nordhausen women were called to duty for long hours in the streets, stacking, moving, and cleaning reclaimed bricks and building materials. The city leaders complained that the better-situated women were able to get excuses from their doctors and were not seen at the work sites. "Herr Klemann is of the opinion that women who have lived well in the past twelve years and have several pairs of shoes can certainly take part in this work," read one statement in the Antifa Council minutes.[10]

Denazification

The Allies and most of the leadership of the reconstituted Nordhausen government recognized that the youth had been indoctrinated by the Hitlerian philosophy and needed a great deal of attention if they were to be a part of building a new Germany. Young Nazis, having witnessed a ceremony for Albert Kuntz, painted on the posters and on windows on several streets a swastika accompanied by "He is dead; we still live" and "We will still triumph." The Industrial Advisory Board, made up of workers, owners, and managers, decided that draconian measures were needed, including a denazification of the local neighborhood administrations and businesses. The three young men accused of having written Nazi slogans on city walls were expelled from their homes with all their belongings and remanded to the police.[11] Thereafter, much harsher measures were taken throughout the city to stop any sign of Nazi propaganda or activity. Explicit laws were enacted to legalize the handling of all those suspected of being "close to the Nazis."[12]

Plans for youth work were put into place that included innovative humanities projects, such as poetry houses, music programs, theater, and parties. The new administration also planned to build interest groups or clubs that would meet around the city and give the youth a free choice of belonging to different kinds of groups. The youth work was under the guidance of the SED and planned to "provide discussion evenings on a broad basis. The leader should take particular care not to fall into slogans, but must take this bitterly serious in consideration of the problem." The goal was to create a system that would develop the character of youth through humanitarian means, so that they would have a democratic respect for their fellow man. In the process, they should also be engaged in the work of rebuilding the city.[13] In many respects, this did not differ in its goals from similar programs set out in West Germany at about the same time. Both separate regimes were anxious to guide the youth away from their Nazi ideology, although both sides hoped that they would be led to the dominant beliefs of the reigning governments.

Many of the townspeople were satisfied with the new local government and enthusiastic about its emphasis on fairness in dividing the resources and in addressing very real problems. Many, however, also feared the Soviets who now held the ultimate authority in Nordhausen.

People who had been functionaries in the concentration camps and Nazis with more prominent positions could be rounded up and taken to "special camps" (*Spezial Lager*) of which there were about ten throughout the Soviet Zone: these camps were not unexpected, for the possibility of "interning" people in camps was written into the Potsdam Treaty, which stated that "Nazi leaders, influential Nazi supporters and high officials of Nazi organizations and institutions and any other person dangerous to the occupation or its objectives shall be arrested and interned."[14] The Soviet camps were in undisclosed locations, and the prisoners were not allowed to contact their families; they simply disappeared, in most cases. The Western Allies also set up camps, some under very bad conditions. These camps were not secret, however, and prisoners could receive packages from home. The prisoners were generally not kept for years, as were prisoners in the Soviet Zone, and were fed somewhat better than those in the East.

The Buchenwald and Sachsenhausen special camps were created on the sites of the former Nazi camps. Buchenwald was already tied to Nordhausen through Dora's initial status as a subcamp and the delivery of prisoners for Mittelwerk. This camp was once again in service only months after it had been liberated from the Nazis, and had a particular meaning to the population of the city of Nordhausen. Special Camp 2, at Buchenwald, opened for new prisoners on August 22, 1945. By the end of 1945, it had 6,000 prisoners, mostly from the area around the camp and the state of Thuringia. At its height, Special Camp 2 imprisoned more than 16,000 people, but this number declined because of its high death rate and the deportation of some of the prisoners for slave labor in the Soviet Union. The conditions in the special camps were hideous and totally inhumane, but could not be used as a deterrent to others, for the camps were kept secret. Over the course of the period August 1945 to February 1950, 28,455 prisoners were held in Special Camp 2, of whom about 25 percent did not survive.[15]

Prisoners taken by the Allies in Germany did not have to have a legal hearing, were not necessarily offered a chance to defend themselves, and could be held without proof of any wrongdoing. However, if it was assumed that they posed a threat, preventative detention could be ordered. How many of the prisoners in the special camps were actually guilty of war crimes or had been in high-ranking positions in the Nazi apparatus is not known. Often those suspected or denounced were picked up on the street and were not able to inform their families of their abduction. Others were removed from jails or the workplace.[16] It was a time rife with denunciation and suspicion. Therefore, in addition to the real perpetrators of Nazi terror, many more were incarcerated in these old Nazi camps due to mistaken identity or a neighbor's vengeance. The death toll was huge, caused not only by the physical cruelty of the Nazi concentration camp system, but also by malnutrition and disease and a kind of psychological torture of extremely confined space, monotonous meals of gruel, and enforced idleness.[17]

In the midst of a new beginning and positive activities to interest and engage young people and adults and to lead them into hope for the future, there was also a dread of falling out of favor with the new people in charge. Like the Americans, the Soviets assumed that Nordhausen was a place where the guilty could be found hiding among the common folk, and the tension was high, along with the joy and relief at the cessation of war.

A camp for former Nazis was also established in the Nordhausen area. Called "Hanewacker," it held between 150 and 200 prisoners and was the topic of many discussions among the Antifa Council because of a "lack of clarity" stemming from uncertain incarcerations, length of sentences, and legal recourse for the prisoners. One of the members of the council suggested that "with the internment, there must be the appearance of legality. There should be a kind of 'Peoples' Court' made up of representatives of the four political parties. That would create the appearance of legality and we would be covered."[18]

The camp evolved into a holding area for many different groups of people: teachers who had taught under the Nazi system, old Nazi loyalists, the work shy, those who opposed the new regime and expressed displeasure with it, refugees who had no fixed address or work, and those lost in drunkenness or despair. Hanewacker seems to have had a relatively short life.

The rigid adherence to doctrine as it was developed, however, made itself known, particularly to those who were outside the mainstream. Dora Birnbaum was one of these. Her son was killed in battle early in the war, and she found solace in the midst of her grief by becoming a member of the Jehovah's Witnesses. Her membership was forbidden by the Nazi government, and she was arrested in 1938 and went through a number of prisons and concentration camps, arriving at Dora with the transports from Auschwitz in time to make the terrible trip to Bergen-Belsen. After the war, she lived in Nordhausen and received a certificate as a victim of fascism (*Opfer des Faschismus*), for which she received extra food rations. The following year, she was told to sign a petition condemning the U.S. use of atomic weapons. To sign a petition was against the tenets of her religion. Because of this refusal, her status of victim was revoked, and she lost her pension and ration cards. Her family had to move to a small apartment. She died in 1966 without recognition of the more than seven years she had endured in concentration camps.[19]

Reparations

The Antifa Council began to formulate procedures to handle some of the issues of the Nazi legacy in the city. The GDR was responsible for the reparations to the Soviet Union, and none were paid by the Federal Republic of

Germany (FRG). For the first postwar years, reparations throughout the Soviet Zone were handled on less than an organized basis. There was extensive plundering of personal goods, removal of industrial machinery, and quotas for handing over foodstuffs, grain, and even seedling potatoes. The Soviets had determined the cost of destruction to their land through Nazi imperialism was $138 billion and had tried to recapture $10 billion of that sum by having such a provision for restitution entered into the Potsdam Treaty, but the Western Allies would not agree. Informally, it was agreed, however, that the Soviet occupation of the zone would continue until the $10 billion in reparations had been met.[20] According to at least one estimate, the reparations that the Soviet Union finally received in 1935 dollars came to $19.3 billion. The Soviet Union extended millions of rubles of credit to East Germany as well. Some of those debts were repaid and others forgiven.[21]

The Nordhausen Antifa Council soon began to address the takeover of Nazi properties. It is not clear how decisions were made to divide the proceeds, but most likely it was through the occupation forces. The Soviet Military Administration would receive 60 percent of the value and the state 40 percent. Some of the state's money would be distributed to the businesses and companies involved as compensation.[22]

For those property or business owners who did not readily cooperate, the consequences could be dire. In one instance in 1952, two mill owners in the Nordhausen suburb of Krimderode, Kurt Jericho and Kurt Miller, were reluctant to give over their business to the state. They were charged with providing a by-product of the ground flour to their customers, resulting in the seizure of their mill and a sentence for each of them of three years in prison. They were referred to in the hearings as "enemies of the state." Miller escaped to West Germany, but Jericho came back to Krimderode, where he was allowed to remain in his house next to the mill, but could no longer own it.[23] These harsh measures led others to be cooperative or to leave the Soviet Zone for the West.

The members of the council, acting as representatives of the city, campaigned for a greater food ration for themselves, but were turned down by the state. Their argument was that their work as council members took many hours away from the time in which they could be gainfully employed. Food provisions were very short, and the entire town suffered from problems of supply and distribution. Schools were also unheated, and the children had no school supplies. In general, the first postwar winter was hard for all the inhabitants of Nordhausen, very hard.[24] In part, this was a reflection of the terrible state in which the Soviet Zone had been left by the ravages of war, the intense bombing of cities, and the pillaging of the towns and countryside by exiting soldiers and former slave laborers. The number of animals available to farmers was down 25 to 50 percent from prewar levels, causing great hardship in meat and milk production and distribution.[25] While the Soviet Zone had enough arable land and could have fed the people in East Germany adequately, much of the harvest was sent directly to the Soviet Union or used by the occupying soldiers themselves.

Behavior of the Soviets

The first form of Soviet military administration was the Kommandanturas, a series of fiefdoms established under the direction of a *kommandant* for a given region. Corruption and favoritism were rife.[26] By the time the Soviets took over Nordhausen, this system had been modified, however, and the Soviet Military Administration took charge.

Throughout Germany, Soviet troops committed crimes against women in huge numbers. Some of the commandants were able to bring this violence under control, but others either could not or did not care to be involved. In all, ninety thousand women in Berlin sought medical attention for rape, and the Western Allies recorded eighty-seven thousand rapes in three weeks of Soviet troops being in Vienna.[27] The records of Nordhausen remain silent on this topic.[28] In all of the minutes of meetings of the local government, there are occasional orders mentioned coming from the Soviet commandant, but no word of appreciation or affection for the Soviets by the Nordhausen people. Women of Nordhausen spoke of the danger the occupying troops presented them, but there are no official records.[29]

Recognition of the KZ and Nonrecognition of the Bombing of Nordhausen

The new regime was in no mood to tolerate the old Nazi loyalists or the appearance of neo-Nazis among the citizenry and began by dealing harshly with them. Many citizens of Nordhausen were also depressed and sad when they reflected on the years of the war and had thoughts they wanted to share. One such letter of remorse and guilt appeared in the local paper in January 1947 from a Nordhausen citizen who thought back to the meaning of Hitler's assumption of power on January 30, 1933:

> Remembrance on January 30. We don't forget it so easily.
> It is the same date as then, in 1933, and the folk should "wake up." How much it is rekindled first 12 years later . . . [I]t leads to the naked truth and terrible knowledge.

However, another memory comes to mind on this date . . . It is the date, and it lasted 10 days long: open cattle car trains arrived in Nordhausen from Auschwitz III—Monowitz in a grim cold. This trip! There was nothing to eat, nothing to drink, not even a piece of frozen bread. Pressed together in each of these wagons were hundreds of concentration camp prisoners standing before us, that gruesome picture of death through hunger and freezing.

And then the train stopped, this death train from Auschwitz in the station at Nordhausen, have not many of you seen it? Haven't you glimpsed the crying mass to whom you gave a piece of bread or a drink of water?[30]

And another with no date from a reader of the Nordhausen paper:

I have seen for myself how the men were treated here in our little concentration camp. Almost every evening, the men were piled into wheelbarrows and dragged back to camp half dead. One looked at them and knew that they did not even get the bare necessities to eat. It was understandable that they took cabbages and beets from our fields. For that, they were slugged by their overseers and guards.

How often have I looked out my window and watched and said to my wife that we are all guilty in this crime because we tolerated Hitler taking over our government.

Once my wife wanted to give a poor prisoner a piece of bread, but the guard yelled at her and threatened that in a short time she would have to appear before the commander and be questioned by the Nazi party. This man really wanted to lock her up.[31]

The feelings people had about the bombing of Nordhausen and the tragedy that had befallen their own families were not accepted in the first years as openly as later. There was always the fear on the part of the occupiers that these feelings would lead to a rebirth of Nazi ideology. The bombing must not be seen as placing the Nordhausen population in the position of being victims. It was still important that they saw the Germans, if not themselves personally, as the perpetrators.

With the first anniversary of the freeing of Buchenwald, Communist speakers who had suffered in the concentration camps were invited to speak. On April 13, 1946, Werner Eggerath and Rosa Thäilmann spoke of their time in Buchenwald and Ravensbrück, respectively. A few months later, a large stone with an inscription was dedicated to Albert Kuntz in front of the Nordhausen railroad station. "Tens of thousands of decent, honest anti-fascists from all countries lost their lives for their political ideals against the primitive Nazi bandits. This memorial will be a warning regarding the past! A call to constant watchfulness in the future!"

The history of the camps was being written as the history of Communist incarceration, heroism, and rebellion. That history was more relevant for the first years of concentration camps, when, indeed, most of the prisoners were politically active leftists. After 1938, however, Jews became a large or overwhelming population in the camps. After 1939, when the war began, there were increasing numbers of prisoners of war, as well as those determined to be a burden to the state, including all kinds of minorities—ideological, religious, physical, social, or ethnic. By 1942, almost all Jews had been removed from Germany to death camps in the East. Those who survived were sent back to Germany in 1944–1945 in an effort to use their labor until exhaustion or disease and starvation claimed their lives. This part of the history, if mentioned at all, was produced as an aside in the antifa literature.

The fourteen thousand refugees left the barracks on the land that had housed the former Mittelbau-Dora in 1946. The Soviets removed remaining equipment and missile parts, then blasted the tunnels shut in the summer of 1948, so that none of the curious could trespass.[32] A few holes remained around the Kohnstein, and occasionally an adventurer would be lowered down to explore the tunnels, which were filling with water and rusted parts of rockets. This was clearly trespassing on government property now, and it was becoming clear that running against government restrictions had serious consequences.[33]

Groups of women cleared the weeds from the *Appellplatz,* the area where the prisoners had stood for hours in all weather twice a day to be counted. Several of these women remember to this day that while they cleared the large empty space of weeds, it was a time in which they thought about the prisoners and their travails.[34] At least two of these women remain actively involved with the memorial more than sixty years after the camp's liberation.

Nordhausen Mahnt

Very little was said publicly about the bombing of Nordhausen. It had been carried out by the Allies, but not specifically by the Soviet Union, so perhaps it was thought better to let the message of German guilt settle without discussing other wartime crimes against civilians. Public assemblies centered on the heroes of the concentration camp and the losses there, not on the city and its devastation.

In the minutes of the Antifa Council of March 8, 1946, the representatives discussed a public meeting in the central square of the city (*Marktplatz*) to remember the victims of both the concentration camp and the bombing of

Nordhausen. They would plan that all the businesses would be closed for the time period. In a following set of minutes from the same year, undated, the request is mentioned as having been denied: "The rally for the destruction of the city on April 4 is forbidden by the Russians."[35]

A possible exception was the interesting effort by the Nordhausen government to mount an exhibit called "Nordhausen Mahnt." *Mahnen* is a German verb meaning both to warn and to admonish. This is an important word in regard to memories of the Third Reich, for it carries with it several assumptions. First, in admonishing, there is understood to be a perpetrator. Second, by warning, there must be the possibility of the deeds reoccurring. But who are the perpetrators, and who are those we must watch to be sure they do not do "it" again? It is a strong word, but very ambiguous. It lends itself to a discourse of unease.

The exhibit was developed under Nordhausen mayor Hans Himmler. He had been imprisoned in the Third Reich, and his wife had been in Ravensbrück concentration camp at the end of the war due to their anti-Nazi activities. "In 1949, he was the initiator of the exhibit, 'Nordhausen Mahnt.' This exhibit was supposed to bring attention to the very damaged city and the reasons for that damage that must never come about again, but also to the reconstruction due to the hard work of the citizens under the SED." Indeed, the hard work had resulted in a new infrastructure for the inner city, a new city hall (*Rathaus*) with a venue for city events and dinner meetings (*Ratskeller*). Finally, Mayor Himmler became known as the "theater father" of Nordhausen, as he convinced the Soviet authorities to agree to reconstructing the Stadttheater.[36]

In announcing the exhibit, Mayor Himmler put out the following statement:

Nordhausen mahnt . . .
   All those who through the bombing war lost their loved ones, all those who through the bombs of the Americans lost their businesses, all those who five minutes before the end of the war lost their last belongings, their dwellings and their household goods. We think upon the need to fight with all their might for democracy, for peace, and against war.

Nordhausen mahnt . . .
   All places that were not attacked, all cities and all places and all regimes that were responsible, for Nordhausen alone will never be in the position to create what took centuries to build and in a few minutes was destroyed. That requires the solidarity of those who have not lost everything and the support of all those jurisdictions [who do not have to rebuild].

Nordhausen mahnt . . .

Also the people of the city, that they think about the fact that the city government alone cannot accomplish everything that would provide a good life, for that is the job of the total population of the city. Together we have suffered, together we have lost everything, and together we will and we must rebuild in the year 1949.

Nordhausen mahnt . . .

Every part of the population to think about the two-year plan that is part and parcel of our economic recovery. We will fulfill and more than fulfill these goals, for they serve not only to raise our standard of living in themselves, but serve to [ensure] the rebuilding of the city Nordhausen.[37]

The exhibit ran May 6–27, 1949. The local newspaper praised the idea and added many other accomplishments to the list of those already mentioned. There was pride in what the city had done to rebuild and a call for more effort and more sacrifice, even as things were improving for the people of Nordhausen.[38] The cold war was also reflected in the only blame attributed in the exhibit: the American bombs. The beginning of the vague expression of anger at those who make war left open the question of to what extent the German people were part of the perpetrator group. What was clear was that fascism, meaning military, capitalistic warmongering, was not wanted, and those who represented this ideology were not wanted in the GDR (*unerwünscht*).

In 1950, there was a demonstration on the fifth anniversary of the bombing of Nordhausen attended by thousands of people. It was declared under the positive note "Nordhausen Rebuilds" and enjoyed the sponsorship of the city and the SED.[39]

Remembering the Concentration Camp at the Original Site

On the first anniversary of the liberation of Mittelbau-Dora, April 11, 1946, a small ceremony was held in front of the crematorium.[40] As commemoration, a simple wooden marker, "Lager Dora," was placed as a remembrance without elaboration. Refugees were still living in the camp's barracks until 1947, but only the crematorium and the small firehouse remained as solid buildings. Within a few years, all the barracks were gone, taken apart for use in construction. With the refugees rehoused elsewhere, the site cleared of evidence of the rocket assembly, the tunnels blasted shut in 1948 by the Soviet occupiers, Mittelbau-Dora within a few years became a no-man's-land. A few people tried to keep the weeds off the *Appellplatz*, but the grounds were unsightly.

Later in the year, in December, a ceremony was held at the railroad station where a plaque was placed to honor Albert Kuntz, the first of many ceremonies honoring him as the most prominent of the Mittelbau-Dora prisoners. Hans Himmler, the mayor, spoke with deep feelings about the purposes of the plaque to both recognize and honor those who fought against Nazi power. Albert Kuntz was among the first anti-Nazi leaders and spent all of the years of the Third Reich in prisons and camps. But the mayor, himself knowing the pain of years in prisons and camps, continued in his speech to be inclusive of "communists, socialists, Catholics, Jehovah's Witnesses, men and women of July 20: they gave their all for freedom and peace and paid with their lives."[41]

What is missing in this first speech and in those that followed is any mention of Jews and the numbers they represented not only in the camp but in the Nordhausen losses. One could say that religion was not to be mentioned by the new Communist state, but the mayor had referred to Catholics and Jehovah's Witnesses. The idea of a Jewish genocide in Germany was not acknowledged, a black hole and a black mark against a person and a state that denied the most vicious truth of the Nazi era.

The school superintendent in Nordhausen reported that the upper-school classes were already visiting the concentration camp site and taking tours that included the crematorium. "They were shaken as they looked at this oven," he reported. "The number of dead, even the ashes and the remains still there, serve those who come after as a warning and must remain."[42]

Former prisoners of Mittelbau-Dora came to see the land during the early years following the war. Their pictures are found in various archives, but little note was made of these visits. The next mayor in Nordhausen, Fritz Giessner, was also a product of Nazi prisons and camps. He, like Hans Himmler, felt great empathy for the returning prisoners and personally took them on tours of the camp and hosted them with great sensitivity.

The First Mittelbau-Dora War Crimes Trials

It was a few years before war crimes trials were instituted. Those responsible for perpetrating the terrible suffering and enormous numbers of deaths among the prisoners in the Mittelbau-Dora camp were among those who should have been brought to justice, but were they? This question is answered through the records of the war trials and the biographies of the rocket scientists. It is often incomplete and also disappointing.

The eyewitness accounts of U.S. soldiers and officers of the armed forces, the congressmen and senators who followed them into not only Mittelbau-

Dora but also Ohrdruf, Buchenwald, and other camps, were indelibly branded with the sights from a different world, sights of unspeakable misery and raw extermination. These images were transmitted in two dimensions to newspapers and journals throughout the world, so that they became well known as the German crime of not only the century but also historical proportion.

The images and knowledge cried out for punishment, but a few events intervened. For the first few months after some of the perpetrators were captured, the war was still being fought both in Europe and in the Pacific. A few of the camps were quickly put to use again by the Allies as holding areas for those believed to be guilty of Nazi crimes or posing a threat to the newly established occupation forces. In the former Nazi camp Dachau, U.S. forces founded such a camp, while in the Soviet Zone, Sachsenhausen and Buchenwald were used for this purpose.

The Bergen-Belsen Prozess (Trial) was held under the auspices of the British Military Court and took place in 1945. Twelve SS members and some prisoner-Kapos were charged with crimes that occurred during the death march from Dora to Bergen-Belsen, which was a large camp that by April 1945 no longer sustained the lives of the prisoners housed there. It was one of the end stations of the various marches. British soldiers who freed the camp were every bit as shocked by what they found as the American soldiers were when they discovered the Boelcke-Kaserne in Nordhausen. The outcome was that twelve SS members were hung, five were dismissed, and four received long sentences.[43]

In the early summer of 1947, intensive preparations began for the so-called Nordhausen Prozess in Dachau. This was the only Mittelbau-Dora trial led by the Americans. Two dozen people were charged, including fourteen guards, four Mittelbau-Dora prisoners who had behaved in a criminal manner, and the director of Mittelwerk, Georg Rickhey.[44] The trial began on August 7, 1947, and lasted until December 1947 and was hindered through the difficulties of obtaining witnesses from the ranks of former prisoners. Many were too traumatized to appear in court and face the accused, some were frightened that the public would find out that their own behavior had been influenced by the extreme starvation and deprivation they encountered in the camp, and still others were simply too ill.

Conducting the trials in Germany was difficult for a number of reasons. "Nazism permeated German society like a pervasive cancer, scattered through the body politic as if someone had thrown a handful of fine sand. Before 1945, some six million people belonged to the Nazi Party, with millions more involved with affiliated organizations. Arguably, it was this contrast which made it impossible to carry out a radical purge in Germany, even before the Cold War made it inexpedient."[45] The result of the trial was relatively mild sentencing compared to other postwar trials. However, the testimony of the former prisoners became a part of the standing record, which had a value all its own.

Hans Möser, an SS officer in charge of the "Protective Custody Camp," was sentenced to death and was, indeed, executed at the end of 1948. SS officer Heinrich Detmers was found guilty of crimes in both Dachau and Mittelbau-Dora and was sentenced to fifteen years for the Dachau crimes and an extra five years for those committed in Mittelbau-Dora.[46] Another SS officer, Otto Bringmann, who had caused terror in Ellich-Juliushütte, was sentenced to life in prison.[47]

Former prisoners who had worked as *Kapos* were also sentenced. Such was the case with Richard Walenta, who because of his gruesome activities in Ellrich before the end of the war had even been sentenced by the Nazis to life in prison and had been kept in the bunker. SS Officer Erhard Brauny, who was partially responsible for the massacre at Gardelegen, was sentenced to life imprisonment as well. Other *Kapos* received sentences of shorter periods.[48]

None of the professionals were sentenced. Georg Rickhey was brought before the court but found not guilty, most likely because of his close ties with Arthur Rudolph and Wernher von Braun, who were already in the United States. They were all excused as primarily "technical personnel," although they had ties to the fate of prisoners.[49]

Of those sentenced in the Dachau trial, only Möser and Walenta received full sentences. Detmers's sentence was commuted in 1951, Bringmann's in 1958.[50] The casual way in which Rickhey was excused made it clear that those of technical value would have a new chance in the United States. A Nazi, his testimony was always presented from the standpoint of technical issues involving the A-4, and his interaction with prisoners was ignored.[51]

Other trials that focused on other camps included defendants who had also been in Mittelbau-Dora. The "Auschwitz Trial" held in Luneberg in 1945 brought thirty-three SS members and eleven *Kapos* before the law. Twelve were SS officers who had been in Mittelbau-Dora as well. Three of them were sentenced to death and hung. In Berlin-Pankow, in 1947, a trial was conducted by the Soviet Military Tribunal and was primarily concerned with the camp Sachsenhausen. Of the sixteen defendants, two had been in Mittelbau-Dora's outer camp Ellrich. Two were convicted and sentenced to years in Soviet prison camps, where one died and the other was released after nine years to the FRG.[52]

Conclusion

After the war, Nordhausen had cause to be proud of its rebuilding campaign and the progress it made in reestablishing the infrastructure. It also developed new political structures that had a large contingent of former concentration camp prisoners and others who had been targeted by the Nazis. Their early attempts at humanizing the sociocultural life of the city through educational and arts programs were counterbalanced by Soviet-inspired crackdowns of those not in agreement with the new system. There was still reluctance on the part of the occupying forces and, thus, the town leadership to recognize the bombing of Nordhausen, and there remained little opportunity for the townspeople to mourn the immediate dead of their own families in any public way.

Denazification took place under the gaze of the Soviets, but the Germans who had leadership positions were themselves anxious to wipe out the vestiges of fascism. In the name of security, they took harsh measures to quell any sign of the old regime. War trials took place in western Germany with different groups of defendants coming before a variety of tribunals. Some death sentences were meted out, but most of the defendants received relatively light sentences and were assigned little responsibility for the thousands who died under their watch. All technical people were dismissed from prosecution; many were already in the United States, where they eventually made good careers for themselves in the American space industry, even rising to great public esteem.[53] Other technical people were taken to the Soviet Union, where they worked in relative isolation for a number of years before being returned to Germany. Both countries extracted what they could from the tunnels of Mittelbau-Dora, the Americans retrieving paperwork and missiles and the Russians removing everything that was remaining "down to the rail tracks and high-tension wires."[54]

6. The Mahn- und Gedenkstätte in the GDR

The early years following the war were filled with work and hardship for the people of Nordhausen, but they settled into the new reality and actively engaged in rebuilding the infrastructure of the city. They also developed the permanent structures of government and city life under the watchful eyes of the new state and its Soviet sponsors. In this flurry of changing perspectives, the camp at Mittelbau-Dora engaged the imagination of the new city leaders and a core of dedicated citizens and party members who wanted to keep the reality of those years alive.

For many, the anxiety about a new round of fascism was not a political ploy but a real fear. The trust among the Allies was broken, and it was no longer a time for compromise and making adjustments to one another. The battle for hegemony in Europe was very serious. For those who had been in prisons during the Nazi years, like Werner Eggerath, who became the first minister president of Thuringia following the war, such memories were often more real than the life around them. Nothing was more important than keeping the pledge "Never Again." For some of the other townspeople, the occupation was a welcome relief from the bombing, and hopes for normalization flourished.

The Establishment of the German Democratic Republic

There was no clear date when Germany would be free of foreign occupiers. The Allies themselves could not decide when it was safe to leave Germany to its own devices. Should it be split, or should it be united? These were serious questions in the postwar years that had long-term consequences not only for Germany but for the economies and security of the Allied nations as well. The arguments were that, on the one hand, if the country were united, the industrial West and the agricultural East could share resources and become trading partners or, better perhaps, consumers of each other's goods. On the other hand, "the Soviets were interested in maintaining maximum flexibility to accommodate to a four-power agreement on the unification, demilitariza-tion, and neutralization of the country. The Soviets were too desperate for a share of West German coal and mineral resources and too worried about the integration of West German industrial power into an American-dominated Western condominium to give up easily on hopes for a neutral Germany."[1]

The question of which side would control the politics of Germany was critical and in contention on all sides, for each feared the other would have greater influence. Behind the scenes on both sides, some policy advisers were recommending that Germany remain divided. The underlying hostility of one side to the other grew as peace was established. The mutual suspicion of intent and motivation undermined any possibility of continuing the coopera-tion that had existed in wartime. The West instituted currency reform in 1948 that was rejected by the East. Shortly thereafter, the Soviets blocked the air deliveries of food and other supplies that America, France, and Britain had been sending into their Berlin zones. The Berlin Airlift proved that Berlin could survive even without land transport.

Nordhausen and the Cold War

Now the cold war began in earnest. With relations broken, "the U.S. had become convinced that all German agencies and a central German gov-ernment would only serve the extension of Soviet influence throughout Germany. This assessment was the basis for American policy which led to the establishment of the two Germanies."[2] In May 1949, the Allied Military Government approved the constitutional document called the Basic Law, paving the way for the establishment of the Federal Republic of Germany in West Germany. In October 1949, the German Democratic Republic was established in the East.

With the emergence of a new state that was more independent of its Soviet occupiers than it had been, although certainly not without strong and often contentious ties, the GDR could envision both its past and its future. By 1950, at the behest of the survivors, a small area in front of the crematorium was paved, and a symbolic grave of ashes was erected. The hamlet of Salza, just outside of Nordhausen, organized a memorial for the camp in 1951 and placed a commemorative stone near the road leading to Mittelbau-Dora. French survivors came to pay their respects. More visitors came to Nordhausen each following year to see the site of their imprisonment.[3]

In 1958, the national memorial in Buchenwald (Mahn- und Gedenkstätte Buchenwald) was dedicated, with thousands of survivors, family members, and citizens present on the grounds. There were six hundred citizens of Nordhausen present along with five hundred from the region. These eleven hundred were transported by bus to the site about an hour away. In a call to Nordhausen residents to take part, Mayor Himmler said: "It is a great honor and duty to stand among the 5,000 people at the memorial Buchenwald beside delegations from 17 countries and show that we are putting forth our entire energy for a Europe free of atomic weapons, for the retention and solidifying of world peace. Down with the fascist warmongers! The peoples' friendship lives! Everything for the peace and the socialist future of our land! [Heimat]."[4]

This was the beginning of large gatherings to remember the past and to present the values and goals of the future to the people of the GDR. When survivors then came to Buchenwald, they had a place to meet, museum-like exhibits to visit, people who would talk to them. Many wanted to make the trip to Nordhausen as well, but the roads were somewhat uncertain. The staff of Buchenwald then made it possible for these trips to take place, and the mayor of Nordhausen, Fritz Giessner, led the groups through the Mittelbau-Dora grounds.[5] Increasingly, the groups complained of the terrible state of the overgrown Nordhausen camp.

There was always some vandalism around the site of the concentration camp, but in 1956, the crematorium was vandalized. Nordhausen's Antifascist Resistance Committee (Komitee der Antifaschistischen Widerstandskämpfer) made complaints to the government, and the country's minister president, Otto Grotewohl, promised twenty-five thousand marks to build up a presentable place for memory. The city of Nordhausen decided to add lottery money to that sum. In April 1957, the committee was given twenty-four thousand marks and the responsibility under law to care for the property in the future.

More and more survivors came to Nordhausen in the 1950s. The personal interest of the mayor in their well-being and their stories made it a worthwhile trip for them. Only Communist or Eastern European visitors were able to come, with few exceptions, because of restrictions on visas from the side of the GDR, but also from other countries as well. Although the city of Nordhausen was aware of the former camp, there was not a real venue there for large gatherings, and so it remained a rather separate and unimportant place. Most of the large antifa gatherings were held at Buchenwald.

The exodus of East Germans to the West continued unabated and increased as land reform and lack of consumer goods relative to West Germany became more apparent. Fear of the growing repression of the state contributed to the wish of many to move to the FRG. Those who openly expressed their feelings were subject to imprisonment, expulsion from home or country, fines, and sentences of hard labor.

The border between East and West Germany was closed in 1952 and 1953, and those deemed untrustworthy were forcibly transferred to many small towns in another part of the country (*Zwangsumsiedlung*), where they had to start over under the harshest of circumstances, with a black mark on their records. In the area around Nordhausen, people were removed from twenty-three communities. On the day of the move, the officials were prepared to take over the belongings of the people designated and pack them into trucks for the trip northward. In all, 112 families were on the list to be expelled from their homes from the Nordhausen region, but many fled to the West before the appointed time. Eventually, 14 families and two individuals were taken away. There was a disbelief and abhorrence among much of the population about the forbidding of border crossing by citizens of the GDR into the FRG. Although it was still possible for GDR citizens to find places to cross without being apprehended, it was suddenly against the law, and the consequences, if caught, were not insignificant.[6]

Following Stalin's death in March 1953, both the East and the West were entering a new phase of their relationship. The situation was tense. A few months later, a general uprising in the country over many discontents reached Nordhausen as well. "All self-employed persons forfeited their ration cards and were then forced to buy goods from the much higher priced state stores. Subsidies on foods were eliminated or reduced, and special priced travel fares for workers were all but abolished. Pressure was increased to hasten collectivization of agriculture. A final measure adopted at the Thirteenth Plenium in May 1953 decreed that workers' production norms would be raised a minimum of 10 percent, effective 1 June 1953, to solve the economic crisis."[7]

The workers in Berlin went on strike on June 17, 1953. The outrage over the required increase in output meant, in reality, a decrease in wages. Strikes and demonstrations spread to 272 towns and cities, including Nordhausen.[8] Workers in several large Nordhausen concerns laid down their tools on June 18, 1953. Although at least a thousand workers struck, they were soon intimidated and went back to work the next day. The power of the state and the military support of the Soviet Union were in evidence and increasingly impinged on the lives of people in the GDR.

For those educated in technological fields, job opportunities in the West were plentiful and highly remunerated. Soon the GDR was hemorrhaging population. On August 13, 1961, the border between the East and West Berlin was sealed. The "Berlin Wall" was only part of the no-go zone between the divided Germany that both reduced the outflow of population and stabilized the population, for many at a great personal cost.

Mittelbau-Dora Reaches the Public

Mittelbau-Dora suddenly became fodder for the cold war in the 1960s, when publicity centering on Wernher von Braun exploded on both sides of the Atlantic and also in both East and West Germany. Always a showman, von Braun had gained popular recognition in the United States through television, where his imposing good looks and cheerful manner made him a public figure. The excitement of a space program fueled the public imagination of which von Braun was the iconic image.

A West German–American film, *I Aim at the Stars,* despite its box-office failure in 1960, further enhanced his image and the place of rockets in the international competition in weaponry and the space race. No mention was made of the use of concentration camps and their labor in the development of rocket launches in the 1940s.[9] The German "Columbus of Space" remained without a German past.

Not to be outdone, the GDR's Julius Mader, a journalist and publicist, either decided or was assigned to write a series of articles and a book about the Nazi rocket weapons and their assembly in the Kohnstein Mountain through the exploitation of slave labor. Mader was a well-educated person who had received his master's degree (*Diplom*) in economics and an honorary doctorate. His book, *Das Geheimnis von Huntsville* (The Secret of Huntsville), centered on the role of Wernher von Braun as an SS officer and Nazi insider, who had become the hero of the U.S. space program.[10] In 1967, a film based on the book, *Die Gefrorenen Blitze* (Frozen Lightning), was released to an enthusiastic audience in East Germany.

Mader was a member of the state security apparatus known as the Stasi (Ministerium für Staatssicherheit), engaged for "special projects." He was also a popular writer and author of several dozen books, materials for several of which were taken directly from state files. The extent to which his exposure of von Braun and other U.S. officials was sponsored by cold war motivations or his own convictions is not known.

The Mahn- und Gedenkstätte Mittelbau-Dora

Following the opening of the Mahn- und Gedenkstätte Buchenwald in 1958, the impetus was greater to do more with the grounds of Mittelbau-Dora, and the city leaders of Nordhausen voted to erect a Gedenkstätte Mittelbau-Dora on the original site of the concentration camp. It was not until the mid-1960s that a Mahn- und Gedenkstätte, meaning "a place of admonishment and remembrance," was finally erected on the grounds. A work group (*Arbeitsgruppe*) within Nordhausen's SED had been working on issues surrounding the Gedenkstätte for several years and was helped by the fact that one of their members, Kurt Pelny, had come to Nordhausen in 1960, having completed a master's thesis on the camp Mittelbau-Dora. The thesis was turned into one of the first publications about the camp.

It was not until July 28, 1961, that an order was announced in the Legal Papers of the GDR titled Statut der Nationalen Mahn- und Gedenkstätten.[11] The new statute said that each memorial site was to be under the Department of Culture and would receive its funding through that department. Each Gedenkstätte was to work with the regional organizations, particularly the committees of antifa resistance fighters (Komitee der Antifaschistischen Widerstandskämpfer). Their assignment was to show:

- The fight of the working class and all democratic forces against the threatening fascist danger
- The role of the German Communist Party as the strongest and leading force in the war against the criminal Nazi regime
- The antifascist resistance in the years 1933–45 in Germany and Europe
- The SS terror in camps and its methods of disrespecting human life
- The common fight of all European nations, especially the Soviets, against the SS terror
- The special meaning of the international solidarity and its measures that led to the freeing of the camps
- The return of fascism and militarism in West Germany
- The historical role of the GDR

Through cooperation and financing from the Institute for Memorials (Institut für Denkmalpflege) and the city's Culture Department (Abteilung Kultur beim Rat der Stadt), many improvements were made to the site. In 1964, a sculpture of several figures representing prisoners was placed in front of the crematorium. A long uphill path with stairs to the crematorium was repaired, and plants were set along it to make it more attractive. They added a guided way through the grounds with descriptions of various places of importance. Everything was done to the extent possible with materials that were on hand and with attention to the sustainability of the changes without much future expense.[12]

On August 9, 1964, the new sculpture was dedicated. Guests at the ceremony included Ellen Kuntz (the wife of Albert Kuntz), a delegation of resistance fighters from the GDR, and city officials from nearby Erfurt. An honor guard made up of students stood near the figures, which were covered with a white cloth. At the right moment the covering was removed, and various groups laid wreaths of flowers around the bottom of the statue. The national anthem was played, and then people were free to tour the grounds.[13] For the first time, the grounds were now called a Gedenkstätte.

The SED's Mittelbau-Dora's work group (*Arbeitsgruppe*) continued to lead tours and look after the grounds of the Gedenkstätte, but with interest increasing, due perhaps to Mader's work, and with more resources available, the time had come to think about a more substantial exhibition. Kurt Pelny, an avid member of that group, began to tour the back roads looking for artifacts and meeting people who might have information about the camp. He went on his motorbike making new acquaintances and learning more about the place that would become his life's work. In 1966, enough material had been

Ellen Kuntz, wife of Albert Kuntz, in front of the crematorium with Nordhausen visitors in 1964 at the dedication of a bust of her husband to the Gedenkstätte. (Stadtarchiv Nordhausen)

gathered to open a small exhibit in the crematorium building, and on April 6, 1966, it was dedicated.[14]

Kurt Pelny came from a working-class, Communist family. He had had only a rudimentary education under the Nazis, but, born in 1931, he was too young to become a soldier. His father was imprisoned for a time as an opponent of Hitler, and, thus, the Nazi regime was not going to give Pelny any advantages. When the Communists came to power, Kurt Pelny was in a much better position. No longer was being in an anti-Nazi family a handicap; on the contrary, his embrace of communism was an asset. He was able to continue his education.

Pelny became professionally involved in the youth development movement of the GDR and was employed in the Free German Youth (Freie Deutsche Jugend) organization in which almost every GDR child was active. He led after-school activities, tutored youngsters, and provided training for workers' groups (*Arbeitsgemeinschaften*). Later he worked in homes with children with behavioral and cognitive difficulties. Pelny was very much taken with the philosophy of Anton Semyonovich Makarenko, a Soviet educator and theorist who created children's centers for street children of the Russian Revolution based upon a system of self-government and self-responsibility.[15]

Kurt Pelny's later work in Dresden at the Pädagogische Hochschule ended with a degree in history (*Lehrer für Geschichte*), which required a thesis. He wrote this paper on the secret weapons of Mittelbau-Dora, and it became his first publication.[16] He and his family moved to Nordhausen in 1960, where he found that the mayor, Fritz Giessner, was a man with whom he could work effectively. Having a similar outgoing personality, Giessner played the guitar, and Ellen Kuntz and Giessner often joined in for happy evenings with the Pelnys.

Kurt was a natural for SED assignments and had many positions that spanned the party and the government that were very much linked to the life of the GDR. He did not so much seek out the positions as he accepted assignments. He had served for two years in the agitation/propaganda department of the SED. "Agitprop," as it became known in the United States, was a kind of street theater developed in the 1930s to educate and engage people on the street on issues of politics and social justice. In the GDR, it had another meaning. Far from being a theatrical engagement, it was serious discussion and education in far-flung venues in which the party agent would inform and attempt to convince people of the efficacy and justice of government policies, such as land reform and changes in the school structure.

Kurt Pelny had begun this work from the very beginning of the GDR in 1949 and traveled to towns and villages in order to explain the issues that concerned people from the government's point of view. As a convinced Communist, he enjoyed being on the forefront of engendering change. He was an affable man and a good conversationalist and speaker. After two years serving his required term in the National Folks Army (Nationale Volksarmee), he worked in the county government and the party in various posts. He continued his interest in gathering materials about Mittelbau-Dora and had an ally in this endeavor in Giessner. Kurt was named the leader of the SED's Mittelbau-Dora work group, but still as a volunteer.

When it became possible in 1972 for him to become the director of the memorial, he assumed the position. He was a natural for the job, having dedicated more than a decade of his free time to the collection of materials related to the camp and having already done research on its history. Kurt Pelny and his wife were able to obtain a small wooden blockhouse on enough land to grow a good garden. For the Pelnys, it was idyllic.

In 1972, Kurt Pelny led a small group of fellow workers (*Mitarbeiter*) in cleaning the area of the former concentration camp Mittelbau-Dora, doing some landscaping, collecting artifacts and personal experiences with Mittelbau-Dora from neighbors and townspeople, and welcoming the survivors who could come to the site. There was no money to construct an

Kurt and Irmgard Pelny in front of their bungalow, 1992. (Gretchen Schafft, photographer, Nordhausen Collection)

administration building, so Kurt made arrangements with the supervisors of apprentice programs to do the rebuilding and found electricians, carpenters, and small workshops that agreed to donate their time and materials to improving the Gedenkstätte.

Despite the fact that travel passes were not readily obtained for non-Communists from outside the Eastern-bloc countries, French and Belgian survivors and their families were among the most frequent visitors to the memorial. Kurt also did what he could to encourage visits of Polish, Soviet, and Czech survivors. During that time, he developed real friendships with some of the survivors or with those who, like Leo Kuntz, were living relatives of those who had died in the camp.[17]

Kurt Pelny felt a great need to find survivors in other countries, to collect their stories, and to tell them of his work and ambitions for the Gedenkstätte. He devised a plan to accomplish this goal by becoming a part-time guide for the government travel bureau (Nordhausen Reisegruppen) and planning trips to Eastern countries where survivors lived. In this way he could meet those who knew the history of the camp and learn more about what had happened there.

From the start, Pelny set about forming a working group (*Mitarbeiterkreis*) and building a culture of concern for the history of this particular concentration camp. He was the first major figure in Thuringia active in the camp history who was not a concentration camp survivor. The mayors of the city since the war had both experienced prison and camps, and the director of the Buchenwald Mahn- und Gedenkstätte was also a survivor. Kurt made friends with Leo Kuntz, the son of Albert Kuntz; Franz Kowalski, the remaining Jewish survivor of Mittelbau-Dora; Mayor Fritz Giessner; and soon survivors of many countries.

The staff had little documentation. Martin Bornemannn, a historian who lived on the other side of the border in West Germany, began writing about the camp. He had access to the documentation in the West and other archival sources in Germany, and, after 1977, the full war crimes trial documentation. At Mittelbau-Dora, the sources were more restricted, limited to the Warsaw trials, some files made available by the Soviets, and archives saved by Polish prisoners, particularly Wincenty Heim. Despite those limitations, many politically oriented scholars in the GDR were working on documentation. One such group was under the leadership of Walter Bartel, a survivor of Buchenwald and a professor at the Humboldt University of Berlin. He gathered students into a working group to explore various aspects of the history of the camps, particularly Buchenwald. They began to build the first archive of the camps in Buchenwald. Although their work was ideologically driven, it was a great service to the otherwise empty bookshelves of the libraries within the memorials.

Kurt Pelny, with the help of his wife, Irmgard, began to write short pamphlets about various aspects of the camp and the people who had suffered there for the general public and for young people. A series of these pamphlets was distributed during his tenure that lasted almost until the end of the GDR.

The Second Mittelbau-Dora
War Crime Trials in Essen

The first trial that concerned defendants who had been active in the Mittelbau-Dora camp was more than disappointing to many who had followed it. The trial had taken place as a subsequent trial to Nuremberg and was held under American auspices in Dachau in 1947. Sentencing of the nineteen defendants was relatively mild, with only one death sentence and two acquittals. Other defendants received a few years each. After only five years, those who had gotten sentences of many years were pardoned by the American civilian authorities and went free. There were two reasons for this. First, the United States was ambivalent about the war trials and sentencing Nazi perpetrators. "Those with lifelong sentences served only fifteen years; those condemned to death, but who escaped the gallows, were released after twenty. Few of the rest sat out their prison terms or more than a handful of years."[18] The second reason was the result of the very real opposition to sentencing Nazi war criminals by the population of the FRG. More important, that opposition played out in the politics of the church, both Catholic and Protestant, as both came out in opposition to punishment.[19]

Only one in every ten West Germans supported the war crimes trials, according to a survey conducted in 1952. Further trials faced massive opposition from the Adenauer government, almost all political parties, and the Catholic and Protestant churches. Even seemingly respectable experts on international law, as well as right-wing organizations with mass appeal to veterans and refugee groups, wanted to bury the very idea of trials.[20]

At the same time, the United States was normalizing relations with the FRG in trade and in weapons. Partly, the normalization was rationalized by cold war strategies. Economic interests also had a role, for there were profits to be made in a country recovering from the war in which new consumers were ready to buy American goods. Businesses that had never completely broken their ties to their American counterparts were also again on the rise.[21]

The security goals of the United States meshed neatly with the economic goals. Defending the world against communism in the postwar years and building a robust capitalism in Europe were the twin goals of the Dulles brothers, John Foster and Allen, the secretary of state and the head of the Office of Strategic Services (later the Central Intelligence Agency) under President Roosevelt, respectively.

> [Allen Dulles] believed he could extract economic and military intelligence from the Nazis' partners, sow disorder in Axis ranks, and preserve business and political leaders favoring private enterprise for postwar reconstruction.
>
> Dulles offered cooperative Axis leaders promises of protection from prosecution for their crimes and asylum from the advancing Red Army. The collaborators often faced charges of treason—as well as accusations of exploitation of slave labor, racial persecution, looting, and other offenses regarded as war crimes or crimes against humanity. Dulles also appealed to the class interests of former collaborators to their desire to protect Western civilization against communism and to similar less tangible factors.[22]

One more large trial was undertaken, this time by East and West Germans in a concerted effort to bring Mittelbau-Dora criminals to justice. The Essen trial was held over a period of years, from 1967 to 1970. It was prosecuted by the GDR, but was held in the West German town of Essen without further international involvement. Sessions of the trial were opened by a West German judge, and were under the jurisdiction of West German criminal law and procedure. The interests of the East Germans were represented by the famous East German prosecutor Karl Kaul. Those indicted were free to move around and even take trips within Germany during the trial.[23]

The cold war was well under way, and although the wall had been built in 1961 to stop the flood of East Germans from leaving, there was concern on the part of the political forces in the GDR that witnesses might defect. Therefore, the prisoner-survivors coming from the East were vetted for their loyalty to the new Communist government, for there was fear that they would make claims against it or try to remain in the West, either of which would be a grave embarrassment.[24]

In the intervening years since the American Dachau trial in 1947, there were many eyewitness reports of what Dora had been and meant to the prisoners. More was known, also through the previous trials, of the extent of the murder within the camp and the outer camps.

In the Essen trial only three SS members were brought forward as defendants: Helmut Bischoff, Ernst Sander, and Erwin Busta. Of particular interest in this trial were the mass hangings of prisoners for sabotage in the last months of the war. Bischoff had been the chief of the Gestapo in the Nordhausen area and during the occupation of Poland had been a leader of a special forces group (Einsatz-Kommando) that functioned as a death squad on the Eastern front during the war and before he was assigned to Mittelbau-Dora. He was known to have been in charge of mass shootings of Jews. Sander was under Bischoff in the Mittelbau-Dora hierarchy, but organized the hangings. He was thought to be responsible for the torture and ultimate death of Albert Kuntz, but it was never proved. Erwin Busta also arranged hangings, both on the roll-call square and in the tunnel.[25]

The lawyers from the GDR were skilled and led by the experienced Kaul, himself a Jewish survivor of the Third Reich. He was held in low esteem by the other side because of his political association as head lawyer for the SED.[26] The preparation of the prosecution team from the GDR was very political and used cold war tactics with the hope of bringing their main concern of monopolistic capitalism into the hearings. In this they were frustrated.

The most deeply disappointing outcome, however, was the dismissal of charges against Bischoff due to his health. In fact, the rise in his blood pressure could lead to his death, so the hearings regarding him had to be stopped.[27] The other two defendants received sentences of between seven and eight years, which they never had to serve.[28]

An Expanded Concept for the Gedenkstätte

In 1978, there was a major impetus to develop the Gedenkstätte further. By now, there was a speaker's podium of dominating proportions over the *Appellplatz,* a description of many important places around the grounds, and a small exhibit in the crematorium. Two original buildings remained in fairly good condition: the crematorium and the fire station. In addition, an all-purpose building had been built in 1972 as a one-story structure at the gate of the Gedenkstätte. It had a large room for meetings and for showing films, separate rooms for administrators and staff members, and a library and archive.

An enlarged concept for the museum was developed by the SED and the Communist survivor group. This conception raised Gedenkstätte Mittelbau-Dora to a Level I museum of the GDR. It was declared to be of significance far beyond Nordhausen—indeed, for the whole GDR. The multiple goals for the new memorial site were simultaneously political, ideological, scientific, and educational. It would show how fascist Germany had used its technical power to spread imperialist capitalism. It was critical that the antifascist forces under the leadership of the Communists be put in a context of patriotism and multinational proletarian action. This would be put together in a knowledge-able demonstration of political-ideological work put into practice.[29]

The model of the Buchenwald exhibit stressed the illegal party organizations, the international camp committee, the national committees, and the

A young couple marries in front of the crematorium at the Gedenkstätte in 1977, dedicating themselves to antifascism. (Stadtarchiv Nordhausen)

commandos. Although most of the prisoners in Buchenwald were unaware of such actions, the emphasis on the international camp committee obtained even less for the prisoners of Mittelbau-Dora than those in Buchenwald.[30] When Buchenwald was originally built in 1937, it housed primarily political prisoners. Its population changed through the years, taking on large numbers of Jewish prisoners following the November 1938 pogrom known as the "Night of Broken Glass" (*Kristallnacht*) and, beginning in late 1939, an increasing number of non-German resisters and prisoners of war. The full range of Nazi prisoners, including every kind of minority population, was also represented in large numbers.

In Buchenwald, there is no doubt that the resistance led by Communist prisoners existed and defined the camp, if not for the majority of prisoners, at least for many. In Mittelbau-Dora, there was a small group of resisters of perhaps a few dozen prisoners, who attempted to build an international organization within the camp. They certainly could not all meet together, and the organization must have been loose. The possibility of organizing in the same way as those prisoners in Buchenwald had done was minimal. The conditions were just too brutal at Mittelbau-Dora for all but a very few prisoners to be concerned with more than survival: the camp was spread among the main camp and forty-three outer camps, the prisoners were composed no longer of the political groups that had populated the concentration camps of the 1930s, and very few of the Dora prisoners had been Communists.[31]

The indications that there was indeed an international resistance committee within Mittelbau-Dora composed of German, Czech, Polish, French, and Soviet citizens were found in the records of sabotage among prisoner memoirs, the number of prisoners arrested from November 1944 through March 1945 by the camp's SS, evidence at the war crimes trials, and the oral history collected at the time. Kurt Pelny recorded this evidence in a small book that presents the chronology of events. The goals of the international committee were to defeat the regime's plan to eliminate their opposition through murderous work, to institute work slowdowns, and to systematically disturb the viability of the weapons being produced.[32]

Jan Čespiva, a Czech doctor working in the sick bay, was arrested because an informer had found evidence of a radio in his office and reported it. Otakar Litomisky gives the credit for the radio to Jan Chaloupka, another Czech prisoner who built a radio receiver that could receive broadcasts from Moscow and London.[33] The massive arrests of the group over a period of months ended with the hanging of more than fifty Soviet suspected saboteurs. The camp administration in late 1944 and early 1945 arrested, tortured, and murdered many of the ring leaders, including Albert Kuntz.[34]

Individual sabotage is reported in most of the memoirs from Mittelbau-Dora survivors. "I observed over the whole time of the existence of the Dora camp, that the Czechs carried on a systematic sabotage. . . . They had to observe calmly that one could make something wrong. . . . [T]hey must observe calmly that a machine could be damaged even when it would be possible to correct the error."[35] Another view in a prisoner's memoir is less sanguine:

> Sabotage is a damned risky effort when prisoners are working on large pieces, especially when they are of different nationalities. The animosity between groups is so great that systematic sabotage is quite dangerous. . . . But in the right group, the mistakes and accidents that could be repaired with a little effort are silently passed along by tacit agreement. In fact, any change in the working pace in order to repair the fault would immediately attract the attention of the German Meister who might cry out, "Sabotage!" So, mum's the word, and the group continues working as if nothing at all had happened. . . . The beautiful rocket won't reach targets of strategic value or dense population. Instead, it will destroy itself in a market garden or, at worst, on or near some unfortunate, isolated human habitations, but, after all, that is war.[36]

By the 1970s, it was not only the political organization that dominated decisions about how the Gedenkstätte would be designed, but also the pres-

Ceremony at the *Appellplatz* on the Day of Victims of Fascism in 1974 at the KZ Mahn- und Gedenkstätte Mittelbau-Dora. (Gedenkstätte Mittelbau-Dora Archiv)

A new exhibit at the Gedenkstätte in 1982. Kurt Pelny, director, is on the left, and Franz Kowalski, Mittelbau-Dora survivor, is in the front, second from the right. (Gedenkstätte Mittelbau-Dora Archiv)

ence of many survivors who were active and wanted their stories told and taken seriously. Many spoke to Leo and Ellen Kuntz, who were anxious to find out what they could about the life and death of Albert Kuntz. They spoke to Kurt Pelny and to others on the staff of the memorial, who came to know and respect them and what they had experienced.

The guidelines set by the SED, despite the discrepancies, were followed to some extent. There were displays of the Nazis who had retained prominent positions in West Germany, the von Braun images from American films, and the continuing weapons production of the same companies involved in the Second World War. However much these images and statements were aimed at fostering anti-West, anticapitalist sentiment, they were still true, and the information was not readily available elsewhere.

But events and people who did not fit the heroic mode were omitted. Where were the Jews who had come into the camp more dead than alive in the winter of 1944–45? Where were the descriptions of nonpolitical or even nationalist prisoners from France, Belgium, the Netherlands, or Poland? The majority of prisoners in the camp were not reflected in the concentration on heroic Communist personages. However, in the small fire station there was an exhibit of the handicrafts created by the prisoners and the important poem by Julius Fucik, found in the introduction to this book, that urged visitors to look at all the prisoners, not just the heroes who had names that all would recognize.

Development of a Gedenkstätte Work Culture

Over the years, a specific work culture developed within the Gedenkstätte. There were grounds people, building engineers, carpenters, librarians and archivists, and administrative staff. They met several times a day for coffee or lunch or just to talk about plans. For the most part, the atmosphere was positive. There was little feeling of competition, as the wage differentials were not great. They had a mutual responsibility and became tied to the survivors through their own experiences and a feeling of respect.

For instance, one of the workers had lost his father in the war. His mother, caring for several children without support, was ordered to go to work in a munitions plant. She could not leave her children, she felt. A representative of the Nazi state came to see her and gave her a week to find support for herself and the children or they would all be taken to camps and orphanages. She begged an uncle to take them in, which he did, and they were spared. Another staff member had seen the camp as a child and had watched the prisoners digging a ditch, falling over from exhaustion and being beaten by guards. The guards spied him and yelled that if he didn't move away they would kill him.

Most likely most Germans living near camps had witnessed more than they cared to remember. However, members of the Mittelbau-Dora working group were encouraged to remember and to think about what the Third Reich had meant to so many. They had lectures from Soviets about the effect of the Third Reich on the Soviet Union. To enhance their understanding, Kurt Pelny planned trips to the outer camps and other memorial sites and shared the history of Mittelbau-Dora as it became better known. They had no source of transportation other than trains or buses, so they went together, meeting at stations or bus stops.

The staff members were encouraged to make themselves available to schools and factories, where they gave lectures and talks about the camp. The hours were flexible, and the working atmosphere was generally not stressful, so evening hours were not viewed as a hardship. When the work was difficult or if the staff was feeling bored during a period of time, Kurt would provide a surprise of some kind: ice cream brought in by car on a hot day, a cultural event, or a party. The staff had a regular program for parties, picnics, trips, and other events. One of the grounds people, Wolfgang Köhler, was the jolly leader of "quiz shows" for the staff; a walk in the woods, only to find a pot of boiling sausages at their destination; or dance parties. The staff had its own vacation spot, a trailer set up not far from Peenemünde on the Baltic Sea in the midst of a beach colony that could be reserved with advance notice by staff and their families. Although none of these events or benefits would impress today's workers, in the context of the postwar GDR, they were a source of real pleasure and, for many, made the job special.

Some of the staff were members of the SED, but many were not. Wolfgang was an independent, not belonging to any party. One of the secretaries also remained independent. Others may have been members in name only, but were not enthusiastic. Until the late 1980s, none was in active opposition: that would have been cause for dismissal and possible punishment. At least two of the staff had relatives who were viewed as oppositional to the government, but that did not appear to cause trouble for them.

Once a month, there was a political meeting at the Gedenkstätte for the staff. At that time, they discussed their schedules, the cultural programs, and problems within the Gedenkstätte. People stated their preferences for vacation time and asked what places (*Ferienobjekte*) were available to them. If

Christa and Wolfgang Köhler, 1996. (Gretchen Schafft, photographer, Nordhausen Collection)

Kurt had been to a meeting with survivors, he would hold a special meeting (*Arbeitsbesprechung*), and if survivors were planning a trip to the Gedenkstätte, he would assign special jobs to staff members. There were a small number of prisoners' records available to the staff, and they were used to answer the visitors' questions about specific people who had been in the camp. For many visitors, the concern shown by the staff made up for the paucity of information. Increasingly, political issues were on the agenda, and someone from the SED might come to be sure everyone was on the same page. Over time, not everyone was.

The Gedenkstätte was used for groups, as well. Some groups were well represented by the SED and had political meaning. For instance, the Free German Youth and the recruits to the Nationale Volksarmee regularly held ceremonies at the site. They also helped with cleanup days and other events. Church groups regularly met around Easter to walk the stations of the cross through the area where so much suffering had occurred, and volunteer groups of West German youth came occasionally for work camps and meetings. Groups not specifically sponsored by the SED were held in suspicion, and notes were taken by police spies who added them to the files on individuals who were under surveillance.[37] Classes from local schools made afternoon

Volunteer young people cleaning the Gedenkstätte grounds in 1983. (Gedenkstätte Mittelbau-Dora Archiv)

trips to the Dora grounds. There, they did some landscaping and cleaning, a welcome change from their classrooms, but they did not usually assign political meaning to their activity.[38]

The staff of the Gedenkstätte was well aware of the GDR propensity for spying on its citizens. Some felt it was a security that they could welcome, a way to always be safe from those who might want to do them or their country harm. Others were oppressed by this constant presence of strangers in their lives and the demands that were placed upon them at times. Wolfgang Köhler, for instance, had been found with an illegal firearm in his house, a rifle left over from a grandfather who enjoyed hunting. Taken to the police station, Köhler was asked to be an informer in return for having the charges dropped. Later when telling this story, he claimed that he was unprepared to do this. His wife was then pressed into service. She should go to one of the churches nearby and listen to the sermons and conversations of parishioners and report any antigovernment sentiment expressed. In the same conversation, she said that she found it impossible to carry out this assignment. She was not used to going to church and found it so dull that she fell asleep and never had anything to report. Eventually, she just stopped going, and no further problem came their way. Their son was not so lucky, however, for he was harassed by the state apparatus for his beliefs and associations, and many doors were closed to him over the years. For him, the state and its bureaucracies presented a constant threat.[39]

Conclusion

There was so much to do following the end of the war that one could hardly envision the future for Nordhausen. Yet at the same time, as streets were being cleared, work started again, educational institutions were re-created, and new values were introduced. Leaders of the city were coming together to decide how to take care of the determined Nazis who remained around the city, how to develop a workable political system, how to provide fairly for all those who needed the basic elements of life. While decisions were often made on the basis of ideology and political considerations, the town was remarkable in its energy and purpose, having been 80 percent destroyed in the last days of the war by strategic bombing raids. Life did begin again.

Although having taken authority over Nordhausen in 1945 as agreed upon at the Yalta Conference, the Soviets stayed out of sight for the most part. They held all the cards, but played them judiciously in Nordhausen. They, like the short American occupation before them, did not allow the people to mourn their own dead in public. Eventually, an exhibit could be mounted mentioning the terrible destruction the city and families had experienced, but it was carefully framed within an optimistic and encouraging picture of "tomorrow in the socialist world."

At first, the site of the concentration camp was forgotten in the immense duties that had to be assumed by each person just to keep going. However, before too many years, the remembrance of the camp fitted the guidelines set out in conjunction with the Soviet Union. The memorial fitted into the political education that the leading political party wanted to impart to the postwar generations. It was slowly rebuilt in a mixture of respect, reverence, political will, and obfuscation. It was a site of community gatherings and ceremony, some taken seriously by the citizens and some mocked. Some of the sanctioned activities and the people taking part in them at the Gedenkstätte were closely monitored for signs of danger to the state's interests.

The issue of German guilt, so much a part of Western remembrance, was completely absent in the East. The GDR built a story that separated the good from the bad, not by country, but by political persuasion and economic ideology. For those on the right side of the fence, it felt right and good. For those on the wrong side, it irked or, worse, rankled.

The complete loss of Jewish life in the city went unremarked. There was no guideline in the regulations for the Gedenkstätte to mourn their disappearance and no attempt to explain it. For the few Jews who remained in Nordhausen or came to settle there, no obvious discrimination was noticeable, but religion in general had no role in the new state and was only barely tolerated. Those who sought to practice seriously any religion were held in suspicion.

A vague discourse of potential individual guilt, seen in the frequent use of the word *mahnen* carried with it both a warning and a sense that things could turn at a moment's notice. It also carried a message that urged citizens to be aware and responsible. In many respects, the GDR years encompassed all of these admonitions, ambivalent as they were.

Von Braun's path was not as smooth as before the films, and he was called to give testimony before Congress, but his importance to the U.S. space program insulated him from prosecution. The Department of Justice's Office of Special Investigations, founded in 1973, was in charge of finding and prosecuting Nazis guilty of war crimes. It learned that the United States had kept a file on von Braun. Arthur Rudolph, the production manager of Mittelbau-Dora, was expelled from the United States after many years and stripped of his NASA pension, but von Braun died before they could take action against him.[40] Those most responsible for Nazi crimes in Nordhausen were not given the full measure of punishment for their acts. The survivors suffered at this knowledge and their own continuing lack of voice and power to find justice.

7. The Wall Comes Down

Nordhausen had not existed in a vacuum; it was highly influenced by the national policy makers and had to work largely within that framework. Indeed, the national government was not entirely free to make its own decisions, for it was a country that, as often asserted in the West, was a "satellite of the Soviet Union." Nordhausen, like other small cities, was on the end of a chain of command, impacted by what was occurring internationally and nationally, but also shaping its own local future. In the 1980s, the situation became critical.

Germany had experience in transitions. The denazification of the Third Reich had left a trail of procedures that could be used: get rid of the teachers, fire the administrators, examine the people who were close to the state apparatus (*staatsnah*), expel sympathizers of the previous regime from their jobs and remove their privileges, punish a few, reeducate the masses. The discourse and rhetoric must also change in public institutions like the Gedenkstätte—perhaps particularly the Gedenkstätte. By the end of the 1980s, these procedures began to come into play.

The Gedenkstätte Loses Its Leader

Dissatisfaction and unrest had become more open by the mid-1980s, and the entire Eastern bloc was sensing that Gorbachev was going to make big changes in the Soviet system that would soon impact the GDR. At the twenty-seventh party congress, in the spring of 1986, he announced his new conceptions: "perestroika" and "glasnost." These reforms would relax relations with the West, give parliamentary rule a larger role, and give state offices more power while reducing the power of the party. The reforms encompassed more individual freedom of expression, free from repression.[1]

The GDR was in a peculiar situation. If the people compared their living standard with others in the Eastern bloc countries, they were very well off because of their industrial base and agricultural sufficiency. However, common necessities of life were often missing, and stores were not well stocked. It was a common practice among the people, though unwelcome to the SED leadership, to watch television programs coming from the FRG. There, the comparisons between East and West were apparent to GDR viewers. Visits, although restricted, did occur between relatives from East and West Germany, and word of mouth increased the feelings among the populace that they, living in the GDR, were the poor cousins. With the increased freedom of expression in other Eastern and middle European countries, people began to complain more about how things should be reformed.

The discussions within the Gedenkstätte often became heated and divided between those who favored system reform and those dedicated to retaining the system safe from threat. Where goodwill and a team spirit had prevailed, the staff was now divided; hot tempers and harsh words were not uncommon. Kurt Pelny may have considered his own political position when he decided to leave the Gedenkstätte, but he had other reasons as well. He suffered from the injuries he incurred in a motorcycle accident in the late 1950s, and by the late 1980s, he had trouble standing and walking for more than a few minutes

Nordhausen's Töpfer Street with the department store Töpfertor, downtown, in the GDR period. (Stadtarchiv Nordhausen, no date)

at a time. He stepped back and retired in 1988 without a successor at hand. He left a gap filled by the staff (*Mitarbeiterkreis*) until a new director could be found.

Euphoria and Hardship

Dr. Peter Kuhlbrodt was assigned in September 1989 to be the new director. He was a teacher in the Nordhausen high school (*Gymnasium*) with a doctorate in history. He had been raised in the nearby town of Ellrich and remembers seeing the "zebras," as the townspeople called the prisoners. He did not know the context when he was a child. As a teacher, he was obligated to take his students to the Gedenkstätte to do work on the grounds, but he did not approve of the political tone that accompanied such visits.

Peter Kuhlbrodt was not a "150 percenter," a reference to those who were more than willing to hold the line and ignore or explain away most of the excesses and failures of the GDR. His father was a target of the Communist regime as someone who had had an important position in the Third Reich and had escaped to the West. Peter Kuhlbrodt had seen Leo Kuntz become the center of attention due to the heroization of his father, while the Kuhlbrodt family was shattered. It hurt personally, and he did not agree politically.

Kurt Pelny's secretary knew the Kuhlbrodt family and was aware that Peter had finished his studies in Leipzig and was back in Nordhausen. As a major functionary in the Nordhausen SED leadership, she suggested that Kuhlbrodt be the successor. He was not prepared for the political stress within the Gedenkstätte and the obligation as director to speak to the city leadership of the political work of the memorial.

At this same time in 1989, the open rebellion against the ruling government began in the GDR. On September 11, the Hungarian border was opened to people wanting to leave the GDR, and a way through Hungary to Austria and on to the West was now clear. One of Berlin's newspapers reported that within the first two weeks, twenty-six thousand GDR citizens had fled their homeland over the Hungarian route.[2] News was restricted through Eastern state-run television and radio channels, but was nevertheless immediately known through word of mouth or news from the West.

Wolfgang Köhler, who had been a force for fun and good sense among the Gedenkstätte staff, found that he had to make a decision with very personal consequences. As the border opened and East Germans could find sanctuary in Hungary and a way to the West, his son, a medical doctor, decided to take the chance and leave with his young family. He needed his parents' help to store belongings and gather money for the trip. For the first time in his life, he openly told his parents of the repression he had experienced over the years and the toll it had taken. As a medical doctor, his chances had been seriously circumscribed by the government because of his activities in alternative peace groups. Christa Köhler, Wolfgang's wife, said, "It was the first time he had ever really talked to us since he was a child. He poured his heart out. We hadn't known."[3] The parents entered the conspiracy and moved their son's family things into their house in order to allow them to depart with a minimum of baggage. When it was over, and the son safely over the border, Wolfgang and Christa pretended to be surprised. They were painfully aware, however, that their relationship with their beloved grandchildren might be lost forever. Wolfgang pretended to his fellow workers at the Gedenkstätte that he was disappointed in his son, but secretly he supported the decision.[4]

Others used their new opportunities to travel westward as well, and soon there was a stream moving eastward in order to get to the West. Those remaining in Nordhausen demonstrated, watched the national movement grow, formed local groups supporting new political forms, and met privately to discuss the future.

The Citizens Movement (*Bürgerbewegung*) in Nordhausen

Local Protestant churches were the first to reflect the national movement as they began in the fall of 1989 to lead "intercession services" (*Fürbitteandachten*). New political groups—the New Forum (Neue Forum), Democracy Now (Demokratie Jetzt), and the Democratic Awakening (Demokratischer Aufbruch)—each gathered people to their meetings, attempting to create a political platform for the whole GDR.[5] Churches were the safest and easiest places to meet, as few people had large-enough apartments and public space was not available to non-state-sponsored groups.

With the direction from Moscow to allow freer discussion and open debate, people were willing to risk reprisals in order to test the waters, despite the fact that the meetings were observed by the state security representatives, and wider efforts were put into place to quell the rebellious mood. However, from September 1989 through October 1989, the die was cast: this was a movement that would not be reversed.

The meetings that had begun in September with twenty to thirty people present grew within a month to hundreds of attendees. They poured out of the churches, and the Reverend Peter Kube and Protestant priest (*Probst*) Joachim Jaeger became leaders of more than their own flocks. The meetings became complaint and accusation sessions (*Klage und Anklage*).[6] The floodgates opened as people spoke of their frustrations. They wanted a free press, radio, and television; they wanted the right to travel beyond the western boundary; they wanted open trials and fair representation in court; they wanted an end to spying on one another; and they wanted a secret ballot.

The demonstrations moved from the church to the city streets on October 24. Taking candles to represent their peaceful intent, the people moved through the streets to the city hall. The next week, they again took up candles and marched to an open area called the August-Bebel-Platz, crowds gathering around an ill-functioning loudspeaker.

Nordhausen was only one of the many cities in Germany that were experiencing street protests and calls from the churches to speak and act for reform. In Leipzig, hundreds of thousands of people were protesting, including some who had come from Nordhausen. One woman reported that after a fear-filled trip by car to Leipzig from Nordhausen, she stopped on the way to the demonstration to buy two toothbrushes that were not available in her own city.[7]

The leaders of the city and party government invited the Altendorfer church group to sit down for a roundtable discussion with them. No political group from the movement was included. The politicians had decided in advance to meet the demands of the church people for open demonstrations and offered a large hall where they could meet, the Hall of Friendship within the theater. The protesters decided that they would take up the offer, but not at the expense of giving up the mass meeting at the August-Bebel-Platz.

On October 31, an estimated twenty-five thousand people gathered at the August-Bebel-Platz. The GDR paper *Das Volk* reported that representatives of the party and the state "apparatus," the head of the local area government (*Kreissekretär*), representatives of the churches, the New Forum, and other men and women discussed the political situation (from the podium) for several hours.[8]

National Events Impact Nordhausen

A few days later, on November 7, people streamed again into the theater's Hall of Friendship. There followed a series of discussions several times a week. However, national events were taking over the local movement. After massive demonstrations in Germany's main cities, a removal of most of the political leadership, and amnesty granted to demonstrators and those who had fled the country, the time was ripe to open the Berlin Wall. On the evening of November 9, guards at the Berlin Wall stepped aside as people on both sides climbed up on it and greeted each other in overflowing enthusiasm. The wall had "fallen." Cars could now drive through the checkpoints.

By November 12, cars were lined up for miles to cross the border into the West. The next day, the new head of the GDR government declared his willingness to start negotiations with the FRG.[9] Shortly thereafter, the FRG offered spending money to those coming over from the GDR. The crowds were huge, on foot and in cars.

With the opening to the West, the discourse on civil rights in Nordhausen changed in tone. Instead of looking for reform of the ballot, less surveillance, and more personal freedom, people started to talk of the possibility of becoming part of the economy of the FRG and gaining its standard of living.[10] The rapid success of the protests in gaining access to the West changed the agenda from reform to reunification.

It was not everyone's agenda, and many looked back on the early fall with mixed feelings. For those in the government, it was a time of anger, denial, and anxiety. And for a sizable minority, the hopes and dreams that had been rooted in the communist ideals that had emerged from the Nazi times or before were lost, leaving a deep depression. It had not been a true communism after all, but only an attempt at a socialist reality (*Realsozialismus*).

Graffiti on wall in East Germany: "Germany united, strong and big, the shit starts all over again." (Gretchen Schafft, photographer)

Among Nordhausen citizens, elation was mixed with disbelief and fear at the prospects of the future.

Peter Kuhlbrodt left his post as director of the Gedenkstätte in the spring of 1990. He was free to fully relish the changes that were occurring. Within a short time, he became director of the city archives, a job well suited to his love of local history, where he was able to make contributions to documenting the history of the city, including the bombing of Nordhausen and the American occupation.[11]

Germany Reunifies

The protesters in Nordhausen had not spoken of ending the GDR. They were certain that they wanted reforms and thought they were possible. With the citizens now taking short trips to the FRG, the tone began to change. Different political groups continued to meet with great expectation of how things would change and a feeling of anticipation of the changes they themselves would make. Some began to see their groups as becoming political parties with platforms that had to be developed. It was a time of unparalleled excitement for those who wanted change.

At the Gedenkstätte, there were strong divisions. Some of the staff wanted to get rid of all evidence that the state had used the site for political purposes. Others were worried about their own futures and to what extent they would be branded by such a drastic change in the political structure. A few worried about their mission and what would become of the place itself and the survivors they faithfully served. Others wanted to do away with the anti-West displays; before he left, Peter Kuhlbrodt used a paintbrush himself to cover over some of the words and pictures he found most offensive.[12]

With the border open, many people from the FRG and other Western countries started to come to look for long-lost relatives.[13] The staff continued to be as helpful as possible, but family members of the former prisoners wanted answers to questions for which there was no documentation. As stressful as it could be for the staff, it was also stimulating for them to meet new people and hear their interests and stories.

For a time, it seemed as if there was no government, no stability, although provisory adjustments were made. Nordhausen's bureaucrats were also busy destroying documents that could be incriminating, including Stasi and other government files. People became inventive in figuring out how to get rid of things, just as the Americans and the Soviets had been in the past fifty years.[14] Those on the wrong side of this fight spoke of the need for purposeful optimism (*Zweckoptimismus*) to cheer themselves up, evidently referring to previous times when life was hard and a certain view of the future being better was required.

Franz Kowalski was one of the people who saw some good coming from the changes, but he was worried about his children's possibilities under the new government. He had been a political personage in Nordhausen, often taking part in the city leadership, always available to Jewish survivors who wanted to say kadish, the prayer for the dead, and a close friend of Kurt Pelny. He had experienced everything from Auschwitz to Mittelbau-Dora and survived his imprisonment and all that it meant. This change was un-expected and offered new challenges to him. Speaking to Kurt Pelny in his little garden one day, he said, "My children may lose their jobs because I was active in the party. But the good news is, my grandchildren will be able to learn Hebrew!" He repeated his opinion to a newspaper reporter at about that time: "My grandchildren are now learning Hebrew. That's something to be happy about, isn't it?"[15]

Franz Kowalski's multifaceted loyalties to the GDR government, to the an-tifascist ideals, and to the Jewish tradition were not so unusual. Others in Nordhausen had maintained comfortable church ties while being loyal GDR citizens. A leader of the protest movement said in an interview: "I grew up in the socialist schools and had to deal with the theme of communism. I read Marx, Engels, and Lenin, but not the entire works, just excerpts. I was very interested in them, even with my protestant background . . . and I thought Christianity and communism are both terrific. Because the person (Mensch) is surely not only judged on his heritage, but simply as a being created by God."[16]

Events moved quickly, and by December 1989, the government leadership of the GDR had made many concessions to the protest movement including removing from the constitution the dominant role of the SED, lifting travel restrictions, stopping excessive exports of food and consumer goods, and forming a new ruling coalition headed by a Christian Democrat. A new party was formed called the Party of Democratic Socialism under the leadership of Gregor Gysi to represent the reformers of the SED of which he had been a temporary chairman.

Gedenkstätte Reconceptualized

After a few interim administrators at the Gedenkstätte, new leadership was found. Dr. Cornelia Klose, who was an educator by training, took over the reins in this turbulent time. Like Dr. Kuhlbrodt, she had had no experience in running a museum and no particular information about the camps except for what she had received through her GDR education.

When Cornelia Klose was selected, she found the Gedenkstätte in a state of disarray. No one knew what was to be kept or thrown out as outdated material (*Altlast*). She put a stop to burning documents, posters, old books and pamphlets, and display pieces. The people who were both a part of the reform movement and those who were opposed to it were still working side by side.

There was an attitude of uncertainty and unrest, not only in the Gedenkstätte, but in the GDR generally; Nordhausen was not immune from it. GDR police had old-fashioned cars that were not able to achieve high speeds, while criminal elements from the West were often equipped with models that could win any race with the authorities. Robberies increased, even at the Gedenkstätte, and people became more anxious and more suspicious. The price of concentration camp artifacts skyrocketed on the black market, and none of the memorials were equipped with security technology.

For those who had waited for political change, no amount of unrest could disturb their joy and elation. People met spontaneously and began to talk openly about the future and to plan for change. For many others who had not been active in the "quiet revolution," it was frightening to be without the security of the old system and to face an open society with a minimum of police presence.

New challenges arose where one would least expect them. One person said, "Traveling to West Berlin was exciting. The stores were filled with goods that we had not had on our shelves. Going into the stores was a different story: it was terrifying for me. I could imagine going into the stores with no door handles, those that opened automatically, but I could not believe that they would open from the inside so that I could leave. It took awhile before I tried to do it."[17]

On October 3, 1990, four months after Dr. Klose had begun her tenure at the Gedenkstätte, the reunification of Germany was finalized. Most Germans on both sides of the former wall celebrated, while others, Germans and non-Germans, wondered what a large Germany would mean to the world once again.

Reeducation

Peter Kuhlbrodt had started the reconceptualization of the Gedenkstätte, but had not been in the leadership long enough to finish the job. He had removed some texts, the bust of Albert Kuntz, and the plaque above the door to the crematorium building that read, "7,000 resistance fighters of many nations were murdered and burned on this spot. The living must deal with it."[18]

Cornelia Klose, under the direction of the city's government agencies, began to sort through the staff. Each was asked to sign documents stating that they had not taken part in any domestic spying activities. A few did not sign. There were other reasons many could be released from employment at the Gedenkstätte: they were already older and eligible for preretirement (*Vorruhestand*), they were no longer needed, or they were redundant. Those who remained were the younger men, those who had opposed the Communist regime or could make that claim, and those who showed great willingness to work within the new system.

Wolfgang Köhler was devastated by the news that he was through at the Gedenkstätte. He could not believe it and talked about it endlessly with his friends and his wife. He had never been a Communist. He knew the ins and outs of the old buildings, and he believed that he could still do the work of a younger man. In reality, skilled as he was, he probably could not keep up with the work any longer. He was older and not in good health, and he had often rested on the bench in front of the crematorium for long periods in the afternoon.

No one asked Kurt Pelny for advice or for his opinion. People on the street often crossed to the other side to avoid speaking to him. His family remembers that he was ordered not to appear at the Gedenkstätte (*Gedenkstätteverbot*), but there is no record of it. The contacts he had made, the materials he had gathered, the books and pamphlets he had written were not available.[19]

People were brought in from the FRG to work in many government agencies, banks, and schools. The Gedenkstätte also had some new faces as it lost the old. Most important, the leadership of the Gedenkstätte was not alone in the hands of Cornelia Klose, but under the advice and guidance of a historical commission made up of historians from the FRG. No GDR historian was asked to participate. The commission began shortly to write their own pamphlets without SED ideology. Themes like resistance, monopolistic capitalism, heroism, and international solidarity among the prisoners were replaced. In their stead came an emphasis on prisoners from Western Europe, the specifics of rocket production, religion in the camp, and the liberation.

However, Cornelia Klose also became aware of the place of industry in the history of the Gedenkstätte and spoke out to the newspaper about the more than one hundred firms that worked "hand-in-hand with the Nazi doing their dirty work (*Schergen*)." Therefore, she reasoned, the people of Nordhausen, who worked at the camp as civilians, knew about the camp. "I am of the opinion that the city of Nordhausen literally lived off of the camp."[20]

With the historical commission in place, it was time to create an advisory board of interested parties involved. The government of Nordhausen, certainly with advice from the Gedenkstätte and the historical commission, invited a variety of survivors, interested parties, church leaders, representatives of the national and local Jewish organizations, and city and state leaders to take part. The main topic on their agenda was the opening of the tunnels for visitors. The Jewish representatives were clear that this enlargement of the Gedenkstätte offerings should not glorify technology over the horror that befell the prisoners. They met a few times a year to comment upon and approve the plans of the historical commission, to plan events for survivors and others at the site, and to set out their own agendas.

Not all who wanted to join the advisory group were invited. No criteria were announced for the selection, and no reason was given for exclusion.[21] None of the previous people who were active under the SED government were invited. Franz Kowalski said in a newspaper interview, "I've heard that they now want to have an advisory council, but do you think they have invited me to work with them? Nah." Kowalski had worked before with the Gedenkstätte. He had led the first group through the site and did not understand why today no one wanted to have anything to do with him. He was not about to advertise his unhappiness with the situation, though. "If they don't come [to me], I'll take my experience with me to the grave."[22]

The French wanted the staff to know that Mittelbau-Dora was one of the largest French cemeteries outside of France and felt the Gedenkstätte should "show the suffering, the will to survive, and the resistance of the people during the production of the rockets." In summary, they urged that the "memorial Mittelbau-Dora should become a Europeen [sic] place for memory, a Europeen education place, a place where all generations can meet."

Both the literature of the East and that of the West tended to be short, inexpensive handouts for visitors of the site. Both recognized the terrible suffering of the prisoners. The GDR had recognized that suffering in the spirit of heroism, the now-encompassing FRG recognizing the victimization of the prisoners.

Both the GDR and the FRG governments saw the value of the Gedenkstätte for civic education. It was led by the SED and the Culture Department of the city government under the GDR, with oversight of the national organs of historical preservation (Denkmalschutz). Under the FRG, the civic education was under the central direction of the Regional Center for Political Education (Landeszentrale für politische Bildung) and its provincial branches, as well as the Thuringia and Nordhausen government agencies for culture, historical preservation, ecology, and other appropriate offices. Many nongovernmental agencies became involved in an advisory role, such as prisoners' groups, national and regional Jewish groups, and various church groups.[23]

New Groups

Now that the Western European survivors were heartily welcomed into the activities of the Gedenkstätte, they formed organizations across national boundaries. The European Committee Dora-Ellrich-Harzungen "For the Memory" (Comité européen Dora-Ellrich-Harzungen "Pour la Mémoire") became the largest and most influential.

Efforts were also made to bring survivors from the Eastern countries to the events at the Gedenkstätte, and the city helped to raise money to pay their way. Many were impoverished with only the Soviet Union available to help rebuild their countries. The Soviet Union had to deal with its own devasta-

Linda Hunt, American journalist, and Yves Béon, survivor of Dora and author, together in 1995 at a ceremony of remembrance sponsored by the city of Nordhausen and the Gedenkstätte. (Gretchen Schafft, photographer, Nordhausen Collection)

Polish survivors of Mittelbau-Dora at the fiftieth anniversary of liberation, 1995.
(Gretchen Schafft, photographer, Nordhausen Collection)

tion and had little to offer. Yet several former prisoners came from Poland
and Czechoslovakia, where survivor organizations were very well attended.
The Roma groups from Germany were well represented by very personable
families who spoke freely to others, but stayed largely to themselves.

Cornelia Klose and the staff were very gracious to the older men and
their families and tried very hard to make them comfortable. The city of
Nordhausen provided some funding for nice meals and lodging for those
who came for anniversary events. The men responded to this kindness with
genuine affection, for the director in particular. They became well known
to the staff, and their stories were shared, thus educating and sensitizing the
staff at the same time.

The first mayor of Nordhausen after reunification was Manfred Schröter,
a Nordhausen native who had suffered for decades under repression from
the former government.[24] While still in high school, he had refused to write
an essay condemning the FRG's Chancellor Adenauer and was expelled.
He had to work in a factory. After winning prizes for his productivity and
taking night classes in order to get his high school diploma (*Abitur*), he was
finally allowed to go to medical school. As a prominent citizen of the city,
but one with contrary views to the government and a church member, he
was watched constantly. He avoided most sanctions until he spoke up in a

Jewish survivor with wreath at an outer camp of Mittelbau-Dora during
the fiftieth anniversary of liberation, 1995. (Gretchen Schafft, photographer,
Nordhausen Collection)

parent-teacher meeting and objected to mandatory military practice for high
school students. Almost immediately, Dr. Schröter was relieved of public
medical duties and had to use private means to continue his practice.

At the same time, Manfred Schröter was an avid "hobby historian," and
wrote of the bombing of Nordhausen and of the Jewish citizens who had
been expelled in 1938. The first book was allowed through the censors, but
the second was criticized and delayed in its printing. With the new government, Mayor Schröter was able to publish, govern, and educate the city about
the loss of its Jewish population. He was known to treat people fairly, and
was civil to all of the citizens, even those representing the ideology that had
caused him such pain.

Another change in the Gedenkstätte culture was the institution of the
group Youth for Dora (Jugend für Dora), made up of young people who
had an interest in the history of the concentration camp and wanted both
to learn about it and to help with its current activities. Previously, school
classes had done the same under the antifascist banner. Now, the groups
were much smaller, but very sincere. They met and planned work camps
and meetings with survivors, and were met with great enthusiasm on all

A wife and daughter remembering a former Mittelbau-Dora Polish prisoner, 1993. (Gretchen Schafft, photographer, Nordhausen Collection)

sides. The survivors were generally happy to talk to the "next generation" or the "grandchildren's generation" and used all of their opportunities to do so. Often, the people of Nordhausen were invited into the Gedenkstätte for a coffee hour to meet with survivors and to hear their stories. It was direct education without interpretation.

Some survivors could not bring themselves to come back to the camp. Martin Adler, for instance, had been a child of fourteen when he arrived.[25] He was born in a border area of northeastern Hungary in the Carpathian Mountains in a Jewish shtetl. Beginning in 1941, anti-Jewish laws were in place, and Martin witnessed half of the members of his village taken away to their deaths. Martin's father was conscripted into a forced labor battalion in which he served as a human land-mine detector from 1941 to 1943.

In September 1943, shortly after Martin's fourteenth birthday and despite the hardships the family suffered, the family sacrificed to send their gifted son to a famous yeshiva some distance away. His mother walked with him to take him to his new school.

In the spring of 1944, wholesale deportation of the region began, and Martin returned home from the yeshiva. Shortly afterward, Martin and the remaining people in the village were deported to Sokirnitsa, a ghetto that was located near the train station. Before they left their home, Martin remembered his mother saying, "Why do they have to take us anyplace? This is my home. I was born here. Why don't we die here? Let them kill us here." Martin's family and the people of the village did not stay in the ghetto long before it was cleared, and all of the inhabitants were sent to Auschwitz. Martin's mother had given birth while in the ghetto, but the baby died before the trains were loaded.

Upon arrival in Auschwitz, Martin's mother said to his father: "You take the boy. I'll take the little ones." With that, she and the younger children were herded toward the gas chamber, while Martin and his father, looking capable of work, were sent in the other direction.

The two of them managed to get into the group being sent back to Germany to join the minions making weapons. Loaded into trains, again without provisions, they started the long trip. Martin remembered the guard in the railroad car looking at him and calling him to the front of the car where he gave him a crust of bread and a little room, so that he wasn't crushed by the many people.

Eventually, Martin and his father arrived at Mittelbau-Dora. The exact route and timing were unclear to Martin. Martin was put on the detail that was building the crematorium, as he remembered it. He remembered carrying bricks up the steep, slippery hill. His father was sent out from the camp on a construction commando (*Baubrigade*). Martin was completely traumatized by the violence, beating, and starvation of the prisoners.

A few weeks after Martin and his father arrived in Dora, a prisoner asked Martin if he was from Volve (Martin's hometown). When Martin said yes, the prisoner said, "Well, do you know a guy by the name of Adler that they shot today?" Before the news could sink in, another prisoner said, "You idiot, that's the kid's father."

Martin was found by someone who took him aside and told him to report to the place where clothes were sorted, as he recalled. There, he was protected from the wind and weather and largely from the brutality around him. He survived.

Martin was "evacuated" at the end of the war to Bergen-Belsen, and after three days without any food at all, the camp was liberated. After a few weeks in the surrounding area, he headed back to Volve but was unable to return because the borders were closing. He eventually stayed in a displaced persons' camp in Italy, where he was placed with other children from the camps.

Martin was able to immigrate to the United States, and he landed in Detroit. He made his way, graduated from high school, worked in a pawnshop, and eventually owned his own furniture store. He had a family: wife, son, and daughter. His haunted life was a constant reminder to all of them of his past.

That did not define Martin Adler, however. A highly intelligent man, he read everything he could about the Holocaust and tried to tell others about his experience. He found a few other survivors and made fast friends. He tried to be the most supportive father he could be to his daughter, who, as an adult with a doctorate in psychology and her own family, was his pride and joy.

A peaceful man, Adler sought to find the good in others. He said to one German who had come to see him, "I know if you had seen me then, you would have given me a piece of bread." Another young German girl came to visit him because she had heard of his story and corresponded with him. He invited her to visit and paid her way to come to Detroit. When she went home, she and a few others arranged to have a ceremony for Martin's father, to say a few prayers, and to hang a plaque to Hermann Adler in the crematorium in his honor.[26] Martin Adler contacted the Jewish community in Erfurt, the next larger town to Nordhausen, and made a donation in his father's name. Kaddish, the Jewish prayer for the dead, was said for Hermann Adler.

With these steps taken, Martin Adler made plans to come to Germany and Poland with his daughter, to visit the Auschwitz memorial, and finally to attend the Mittelbau-Dora memorial days on the anniversary of its liberation. Friends helped make the arrangements and then went to Auschwitz to wait for him to arrive. He did not come. He could not. The friends waited for several days in Auschwitz and came to know the camp in its re-creation very well. They no longer wanted to see Martin there. It felt voyeuristic. Sensing the depth of Adler's grief, it was too much for any of them. Martin Adler had made a good decision.

Like many others, Martin Adler could not come to the Gedenkstätte. Perhaps the majority of survivors lived very compartmentalized lives where the camps were tucked away in the recesses of their minds. For Martin, the camps were his primary cognitive focus and entered into every conversation. By interspersing the most horrible thoughts and memories with very funny jokes, he appeared to apologize for hoisting his terror onto the listener. His daughter, in her eulogy for her father, put it this way:

> He was one of the funniest people I have ever known. He seemed to have a joke for every conceivable situation. They were really funny, and he made them even funnier by enjoying them and laughing with you. . . . This is a quote from my dad as he talks about the Holocaust . . . "If I tell you jokes, I won't cry; or maybe I should cry and not tell you jokes." But he did tell jokes, and his love of life and

laughter was remarkable. After witnessing the worst in people, he managed to embody the best: kindness, generosity, selflessness, and love. . . . I think my father embodied the principles of unconditional love better than anyone I have ever met. If he knew you, you felt loved by him; it was that simple.[27]

New Developments

In 1994, the science minister of Thuringia announced the establishment of a foundation for the concentration camp memorials Buchenwald and Mittelbau-Dora, with both directors being equally represented. The foundation would provide oversight of the administration and funding through the state's parliament and relieve the individual memorial staffs from much of the administrative and fund-raising duties that they had had.

Research on the concentration camp was given a major boost by the establishment of a study group (*Studienkreis*) made up of graduate students in former West Germany (*Alte Bundesländer*) who set to work in the pattern of Walter Bartel's group from the 1950s. They were not bound by an overt ideology.

In April 1995, the tunnels where prisoners had labored were opened for the first time since the Soviets had blasted them shut during their occupation. Great interest in exploring them arose from all sides. Film crews suggested supporting explorations by boat through the unknown flooded territory, supporting these efforts with product advertisement, but this was not acceptable. A still photographer took excellent artistic pictures of the remains of rocket parts and showed them in an exhibit at the Gedenkstätte and in a book that he published.[28] Little by little, the tunnels showed promise of a future exhibition that would gather ever more visitors to the site.

Beginning soon after reunification, seminars were held for those interested in the Gedenkstätten and their work. Most of the seminars were sponsored by the Karl Duisberg Gesellschaft and the Topographie des Terrors (Topography of Terror), a museum in Berlin with an educational function, both supported by various funding and the Center for Political Education (Bundeszentrale für Politische Bildung), a federal agency.

The seminars were helpful in explaining the system of the concentration camps and were subsidized and held at different memorial sites throughout primarily eastern Germany. Participants were housed in pleasant hotels and provided with meals for a small, subsidized cost. Also subsidized by the Center for Political Education were books that were given out free of charge to provide the broadest reeducation on such topics as the Nazi past, the specifics of targeted groups, civic values, and other general and specific topics. Without these distributions, the knowledge base of the new reunited Germany would have been skewed. Questions about the negative aspects of this kind of, what one might call, "positive censorship" were never raised: To what extent is a selection of books given free of charge also a form of directing public information and opinion? To what extent and how are the books that are selected vetted? What interests are represented in the selection? Out of what coffer does the money to support the project come?

The seminars were a setting in which all interested individuals could take part and have a voice. One's background and political ideology had no bearing on the welcome one would receive. No doubt, they did much to dampen the feeling of exclusion that left many without a say in the restructuring of individual sites. In the early 1990s, small numbers of survivors also attended. Most of them were politically active, healthy, and alert. There was no facilitation in encouraging participants to get to know each other, and the survivors were not identified. They were almost never given any leading or educational role.

The seminars were led by "experts" on the Third Reich, mostly academic historians. They explained the particular nature of the camps, the administrative structure, or a particular issue that the camp encompassed. Never was a survivor asked to speak, but all were free to ask questions or make comments. A skilled person, always the same one, handled both the administrative functions and the discussions. Although this person was very impersonal with most of the participants and made no effort to be welcoming, some obviously knew him well and joined him in smaller groups for meals and drinks. Survivors were not seen to be in those small groups.

In at least one seminar, an argument broke out as one survivor accused another of being a "murderer." He said that in Buchenwald, this fellow prisoner had made choices that allowed his Communist comrades to survive while others died. The facilitator calmed the accuser down, and the discussion period proceeded. Later, some asked the accused survivor what he thought of that attack. "Well, decisions had to be made. I made some of them. Sending someone to a safer job, a better commando, meant that someone else had less chance to live. Yes, it happened." It was a zero-sum game in the camps. There wasn't enough safety, food, rest, or protection to go around, and without an adequate measure of all of these, one would scarcely be able to survive.

East Germans privately were being called "Ossies," and they responded, also privately, by calling others "Wessies" or even "Besserwessies" (Know-it-alls).[29] This accentuated the differences that were felt on both sides in social situations. One woman at the seminar told us that she simply could not contribute to the discussions. "I have the ideas, but I can't find the words that the others use. They don't think like we do, and we don't talk like they do."[30]

It was a difficult time, this period of change in the early 1990s. Euphoria met with serious social and economic problems.

> The two social and economic systems crashed into one another and shattered cherished fantasies on both sides. East Germans lost their fantasy of the West as a consumer paradise. West Germans lost the familiar notion of a threatening East that had habitually reinforced their own egos. East Germans, grumbling about falling living standards, tell you that former Nazi bureaucrats in West Germany were guaranteed full pension rights after the war by nothing less than the Federal Constitution, but that former East German bureaucrats now receive pensions smaller by 40 percent than those paid to ex-Nazis in the West. In the West people complain that reunification costs West German taxpayers too much money.[31]

The inadequacies and confusion among the police and courts made all of Germany a misery for foreigners in the country, with rising violence, neo-Nazi activity, and inadequate and inconsequential sanctions. Reorganization of the whole system left many gaps. For many people, in the early years of reunification, democracy brought uncertainty.

Discrediting the GDR

One of the most effective ways to discredit the GDR has been to link it with the Nazi regime that preceded it. This could be done through looking for similarities in language, tradition, societal structures, or political intentions. It could also be done by using the GDR as an "abnormal" case and holding the FRG up in an idealized form as the "norm." Bedeviling the GDR was an activity that would be readily funded in early months and years after the wall fell, and, as in the denazification, it had a specific goal of reeducation of an entire society.

The societal institutions of the Nazi era were available in the memories of the GDR citizens, and the intensive spying, harsh punishments, and coercive repression of diversity in lifestyles and the arts were apparent to any unbiased observer. However, what is not acknowledged is the personal space of individuals and groups that lies outside the political and economic systems with their enforcement mechanisms.[32] This is the area of subjective life, where people live "free of manipulation by dominant groups. However much the ruling classes may control the themes and content of politics or the sources of history, the subalterns, that is, the people, will always manage to make themselves heard. In other words, this intermediate space represents the subjectivity, the active source of the political activity of the people and, therefore, the basis on which they act as subjects of history and not just its objects being merely acted upon."[33] It is this personal space that the "Ossies" feel is devalued in much of the current rhetoric. In discrediting the system, the critics also attacked the validity of the interpersonal and interior lives of GDR citizens.

An example of this bedevilment is seen in a study of the German tradition of confirmation for youngsters who did not choose to belong to a church (*Jugendweihe*), a tradition in place throughout the nineteenth century in Germany as part of the Free Thinker (*Freidenker*) movement that had originated in England.[34] The Jugendweihe had a large urban following, where in the early 1930s more than a third of the defined Jewish population were married to Gentiles. Many of these unions did not follow a religious tradition of any kind, but their children wanted to join in the major national event of a confirmation.

In Berlin, at least in the pre–World War II era, children preparing for their confirmation in a church or through a *Jugendweihe* were excused from school classrooms for confirmation classes.[35] In this study, sponsored by National Memorials of Buchenwald and Sachsenhausen, as well as the German Institute for International Pedagogical Research, it was claimed that the *Jugendweihe* was a "specific civic ritual in the political socialization of youth in the GDR [that] integrated an instructional component under the broad rubric of the Jugendstunde, a series of teaching thematics leading up to the formal initiation of fourteen year olds into adulthood with special political responsibilities to the state."[36]

The use of the concentration camp memorials in the GDR for part of the instruction and the use of antifascist heroes to serve as examples (*Vorbilder*) to the youth are presented in the article as a Communist ploy, "in the shadow of the Third Reich." The use of the term *civic ritual* is, of course, descriptive of what it had always been, just as the confirmation in the church had been a Christian ritual. Suddenly, such concepts were placed in a suspicious context and provided ammunition to discredit the GDR's use of an old tradition.[37]

Failing to look at the FRG's rituals of memorializing and commemorating Nazi crimes left the new united Germans with the feeling that only in the GDR did ritual occur. Yet national holidays and the increasing use of speeches by government dignitaries to express remorse and guilt were recognized strategies to bring forward the "normalization" process in the FRG for decades.[38]

A series of "isms" entered the discourse of these early years of reunification: extremism, totalitarianism, and radicalism were some. They all placed
various characteristics at the door of the GDR, often comparing it to the
Third Reich.[39]

Criticism from Jewish activists and intellectuals warned of eliminating
the Holocaust as a unique German event by placing it as just one of many
"extremes." This reduced rather quickly the amount of comparison phrases,
but did not affect other ways of discrediting the regime, such as calling it an
illegal state (*Unrechtsstaat*) or the "second German dictatorship." Any longing
for an extinguished product, cultural form, or habit was immediately labeled
"nostalgia" (*Ostalgie*) and mocked. Looking back was open to ridicule.

Conclusion

The time of the quiet revolution and reunification of Germany was significant
for the redevelopment of the Gedenkstätte. The new government believed
that new values were important to impart to the residents of Nordhausen who
had lived their lives under Hitler's Third Reich (1933–45) and the German
Democratic Republic (1949–89). Once again, the Gedenkstätte was a place
of remembrance and of civic education. What had happened here? What
should we learn from it? How much do we really know, and what should we
explore and research?

Experts and stakeholders were called in to help in two roles: that of historian and that of knowledgeable participant. As before, those active in earlier
regimes were not welcome to take part. They were, however, free to use all
the resources and public programs offered by the Gedenkstätte. This was
very painful for some and satisfying for others. Each director made his or her
own presence felt in shaping what the Gedenkstätte would become. Each was
limited, either agreeably or not, by the sociopolitical temper of the times.

Public reeducation moved ahead through the help of government-spon-
sored programs, some of very high quality. At the same time, remembering
the past in positive terms was as much discouraged as it had been at the end
of the Nazi era. The failure to recognize the differences between the formal
economic and political systems and the lives of individuals and community
groups led to wide-scale undervaluing of people's individual lives and values.
This demoralizing attitude extended to those for whom the Gedenkstätte had
been a large part of their lives.

8. The Modern Gedenkstätte

The anxiety within the Gedenkstätte gradually lessened during the first years after the reunification of Germany as the new director, Cornelia Klose, gained knowledge and understanding of the camp through her work with staff and survivors and became a well-known and well-liked figure in Nordhausen. The importance of the site had grown regionally, nationally, and internationally as scholars addressed the history of the Mittelbau-Dora complex using records and data that had not been available to the GDR historians.

Along the way, the name *Mahn*- und Gedenkstätte Mittelbau-Dora was changed to simply KZ-Gedenkstätte Mittelbau-Dora (Concentration Camp Memorial Mittelbau-Dora). No longer was *mahn* a word to be used. The first memorial had *admonished and warned* about the return of fascism, and the words of Berthold Brecht were often quoted: "Der Schoss ist fruchtbar noch aus dem dies kroch" (The womb from which it crept is still fertile).[1]

Reunification and Normalization

Stresses that were placed upon the director and her staff in the 1990s were not so much local as national in scope. With reunification came a new effort to place Germany in a better light, to normalize it in the community of nations.[2] The FRG had already attempted normalization under Chancellor Helmut Kohl, to little avail. He spoke of the "ups and downs" experienced by societies and the tragedy of war for all the participants, but it was not an acceptable discourse for many.

Trying to place the country among others that had periods of violence from which all suffer came to a head in the ceremony at Bitburg, Germany, on May 5, 1985, in which President Ronald Reagan on a state visit placed a wreath to those who suffered in World War II in a military cemetery that also included SS officers. This drew an outcry from many who rose up in objection to the efforts of placing Germany within the "normal" community of nations and demanded that Germany remain a nation that placated the world by atoning for its guilt and shame. This was better accomplished by speaking of Germany's assistance to Israel and marking certain days for national remembrance of the Holocaust.

Reframing the Second World War as a fight against the Western world's common enemy, communism, was clear in the Bitburg fiasco. "The sequence of Bergen-Belsen in the morning and Bitburg in the afternoon, implicitly disputed the singularity of the Nazi crimes; and shaking hands with the veteran generals in the presence of the U.S. president was, finally, a demonstration that we had really always stood on the right side in the fight against Bolshevism."[3]

In the FRG there had been years of debate among historians about how to approach World War II history. Many believed that World War II should at this date be placed "in the sequence of normal wars" and the Third Reich should be seen "as a tragic but, in the face of Bolshevist aggression, understandable entanglement."[4] Many German historians opposed this point of view. The debate became known as the "historians' argument" (*Historikerstreit*). While some historians were interested in working through history, others came to believe it could be relativized within a broader concept, such as "totalitarianism" or "extremism."

The East Germans had had no real information about the Holocaust, no information about Germany's role in genocide, and no social movement of young people inquiring into their parents' potential involvement in the Third Reich. All questions about the Third Reich had been subsumed under the theory of monopolistic capitalism, with responsibility left at the doorstep of large military-industrial concerns, and their actors. The lack of information and debate made it an easy step, therefore, for many intellectuals to put forth the hypothesis that eastern Germany had been under the totalitarian yoke for almost sixty years, two generations, and that at least a part of the Gedenkstätte should be devoted to this victimhood of the citizens of the GDR. There was little questioning of the FRG's reluctance in the same time period to examine the role of the military-industrial complex in the creation and execution of the war.

The impetus for Germans to look at Germany's key position in developing technology that today plays such an important role in human events was also almost irresistible. Germany had been a pioneer of rocketry and a scientific and engineering leader among nations.[5] To the credit of the Gedenkstätte staff and their advisers, these tendencies were battled and held in check. Speaking to this temptation, Günther Gottmann, the director of the Museum for Transport and Technology in Berlin and an adviser to the Gedenkstätte, described the dilemma of how to portray the history: "Proud triumph of technology or contrite silence about the accomplishment? Neither, but [we need] more careful exhibits of principled ambivalence about technology and technical personnel . . . [the] ambivalence of technology."[6]

Difficulties in Integrating the GDR into the FRG

Deep-seated in German thought, action, history, and everyday discourse was the idea that the countries to the east were inferior, and their people were less intelligent than others. The Nazis had referred to the Polish nationals as subhuman (*Untermenschen*), and that idea found resonance among many Germans despite the fact the surnames were often of Polish origin and many, if not most, German families had Polish ancestry or relatives.

For the GDR to be attached to the Soviet Union and to take on a way of life that to some extent was influenced by them was enough to encourage many Germans to accept the idea that East Germans were a different breed. The more rational explanation for the differences in lifestyle that developed over the years was the fact that citizens of the GDR lived in a very slowly recovering economy in which women were expected to share workforce responsibilities. West Germany, which had massive American aid in rebuilding its economy quickly, followed its traditional path and had a low female employment rate. Women in the GDR, however, became accustomed to full-time work outside the home. They gave up the traditional German standard of household fussiness that required hours of housework every day. For many years, they had old-fashioned coal-burning stoves, simple and often communal laundry and bath facilities, and very limited home improvement materials. Hiring household help was out of the question.[7]

The basic issues with the East German economy are often forgotten in general parlance. The East German mark was not traded on world markets. It had been devalued at the time of the currency reform that occurred in West Germany in 1948. Perhaps most important was the embargo placed on East German goods, making trade viable mostly with Soviet-affiliated states that were poorer than the markets in the West. West Germans often sent "care packages" to their eastern relatives and received "wish lists" from the other side of the Iron Curtain. It was easy for those from the FRG to slip into the mind-set that their benevolence contrasted strongly to the others' poverty.

Most GDR citizens did not see themselves in that light, however. They did not like the deprivations of consumer goods, but learned to live fairly comfortably with the situation. When the wall opened, they were bombarded with advertisements on television and through the mail and overwhelmed with the need to "catch up" and became avid consumers.

After the initial euphoria, many in the FRG began to resent the money, demands, and tax revenues being poured into the East. They began to see the differences more than the similarities with their neighboring Germans. "For the profiling of domestic conservative positions, the wholesale rejection of the GDR was a place of central importance. It culminated in the West German claim to be the sole representative of all Germans."[8]

A new phrase emerged: "nach westlichem Standard." This referred to the acceptable standard of behavior and living expected by Germans in the West and hoped for by many in the East. This idea was so widespread that one German traveling to the West spoke emphatically to his GDR car, a Trabi, with admonition. Driving uphill, he said, "Get the exhaust (*Auspuff*) out of your system now. In a few minutes we'll be across the border, and I don't want you to embarrass me."

The West Germans had been all too aware for years of the blame that the world extended to them for creating a Holocaust and two world wars. Parents tried to protect their children from hearing such things, and many restricted private conversation about the past. The younger generation, after a surge of inquiry in the late 1960s, grew tired of the linkages of Germany to extermination and horror and rejected any idea of collective guilt. The Germans were still feeling much grief, sorrow, and shame about the Third Reich and the crimes that German people committed between 1933 and 1945. Yet there were many escape mechanisms that allowed people to claim that others did the deeds, not themselves or people like them, or that such deeds were committed at different times around the world.[9]

With the opening of the wall, the West Germans now projected many of their own feelings of inferiority and targeted blame on their neighboring East Germans. To many, the East Germans became "the other," vilified and condemned, if not pitied, for their complicity and lack of self-assertion in the face of communism. It was not uncommon for people in the FRG to ask a clumsy waiter, "Are you an Ossie?" or to complain loudly in public about the influx of these unacceptable people ruining the standards of West German society. Even today, one young man born and raised in the GDR and living in cosmopolitan Berlin reports, "The first questions asked at parties are how old are you and are you an Ossie or a Wessie. When I say I am an

Ossie, people can't believe it! They say, 'I never would have guessed! You seem so much like us.'"

In writing some of his thoughts about the differences between the new citizens of the FRG (the easterners) and the old (the westerners), a prominent Nordhausen citizen put it this way:

> Even before the reunification, it seemed to me there was a basic difference between us and visitors from the FRG. I still think it is symptomatic: the "Wessi" feels his importance much more that we "Ossis" do. Their stubborn self-confidence and demanding presence divides us right from the start. In their conversation, no matter what the topic, they use the word "I" at least twice as often as we would. We Ossies, in the time of limited freedom and chronic shortages, experienced and learned something really very special: friendly or neighborly or collegial, at any rate, human solidarity. We found that [the Wessies] did not seek the higher good in the "other" and, therefore, this attitude of looking for the good in others also was not as highly developed as it was with us. Now, with us, we are also losing it.[10]

Ordinary discourse of the FRG almost from the founding of the country was dismissive of the GDR and became second nature to many West Germans. The discourse took, and still takes, many forms. All of the tropes denying that the GDR was a state or denigrating the people within it show that many West Germans think less of their eastern brethren. This situation also leads East Germans to lose confidence in their own history.

A New Director

Dr. Klose left her position as director of the Gedenkstätte on June 1, 2001, to become the director for culture, schools, and sport in the city government of Nordhausen. She was replaced by a man younger than previous directors with a doctorate in history. Jens-Christian Wagner was an ideal choice according to many, for he had done his dissertation as part of the Göttingen group closely associated with the Gedenkstätte. He had volunteered as a guide at the Gedenkstätte while completing his studies.

Wagner was without a doubt an expert on the history and meaning of Third Reich concentration camps, in particular Mittelbau-Dora. He came directly from the Buchenwald–Mittelbau-Dora Foundation, where his particular task was to develop ideas for a new exhibit at the Gedenkstätte in Nordhausen. Dr. Wagner was living in Weimar at the time he accepted the position in Nordhausen and has remained there, commuting a few times a week. Although he is not always on site in the Gedenkstätte, Wagner is fully engaged with it. He set out to increase the knowledge base of the history of the site through publication of his major work, *Produktion des Todes* (Production of Death), and to enhance the work begun by Dr. Klose in working with survivors and youth.[11]

A person open to ideas, Jens-Christian Wagner listened to those who came to him, but did not seek out "old-timers." Many of those do not contact him directly, but complain to others who get the information to him.[12] Aside from greetings on the grounds of the Gedenkstätte, he has never spoken to the family of Kurt Pelny, for example. He did, however, become the chair of one of the hobby-historian groups in the area around Nordhausen (the Westharz region) called the "Trackers" (*Spurensucher*) who did some good work in following leads for regional information about the concentration camp and subcamps.[13] They gave up their meetings after Wagner's book was published; because it was so complete, no further work seemed necessary by the amateur group.

Changes in the Exhibit

There were parts of the exhibit that Jens-Christian Wagner and others believed needed changing, and with the Buchenwald–Mittelbau-Dora Foundation in place, it was possible to make long-range plans to do so. The small original fire department near the center of the grounds had been used for changing exhibits even in the original plans of the Gedenkstätte and more so under the interim directors. It continued to be used this way, exhibiting a range of photo and art displays of interest to the Nordhausen populace.

There is no question about Jens-Christian Wagner's scholarship providing the fundamental information and nuanced analysis that would become the basis of the exhibit of the twenty-first century. However, others were involved as well. The historical commission that had been active before remained in place, with some of the membership changing. Several of the members are experienced museum people. The survivors' committee of seven people could not be as strong as before, as most of the original members were deceased or aged. Most are French, as they had a large number of dead in the camp. Other interest groups still have a voice in the memorial, but a minor one.

The director of the Buchenwald memorial, Volkhard Knigge, a forceful person in his own right, also played a role in redesigning the Mittelbau-Dora memorial. He had gone through the serious issues surrounding Buchenwald during and after the reunification of Germany, and had survived with a good reputation despite the various interest groups who battled to be recognized at the site.

Wagner wanted a more visitor-friendly exhibit than had been installed in Buchenwald, with exhibits that had a very readable text that did not include an overwhelming amount of information. He certainly was in concordance with the mainstream view of the day that the GDR had presented a deliberately biased view of the concentration camp history that should not be repeated.

Heroes or Not?

A moderate liberal himself, Wagner is not afraid of controversy, but he did not see any need to meet everyone's expectations. Leo Kuntz, for instance, wanted his father, Albert Kuntz, reinstated in the Gedenkstätte exhibit as a prominent prewar legislator and a true resistance fighter against Hitler. In addition, he wanted the international nature of the resistance to be recognized, as well as its organization.

Jens-Christian Wagner is more inclined to see Albert Kuntz in the context of the Gedenkstätte as a functionary within the concentration camp structure who possibly both helped prisoners when he could and improved his own position by taking an administrative position in the prisoner hierarchy. Prisoner functionaries were placed in a strange space between collaboration with the SS and assistance to their fellow prisoners. Wagner does not view such functionaries as automatic heroes, and certainly not Albert Kuntz. As there is little direct information about what any functionary, including Kuntz, was able to do to help others, he reserves his judgment.[14]

From another point of view, there was little possibility of any prisoner recognizing the good deeds of others, although most have spoken of a particular person or a small group who helped them get through the horrible ordeal that they lived day after day. With shorn heads, prison rags on their bodies, and a number instead of an identity of their own, even if they could converse in a common language, the prisoners were unlikely to know the name of the person who helped or to be able to identify the person after the war.

This leaves a terrible dilemma: Should the possible self-sacrifice and self-endangerment in which prisoners might have engaged be ignored to prevent heroization of someone unnecessarily or even wrongfully? Do we take a well-known figure and attribute deeds to him without much proof, or that of questionable veracity? Certainly, if the person in question is one who was previously projected in an enlarged role by the GDR, there is no chance that that person will be featured in the same role in the modern Gedenkstätte.

Modern German heroes, interestingly enough, are generally Germans who ranked high in the Nazi administration. The undisputed heroes are those who planned the attack on Hitler in his bunker in East Prussia. For them, there is now a national holiday, although several of them performed loyal service to Hitler until they turned their backs on him, as either they became disillusioned or it became clear Hitler would lose the war.

One hero who was made into a focus of newspaper articles and then the subject of a paperback book was Mittelbau-Dora prisoner Johnny Nicholas. He was not a GDR communist hero, but one discovered by Americans who were fascinated by the history of Mittelbau-Dora.[15] One of the writers, David C. Smith, had been part of an intelligence unit at the end of World War II that examined evidence of war crimes. He had heard of Nicholas and brought the story to a friend of his, who in turn told a newspaperman in Michigan, Hugh McCann. The three authors followed various leads and interviewed survivors of Mittelbau-Dora and even one survivor of Gardelegen, where they believed that Nicholas had perished.

These authors found that Johnny Nicholas was a Haitian national living in Paris during the war doing occasional spying for the British. There he was arrested by the Gestapo and taken to a much feared prison in Paris and then sent off to Germany, headed for Buchenwald. Johnny might have hoped to escape, but being a black man in Germany made this dream an impossibility.

Nicholas was a man who evidently lived by his wits. He had spent his youth between France and Haiti and was fluent in French, German, and English. It is not entirely clear what he was doing at the time of his arrest in Paris during the Nazi occupation. He may have been a spy or even a student. It is known that he studied biology and possibly was a medical student.

Learning the camp system quickly, Nicholas made a persona for himself that, in the records, became a mix of truth and fiction. He claimed he was an American doctor and a U.S. Air Force pilot, knowing that would get him out of hard labor and give him a better chance for survival.

On May 11, 1944, Johnny Nicholas was transferred to Mittelbau-Dora and put to work in the tunnels. After a short time, he was able to pass himself off as a doctor and was moved to the sick bay. There was very little medicine to be practiced there, and it was not difficult to pretend to be a trained physician. The staff had only aspirin, paper bandages, knifes to cut out infections, and alcohol to sterilize them. Some eyewitness accounts indicate that Nicholas was tireless in his attempts to care for the sick, but at least one survivor remembered that he was tough and could throw prisoners down the slope from the sick bay if he was in the mood to do so.

Johnny Nicholas survived the camp, but most likely died in the death march or even, possibly, at Gardelegen. Rumors and legends abound about how he met his end. Those who perished on the death marches did not leave traces of when or where.

Nicholas is now forgotten within the Gedenkstätte, quite different from the time right after reunification when one of the former GDR staff said, "The great, famous American nation should not forget her son. He also earned the right to a special plaque of honor on the wall of our memorial."[16] He was only one of so many Mittelbau-Dora prisoners and survivors who had an ambiguous past. Being a part of this life for several years was heroic.

The Pedagogical Functions of the Gedenkstätte

The Gedenkstätte has always had a mission of resocializing community life and beyond. The first iteration was part of the major resocialization after the Nazi years. Along with schools, public meetings, political organizations, and police and security forces, the Gedenkstätte informed people of new values and suggested the moral stances that would fit with the new government. The messages were created at the top of the hierarchy and filtered down to the masses. It was the responsibility of the people to hear, understand, and adapt to the new values.

The same missions need to be expressed during the years of transition to a unified Germany, but in a more voluntary and more convincing manner. It was not the people's responsibility to hear the message, but, rather, the role of pedagogues to engage young and old and to convince the people that new values and lifeways would be those approved and rewarded. In other words, the onus shifted from the "student" to the "teacher." Again, the Gedenkstätte could play a part in making the change by both showing the citizens the terrible history of the Third Reich and mitigating that by some very positive messages. For example, the juxtaposition of exploitation onto death of work slaves could now be contrasted with a certain pride in German accomplishment in technology.

Even the site of the pedagogy moved. The *Appellplatz*, a very large gravel-covered area that had held many people on mandatory commemoration days, is now hardly used. The beautiful reliefs that are found at one end behind a large podium are decayed to the point of being unrecognizable. Today, the tunnels, reopened and enlarged for visitors, are the high point of a trip to the Gedenkstätte. No place on the grounds displays so openly the contrast between scientific achievement and death. The crematorium presents the visitor with the impression that it would best be forgotten. For several years prior to Wagner's directorship, it had been poorly marked and could have been easily overlooked. More recently, steps to the crematorium have been improved, but the building remains as it was, rather empty and forgotten.

Germany has a highly developed culture of museum pedagogy that is applied to bringing unsavory history to the public in a series of "teachable moments." Few of these events are lectures; they are more performances before smaller groups using a Socratic method. Jens-Christian Wagner wanted to make the Gedenkstätte a learning and documentation center (*Lern- und Dokumentationszentrum*) where teaching and studying would be primary activities. The Gedenkstätte does not set an age limit for young people, but encourages only those over the age of fourteen to take tours and look at the exhibit.

Youth for Dora (Jugend für Dora), the organization founded before his time, continues to draw a modest number of adherents from Nordhausen, but also from the Netherlands, Belgium, and France. The group's goal is to keep the memory of Dora alive with the younger generation and to do so by interacting with survivors and increasing their contacts with those in many countries.

This small group serves some of the functions that the groups of schoolchildren and Free German Youth served earlier in the communist era. They become familiar with the history of Mittelbau-Dora, they meet survivors, and they engage in improvement projects. In addition, Youth for Dora takes excursions to other countries, where they meet with survivor groups or families of survivors. There is, however, no coercion to their participation.

In 2000, the young people developed their own questions for survivors with the help of the staff. They demonstrated how little they knew about these people with whom they wanted contact. One interview was recorded in their publication: "Were there good experiences?" Answer: "None." "What belongings were most important to you?" "My life." "What kind of a future did you imagine?" "I saw no future. The only important thing was to survive." The questionnaire exhibited a certain naïveté.[17]

This kind of enterprise would not be likely to occur under Dr. Wagner's watch. His own knowledge of survivors and the history would deem such questions unnecessary and untoward. Instead, he would be more likely to encourage young people to have unstructured conversations with those few remaining survivors and their families.

The seminars sponsored by the Topography of Terror and the Center for Political Education continue in the Gedenkstätte and other sites around Germany. The publication program and book distribution also are still carried out at public gatherings. The Web site of the center shows that it too is engaged in very serious attempts to change the political culture. In one item taken from a journal titled only "DDR" ("DDR" is German for "GDR"), it states: "The GDR was once upon a time. For many, it is only known only through stories. From the view of historical materials, that through the prism of time appear rather fairytale-like. . . . With all the complexities, there are only a few simple truths. A state that locks up and murders its citizens if they want to leave is not a good state. A political system that gives a small group of old men unlimited power over everything is a dictatorship, even if they give themselves the name 'democratic republic.'"[18] The topics that the seminars now engage are often rather arcane and draw groups of graduate students and people working on very specific topics surrounding concentration camp history. One has the impression that the large topics have been adequately covered and the minutiae are all that is left.

An elderly woman whose father had died in a concentration camp was often a participant over the years. At a recent seminar, she left the meeting room in tears. In the lobby, she said, "All my life, my friends have met every week for coffee and chats. I participated, but always felt my concerns were different from theirs. Only at the seminars did I feel I could express myself and hear from others about the events that changed my life and made me who I am. It was such a relief to have that kind of place. Now, it is over. I don't have anyplace where I can go where people will understand me and what I think about."

During the seminar, Jens-Christian Wagner said that the Gedenkstätte work had taken on a different character as compared with the time before his tenure. "Crying doesn't teach us anything" (Weinen bildet nicht), he stated. This philosophy is an outgrowth of the absence of survivors, for certainly had they been present, such a statement would have been unacceptable. When questioned later about that sentence, he explained, "It was the name of a seminar for young people given two weeks ago, and we meant, it doesn't help to cry; you have to be active. The title was meant to be provocative."[19] Jens-Christian Wagner realizes that there is an age divide in the audiences for the seminars and probably also for acceptance of his approach. Older people do not understand the nuanced messages that are couched in current scholarly work and theory. When they hear this discourse, they misunderstand and are upset by it.

It may be, as well, that the reintroduced use of the formal and informal forms of *you* (*Sie* and *Du*, respectively) are troublesome. In the first Gedenkstätte, the communist expectation was that all people one encountered were "comrades" and could be addressed as *Du*. In discourse with Wagner, it is clear that the distinction is often made on the basis of age. Interpersonal distance from older participants is easily established in a group setting, whether intentional or not, where both forms of *you* are used depending on one's age. Students relate to him easily and call him by his first name and use *Du* when addressing him. This appears to set up a differential among group participants that for some is disturbing.

The Grounds, Tunnels, and New Museum

Jens-Christian Wagner had already been working on the new conception of a reconfiguration of the Mittelbau-Dora Gedenkstätte complex while he was working for the Buchenwald–Mittelbau-Dora Foundation. When he arrived as director of the Nordhausen site, he set to work finding architects and construction firms for the very large project. He had the help and supervision of others, but it remained very much his project.

The results should be examined in three parts: the grounds, the tunnels, and the new museum. Work had begun on the grounds, which were cleaned, pruned, and planted. The descriptive markers were removed and changed where needed, and new direct messages were inserted. Some removal of topsoil had been done, revealing the foundations of various buildings in the center of the grounds. A walkway was improved around the circumference. For people in Nordhausen, the grounds had always provided a place to take a walk, as they are extensive and forested. This feature remained. Nothing was done to improve the existing structures of the crematorium, the fire station, or the small administration building. The roll-call square was weeded, but not changed.

The tunnels were improved with new texts that told individual stories of prisoners and explained what had occurred there. There was no deliberate enhancement of the technological focus. The guided tours also concentrated on the prisoners' lives and their suffering. The tunnels are dimly lit and have a natural temperature of about fifty-five degrees. Some ventilation is provided, and the general impression is eerie and forbidding. Remnants of the prisoners' latrine are visible, and the side tunnels are open enough to picture what might have been in them. At the end of the walkway is a multistoried section in which one can picture the upright rockets being worked on and stored.

Tours of the tunnels are always guided, and groups of a dozen or so people can go together at one time. School classes are also taken through by the staff, not their teachers. The staff seems very well prepared for this tour, which, one would imagine, might present some difficulties with people becoming claustrophobic or frightened. Some tours cover all the grounds and the exhibit and take up to four hours. It is a tiring and intensive effort for staff personnel who appear to be totally engaged in what they are doing.

The museum building was dedicated in the spring of 2005 in the presence of several hundred survivors. On the first floor is the exhibit, an information and book sales center, and an auditorium for lectures or films. It houses a library and archive on the second floor, as well as administrative offices and a cafeteria.

The building set high above the Gedenkstätte is a simple, stark rectangle, but with architectural beauty in its functional lines and airy and sunny windows. Outside, it does not detract from the landscape, and inside it is a comfortable place to work, with views that stretch out over the grounds in many directions. It seems to be perfectly suited to the space and function.

There is a terrace outside the building with a topographical map of the area and a model of how the camp was arranged when it was in operation. One can look down at the grounds and see where various buildings had been.

The museum exhibit is in a softly lit room that takes up about a fourth of the first floor. The main takeoff point of the exhibit is that Mittelbau-Dora and Mittelwerk were an expression of Hitler's call for "total war." This was the final stage of the war, and the camp had been in existence a short time. It is all the more disturbing when one thinks that fifteen thousand prisoners were annihilated in only eighteen months in the camp (another five thousand on the death marches, most likely).

Excellent visuals and some soundtracks help the visitor grasp the meaning of the exhibit. The establishment of the camp, the prisoners' lives, the role of civilian workers, and the late-arriving Jewish prisoners from Auschwitz are shown in sequence. Because of the timing of the camp's founding, it did not have many Jewish prisoners from the beginning and not as many as other camps at the end. The death marches and the abandonment of the camp by the SS are also displayed.

Staffing and Administration

There is a new Gedenkstätte law that has been in effect since 2003. Passed by the Thuringia parliament, it states that the foundation's purpose is to protect the original sites for grieving and remembrance of the crimes committed, to provide scientifically based information, to provide access to the public, and to encourage learning and research into the events that happened there. No quarter is given to the glorification of technology in the statement of goals, but emphasis is on the "misuse of prisoners for the assembly of weapons of extermination." The final goal "is to show the instrumentalizing of the Gedenkstätte at the time of the GDR."[20] In order to do this, it would be useful if the staff and advisory committees would talk to a cross-section of those who were connected in significant ways to the previous Gedenkstätte and have a variety of opinions. Nothing to date indicates that this will be a priority.

Periodically, this effort to show both the history of the camp and the shortfalls of the GDR in the same exhibits causes an uproar. There is always the danger of relativizing the messages of the exhibit, making the Germans themselves the ultimate victims of totalitarianism. This is fought off by lobby groups, but is never settled.

The other threat to the Gedenkstätte is the economic footing of the enterprise. The state of Thuringia and the federal government share equally in support of the grounds and exhibits, but in the past years there have been very large deficits. When the state parliament finds more money to make up the shortfall, most of it goes to the larger and more prominent memorial at Buchenwald.

The Gedenkstätte would like to have a bigger staff, but makes do with eight full-time positions, security personnel, and a receptionist-bookseller. In addition, it usually has several young people doing alternative service to the military and about twenty volunteers who lead tours. One of the ways of handling the large number of jobless in Germany is to provide those without work with short-term employment at the government's expense. There are a changing number of these workers employed at any one time as well.

Conclusion

The modern Gedenkstätte is in many respects a very beautiful place, with wide expanses of open fields and forests. It is, however, a place of horror and terror for those who experienced the concentration camp. As these former prisoners age and are no longer able to come back to the camp, their stories have to be re-created in exhibits and in discourse. This is not always easy and often morphs into other agendas.

Eastern Germany has a constant presence of neo-Nazis who target the Gedenkstätte, but are also found in the city and in and around the schools of Nordhausen. Jens-Christian Wagner does not want to take on this issue at the Gedenkstätte and thinks that is a civic duty for other institutions. He is dedicated to the history. Yet he is often found exploring the issues of citizenship in various ways. He, like Kurt Pelny and Cornelia Klose, has a big interest in explaining the intersections between the city and the camp. To what extent were the citizens of Nordhausen entwined in the life of the camp? Because of denial and of the stigma attached to knowing the answer to this question, evidence is hard to obtain. Yet Wagner has made an admirable try. He has also tied the issues of the camp to racism, violence, and exploitation in today's world and is trying to bring issues of slave labor, group hatred, and authoritarianism into discussions.

The GDR's emphasis on monopolistic capitalism allowed the population to avoid responsibility for what happened in their country. Today's young people cannot take on that responsibility, but they can become aware of what happened at a different time. That is also a kind of responsibility.

There are many aspects of the Gedenkstätte that appear to be very different from the iterations that preceded its current form. Yet many of the symbols, attempts at motivation and conviction, one-sided presentations, and censorship by positive influence of mainstream ideas continue. Differences are found in the open-door policies, the lack of intrusive homogeneity, and the increase in materials and access to them. Once again, using what is available, the staff of the Gedenkstätte tries to draw moral lessons from the tragedy that is their basis for being.

9. Major Themes and Conclusions

In this book, we have presented three phases of the Gedenkstätte Mittelbau-Dora's history in the context of what had happened in the concentration camp and missile assembly plant: the initial memorial under the GDR, the interim memorial during and just after the reunification of Germany, and the restructured memorial as it exists today. We placed the concentration camp events in the context of the last days of the war and subsequent American and Soviet occupations of Nordhausen, a small city that, to a large extent, was shaped by the camp and its survivors. They were a quiet reminder of a time poorly understood and not freely remembered, but one that could also not be forgotten.

During the forty years in the GDR, the Gedenkstätte Mittelbau-Dora framed the history in terms of a citizen's deep responsibility to remember, to mourn, and to idealize the heroes who stood up to fascism. A constant theme was a militant watchfulness for a renewal of profiteering from war, from what Eisenhower called the "military-industrial complex," and for taking peacetime for granted. The guilt for the crimes of the Second World War was someone else's problem: those people and their monopolies still living in luxury and comfort on the western side of the wall.

For the past twenty years, the concentration camp history has been rewritten for those in Nordhausen as a time of crimes against humanity, particularly against Jews and other named groups, a time with few heroes and few tears. In Nordhausen, it is now also remembered that the Germans were technologically advanced, ahead of other countries, including the United States in some areas, their progress achieved through the deaths of millions of men, women, and children.

The Importance of Survivors

Rarely were the people of Nordhausen confronted directly with the contradictions in emphases between the two systems and their varying interpretations of the Gedenkstätte. More often, the differences were presented in new exhibits, in pedagogy, in one side discrediting the other in many different ways. Under communism and noncommunism, exclusionary practices left many without a leading role, but still able to find alternative organizations, journals, and newsletters in which to express themselves. On the fringes, not the center, of the Gedenkstätte work, these outsiders were and still are able to share their perspective with the next generation of Germans. To a large extent, this outcome has been the work of the variety of survivors and the various staffs of the Gedenkstätte who, over time, have insisted that this work go forward.

The prisoner-survivors had no single agenda. Some survivors referred to themselves as "the Mafia" who had worked against the system and come out on top. Those who came to the Gedenkstätte during the GDR years had wanted to be sure that their antifascist stance was recognized. They often came as heroes and had to remind people that they represented ordinary men who suffered and died.[1] Nordhausen's leaders were those who had been among the imprisoned and knew what lessons they wanted to impart and what kind of a regime they were ready to build. Perhaps their hopes and dreams were changed and decimated over the years, or perhaps they went to their graves satisfied that they had conquered their foes and were able to put into place their own dreams of a different world order.

After the reunification of Germany, with relatively little rancor, the survivors of Mittelbau-Dora allowed the Gedenkstätte to display the change of political orientation by giving precedence to a different group of prisoner-survivors. These people formed a new organization and referred to themselves as "the European Committee." The emphasis was on the West, not the East.

Over the years, these survivors came back to the place of their torture for a hundred different reasons, if they came at all. Some wanted to pay tribute to their fallen fellows. Some wanted to test their own strength of will by returning. Some wanted to show their families the site of their suffering. Some wanted to stand among others who understood them and their personal traumas. To place all survivors into an essentialized category, and to stereotype their motivations, experiences, or mental states, is foolish and wrong.

Today, the prisoner-survivors of Dora, the "hell of all concentration camps," are few in number and diminishing. Those who still return to the site do so at a high personal cost, and may come because there they are highly regarded and have friends who look for them. They still have something to impart, to give, particularly to young people. These survivors today are a precious few, however. The director and many of the staff have known survivors over the years, and their stories guide the work to this day. For that reason, the temptation to turn the Gedenkstätte into a tourist attraction, or a paean to technology, a kind of adventure park, or to mitigate its horrible history by comparing the Nazi horror to all totalitarianism has been repelled. The survivors have accomplished that much.

All of the directors and their staffs of the Gedenkstätte have treated prisoner-survivors with respect and kindness. They have each chosen different groups to favor with advisory roles and particular honors, but no survivor has been without honor in the Gedenkstätte. All who found the will to return have been welcomed. It is quite possible that for the survivors, the place itself, rather than the exhibits or content of them, is where the meaning is located. Is there a place to lay wreaths and flowers? Is there a place for quiet reflection? Are there enough benches to make it possible to rest, and is there sufficient handicapped access? These are the issues that confront the elderly visitor.

The Gedenkstätte as a Political Forum

The easiest thing is to recognize the discrediting politics of the "other side"; they are annoying or worse. It is much more difficult to recognize one's own exclusionary practices. In the GDR Gedenkstätte, an ideology was fostered that promoted the idea that there was no collective or individual German guilt, but only the systemic guilt of a military-industrial power that took over political, legal, and governmental functions. Groups chosen by the ruling committees decided how that idea should be embedded in public discourse, including that provided through the Gedenkstätte. The party placed its own trusted and well-tried individual in the position of director at the Gedenkstätte to be sure that this message would be significant, and then oversaw the product to be sure it met the planned agenda. The displays of the suffering and heroism of the prisoners, particularly the communist prisoners, satisfied that goal.

During the communist era, people were brought to the Gedenkstätte in large crowds under pressure to appear, and there they heard the anti-Nazi, antifascist parole that was soon to be mainstream thought in the GDR. The displays showing previous Nazi functionaries, such as Heinrich Lübke, Wernher von Braun, and Arthur Rudolph, drove home to the viewers the continued life and glory of the Nazi world in the West. Lübke was active in

Peenemünde and later served as president of the FRG, Wernher von Braun was a leading star in the U.S. space program, and Arthur Rudolph was a well-paid developer of the Saturn V rocket, which launched the first manned flight to the moon.

After reunification, in 1990, the Gedenkstätte took on a different ideology, one that favored a nonconfrontational separation from ideas that had gone before. Prisoners became those who had suffered, not because they were resistance fighters but because they were gathered up for no single given reason by a totalitarian regime. *Nazi* became *National Socialism:* more specific, but also closely associated with socialism or "real socialism" (*Realsozialismus*), which was a topic much under discussion at the time. Visits became totally voluntary, and more effort was given to thinking about museum pedagogy and the many ways that the site could be used to appeal to numbers of various groups. Guilt was not assigned, and perpetrators were individuals, not capitalist monopolies. The military-industrial complex was mentioned, but not emphasized. Progress in technology was grounded in German science, but came at a price that should never have been paid. Historical fact-finding was highly valued.

Negative censorship, whereby written material had to be approved prior to publication, was replaced by a more open selection of materials from a variety of international authors. Indeed, today the Gedenkstätte and its director are international colleagues of both national German and non-German museum professionals.

The "positive censorship" comes from government entities that provide books and materials that promote tolerance, civic knowledge, and understanding of a unified Germany. However, they also provide books and materials that some believe demonize the GDR. This tends to stifle the possibility of looking at what happened within that system with an open mind. They often promote a post–cold war attitude, as if to dampen and destroy positive reflections on the previous system and conflate the Nazi time period and the GDR under the rubric of "totalitarianism." This can add to generational misunderstandings within families and communication difficulties. Issues that today are related to military-industrial-governmental intersects are not addressed under neoconservative ideology. Issues surrounding the effect of arms production and warfare, arms sales and political hegemony, and non-state regimes and mass murder thus are not usually represented in the new civic education provided through the Gedenkstätte.

The political ideas overtly or indirectly produced and disseminated within the Gedenkstätte culture were mainstream in the communist-era Gedenkstätte. Today, political ideas disseminated within the memorial sites are still mainstream. There are simply two different mainstreams. That is not a nega-tive finding, nor is it surprising. It is realistic. The money for the Gedenkstätte operations was always in short supply and is so today. Thus, funding would be unlikely if the Gedenkstätte programs and displays did not reflect domi-nant cultural modes. Leaving space for discussion, introducing provocative themes, having passing exhibits of alternative concepts may be a creative way of approaching diversity of thought and belief among all the stakeholders of Gedenkstätte efforts while maintaining this middle-of-the-road approach.

The Individual within the Group

Much has been written and spoken about instrumentalization. This is much more a German than an American concept. English speakers would speak of manipulation more readily in describing the use of a setting or event to create a reaction in the participant. In Germany, history of a site like the Gedenkstätte can be "instrumentalized" to create patriotism, nationalism, guilt, anger, or any number of responses. It is usually used as a criticism of the GDR that the memorials served the purpose of legitimizing the state.[2]

There is a limit to which this actually is the case, however. The intention to have a certain impact on the public is mediated by the individual mean-ings that the history has for each person. The instrumentalization is always incomplete, because regardless of how seamlessly the story is told, it will find its individual interpretation in the myriad experiences that make up a person's cognitive response. These individual responses will not be homogeneous within a group, and therefore, there is always space, even if it is private, for those with a different point of view to maintain their own private truth.

An example of private memory crossing the ideology of the state was found in a small group of church members in Nordhausen. Throughout the years of the GDR, nothing was explicitly said about the expulsion of Jews from the city in 1938 and later or their forced emigration to safety or murder in Nazi death camps. This small group, however, remembered and quietly cleaned and maintained the city's Jewish cemetery, although it was not a party-sanctioned activity. They did it with a tacit understanding that they would continue without interference. It was a meaningful place for some in Nordhausen despite the lack of support for their memories or convictions.

And people such as Ilse Kirchhoff, who were keen observers and active participants in the life around them, used that observation not to become dissidents necessarily but to draw their own conclusions. Ilse lived near and later married Hans Hagen, whose father was a Nordhausen policeman in the criminal division. Their lives became tied to the Hermanns, a Jewish family in

Nordhausen. As Kurt Hermann later told of events, on the night of November 9, 1938, his family was awoken by a loud knocking at the door.[3] Luckily, his father was out of town. Kurt, his mother, and grandmother were packed into a vehicle and given a "sightseeing tour" of the city. Their synagogue was in flames, buildings were being smashed, and storm troopers were yelling at the top of their lungs, "Death to the Jews!" and singing songs with lyrics such as "When Jewish blood drips off our knives . . ." The Jews in other cars, who had been subjected to the same "tour," were dropped off at an assembly hall where the police also dumped the Hermanns. Men and boys between the ages of twelve and seventy were taken to Buchenwald, while mothers and children were sent home.

Kurt Hermann experienced the entire horror of Buchenwald in the three weeks he was there, but was lucky to be discharged due to a coincidence and a bit of luck. He made his way back home and rejoined his family. "My mother was able to contact Mr. Hagen, our former neighbor, and asked him if he could help my father who was in the local jail. He promptly did. He went to the jail, unlocked the door of my father's cell, and sent my father home."[4]

Although the family tried desperately to leave the country, none other would accept them. It took Kurt almost a year to find a way out of Germany and across the ocean to the United States, where he began a new life. He was drafted into the U.S. Army in 1942 and was sent back to Germany, where he was assigned to intelligence work in the Third U.S. Army headquarters of General Patton. Under these auspices, he interrogated prisoners of war as the army swept through Germany. "In 1945, while stationed in Freising, a city near Munich, I was able to visit my home town of Nordhausen. I was hoping to be able to collect some information on the fate of my dear parents. The outlook was grim." As he approached Nordhausen, he found that the city had been bombed. "The city of Nordhausen simply no longer existed."[5] Kurt Hermann talked to former neighbors and acquaintances and found that his parents had been sent to Theresienstadt and never heard from again. He later found that his parents had been transferred to Auschwitz and were presumed gassed.

Many years later, a letter that Kurt had written a friend at the time, along with pictures he had taken on that April 1945 trip to find his family, was published in the Nordhausen hometown magazine.[6] He mentioned policeman Hagen in the letter. As soon as Ilse Kirchhoff and her husband, Hans Hagen, saw the article, they got in touch with Kurt Hermann in the United States and began a long and intense friendship with him through the mail and later by telephone. Kurt returned to Nordhausen four times in all, twice while he was a soldier and twice while in Europe before German reunification. He began a correspondence with several people in Nordhausen, including Manfred Schröter and Peter Kuhlbrodt. They make phone calls to one another occasionally to this day. Dr. Schröter was able to find Kurt Hermann's old nanny in a nursing home, and has kept him informed about the rebirth of a small Jewish community in Nordhausen.

In 2008, Hans Hagen died after a very long illness. Ilse had nursed him for many years and missed him terribly. She said, "It was Kurt Hermann who understood and gave me such good advice over the phone about how to get on with my life. He called so often, even more than my children. He has become family to me."[7]

Kurt Hermann has become a citizen of both Los Angeles, where he raised his family and ran a driving school for movie stars, and also of Nordhausen again. Like Martin Adler, he is a man who has great capacity for reconciliation and a store of goodwill that does not seem to fail him. He recently gave all his photos of the Nordhausen bombing to the city archive with directions that they should be available without charge to those with a use for them. Several appear in this book. He was pleased with the reports that students had made a very good model of the destroyed Nordhausen synagogue and that it was displayed at the city hall. He has pictures of that model sent to him by his new Nordhausen friends.

For Leo Kuntz, who learned to know his father in part through the GDR Gedenkstätte, the years have not brought him to reconciliation with the Nordhausen Gedenkstätte. He lived with the image of Albert Kuntz, the hero of Mittelbau-Dora; the new Gedenkstätte made him literally sick, and he was hospitalized for a time. When he recovered, he found other ways to express his opinion both privately and publicly with the postreunification directors, whom he personally respects, and he has found his own public through organizations that share his views. He and his wife have written a book incorporating Albert Kuntz's letters to his wife, and Leo and Leopoldine Kuntz give readings from the letters throughout eastern Germany.[8] The use of today's memorial that does not emphasize the early and often selfless communist opposition to Hitler has not changed his perspective. His own experiences, information, and beliefs are separate from the messages produced externally.

Facts and Objectivity

Everyone wants an objective display when one goes to a serious museum. Many visitors take every explanatory item as an objective fact. Certainly, every effort is made by museum people to produce that effect. However, not everything in the museum storerooms can be displayed: there is not enough room. The selections must have a coherence; there is probably a motif or goal to be followed. The selection of what is on display is objective only in the sense of the planners' mind-sets and the cohesion they anticipate. The cohesion is their imaginary, and in their hopes, it is in the imaginary of the viewers. However, the viewer makes a cohesive story from the fragments that are there; the viewer fills his or her own cognitive spaces.

Tourist culture, of which concentration camp and Holocaust memorials have become an integral part, leads people to expect an instant infusion of history and information upon visiting recommended sites. This can be seen in checklists that some tourists take with them to be sure they have covered the main points of their visit or in the books claiming to inform the reader of "the one thousand places to see before you die." There is a belief that one can consume the history and add it to the store of intellectual wealth, conversational fodder, and notches on the belt of the tourist, so to speak. What is remembered from a museum or exhibit is often cognitively mixed with the quality of the hotel that one sleeps in that night, the satisfaction or dissatisfaction with the lunch, jokes told on the bus, or people newly met. Thus, the memory of the excursion is mired in dozens of small, irrelevant details that color the very information of the exhibits, making them very subjective to the viewer.

The fact that the Mittelbau-Dora Gedenkstätte does not have many of the original buildings of the concentration camp impacts the objectivity of the display. The archaeological fundaments are labeled so that one can imagine where the kitchen, laundry, and other buildings were. One of the barracks has been rebuilt but houses only a spare exhibit, making it seem spacious. The crematorium consists of three rooms and few exhibits. The ovens are still there, but do not seem very ominous in the bare surroundings. The viewer injects a subjective response to the way things are organized. One visitor, an American Jewish woman, at a ceremony in front of the crematorium said, "Look at that! They had the nerve to put a cross over the door!" However, it was not a cross but a vent that had been created at the inception of the crematorium by leaving a vertical and horizontal brick out of the structure for airflow.

One of the values expressed often within the new Gedenkstätte pedagogy is that of *Differenzierung*. Literally, it means to differentiate, but it is used more in the sense of applying nuance to concepts within the concentration camp history. It is the act against essentializing aspects of the past. Looking at the GDR memorials, the criticism is often made that they were not nuanced. Large concepts dominated the exhibits, and while there might have been truth in them, they were not nuanced enough to present an accurate picture of what had happened on the site.

What is not recognized is that there are difficulties in nuancing the history of the concentration camp under any circumstances. First, it is hardly possible to present a postmodern view of the terror and horror that every prisoner experienced in his or her own way. Not all prisoners were heroes. Does that mean that for some, being in the camp was not difficult, nauseating, and frightening beyond expression? Certainly not!

One way of nuancing the display is to present "cool history," without images that promote fright in the onlooker, putting into words instead of visions the conditions under which the slaves lived. The modern Gedenkstätte Mittelbau-Dora has not gone in this direction, but has mixed displays to show as many of the differing conditions as possible and explaining, as well, the outcomes of lives that were once lived in the tunnels and dank grounds and barracks of the camp. It offers information about those who were able to rebuild their lives, at least as far as outsiders can see. However, as the GDR Gedenkstätte could not recognize the heterogeneity of West Germany's leadership, the new Gedenkstätte cannot give credit to the sincere and worthy efforts of the pioneers in the memorialization of the site. This very subjective omission leaves a painful divide within the community and museum exhibit as the Gedenkstätte does not recognize the early efforts to remember the concentration camps.

Nor can the nuancing address the deep, hidden scar left by the bombing of Nordhausen and the reasons that it occurred. The simultaneous event of the liberation of the camp and destruction of so many lives in the city remains a semihidden episode remembered publicly once a year. For a newcomer in the city, there are no reminders of that time except for a monument in front of city hall. The city is a bright, cheerful place with attractive plantings and parks, a rebuilt "old town," and many amenities. Dr. Klose at the Culture Office sees to it that there are many civic activities that engage residents in fun community events and bring them in contact with cultural offerings. Objectively, Nordhausen is an interesting city whose past history of Mittelbau-Dora lives just outside its old walls, and is neither hidden nor suppressed. Many such memorials are hard to find and not advertised in tourist offices. After twenty years, it appears that reunification has worked well here.

Yet Nordhausen is losing population. Industry has not been able to keep up with the need for employment among its youth. The living standard is maintained by expensive government programs that provide a basis of support for the unemployed and underemployed. The industries that had provided a living for Nordhausen residents before unification were shut down in large numbers because of their old machinery, unacceptable levels of pollution, or simply the competition from West German firms. The international economic recession has impacted all segments of the economy and slowed efforts to build up new employment opportunities. The apparent health of the city contrasts with the actual unhappy economic state of many of its residents.

Creating New Forms of Government

Both the old and the new Gedenkstätte contributed to the creation of new governments in radical shifts of values and beliefs. Coming out of the Nazi era, the first memorial was largely influenced by survivors of the Nazi terror. The new government wanted to radically change the order of things, make a secure homeland, share the resources in an equitable way, enhance the lives of those who had been caught in the lower classes with little hope of escape. By placing the sons of the working class in important positions, educating them above others, giving them a voice, they accomplished a significant reversal of class structure, power, and authority. By directing scarce resources first to those who were not Nazi burdened, not too comfortable in their living situation, and removing assets from those who had them in abundance, they quickly moved to equalize a workers' society. To make the homeland secure was much more difficult and caused a remilitarization that many had not anticipated or wanted. The men in uniforms returned, keeping the streets safe, but at a price that was intolerably high to most. Gradually, more and more of the people themselves were under suspicion as "enemies of the state," and there could not be enough spying and informing to make the state safe from its enemies. Not all of this reaction was paranoia, for, internationally, GDR's neighbors did not wish them well. One can argue whether the state collapsed more from internal security concerns or outside threats. Certainly, there was enough of both.

The Gedenkstätte stood ready to reinforce through symbolic means the importance of the state by reflecting the military presence in the oath of office administered there for new military recruits, by militarizing young people's activities on the grounds, and by employing the techniques of oversight to the civilian population when they were present at the Gedenkstätte. In a more positive vein, they reinforced the idea of community by having work crews from the neighborhoods and schools at the site, by inviting newly married couples to dedicate their unions at the memorial to remind them of their duties as citizens of the GDR, and by reminding citizens of the terrors of a fascist dictatorship through the interactions with survivors.[9]

Suspension of Disbelief

Suspension of disbelief is often used to describe the experience of theatergoers or book readers as they become so involved emotionally in what is presented that they no longer are aware of their actual surroundings. In such instances, the participants lose their belief that the performance is a fiction, as emotional triggers mask the reality of their actual surroundings. This usually allows an audience to appreciate works of literature or drama that are exploring unusual ideas. Can suspension of disbelief also occur when one examines a museum display? Does one's critical capacity diminish in the face of extraordinary emotion? Perhaps "cool history" attempts to take the emotion away from the concentration camp memorial experience to allow viewers to come to their own conclusions.

Nationalism and patriotism act to insulate the total range of thoughts and feelings. Military music, calls to arms, presentation of threats to national security, and many other triggers intervene between the facts of the case and one's response to it. If the narrative is strong, the recipient of the message has less agency in determining his or her own belief structure.

The suspension of disbelief is also aided by a viewer's removal from the site of the action. After the bombing of Nordhausen, attention was diverted from the citizens' own troubles to those of the concentration camp. Disallowing discussion and punishing the population for being German in the midst of terrible human crimes, the Allies helped to create a suspension of disbelief in the people themselves, so that they no longer really understood what had happened and who was responsible. The drama and trauma overwhelmed ordinary thought processes and, in some cases, memory. This is rapidly changing, and books about strategic bombing are available in German and English today.

Today, mainstream opinion in Germany is that a gap in understanding of World War II history is due to totalitarian production of knowledge. We have tried to present in this book a wider responsibility; memory from the earliest postwar days has been manipulated and instrumentalized in Nordhausen. Continuing to use the discrediting historical past for purposes other than learning from it serves temporary political purposes, but cannot be good for community mental health.

Nor can ordering the correct response to changes in the system of governance through manipulation of discourse. "Nostalgia," "stuck in the past," and "unrealistic memory" are labels that denigrate individuals' feelings about their own experience and do nothing to empower them to reach conclusions based on information. It is no less "instrumentalization" to discredit people's perceptions and beliefs in the postcommunist period than it was in the communist period. That holds true as well for silencing the past by omitting information about efforts by Gedenkstätte personnel in the communist era to contact survivors, to give them comfort, and to remember them honorably.

Survivors themselves cannot agree on the reality of their experiences, which does not mean that their variability makes them incorrect or not worthy of our consideration. They too have struggled with their own disbelief: Did it really happen as I remember? Did I really behave as I want to think I did? Am I worthy of remembering my fallen fellow prisoners?

Stakeholders and Their Needs

There are many different kinds of stakeholders, and some are in the ascendancy and some in decline. From the beginning, governments have been strong stakeholders. They invest money from their budgets for memorials, they supervise and allow or disallow certain kinds of displays, they appoint or approve of advisory panel members, they direct people toward or away from certain areas of the Gedenkstätte, they encourage or discourage certain groups from taking part in events. This has changed little in the communist or postcommunist era.

The stakeholder group that has changed the most is the survivor group. It changed in two ways: through the groups invited to take special part in the decision-making process of the Gedenkstätte and through its decline due to death and aging. Both of these causes could have been expected, although hurtful to individuals. The Gedenkstätte works within the German culture, and inclusiveness has never been its hallmark. The urge to discredit the "other" is always strong, although great restraint has been shown in the context of the Gedenkstätte Mittelbau-Dora. It would take creativity beyond cultural constraints to show trust and self-confidence in all stakeholders in equal measure.

Another stakeholder group is the tourists. That group has grown over the years, as the Gedenkstätte has had a worthy permanent exhibit and interesting traveling exhibits. The excitement of visiting the partially accessible tunnel in the past decade has enhanced the appeal of the Gedenkstätte. Here, the tourist is confronted with not only the terrible story of German shame, but a potential for national pride that allows one the strength to go forward. Handled well, as the current staff is able to demonstrate, this is a positive development.

Finally, the Nordhausen citizens are stakeholders. They have looked to the Gedenkstätte for almost fifty years as a multipurpose site. Some people use it for its recreational value and take walks along the pathways, looking at nature and breathing fresh air. They have come to learn about German history and the town's role in it. One person expressed the feeling that even though it had a negative renown, Nordhausen's stamp on history sets it aside from other towns of its size: "Things happened here." For many Nordhausen citizens, the Gedenkstätte is also a window to the wider world. International friendships have been formed there, not only among youth in their international work camps, but also among adults who have expressed their remorse to prisoners and tried to show remorse for their suffering. Many have also formed real friendships that take them to other countries and tie them to interest groups that bridge international boundaries.

Stakeholders that should not be forgotten are the people in the United States who have ties to the Gedenkstätte because of their connection to the camp Mittelbau-Dora. They are the survivors, liberators, or their children who have direct knowledge of the history. They are also the journalists and historians who have written about the camp and litigators who have prosecuted the scientists and guards of the camp.

One such person is Eli Rosenbaum, the director of the U.S. Department of Justice's Office of Special Investigations (OSI).[10] Informally, this office was often called the "Nazi-Hunting Unit" of the U.S. government, for since its establishment in 1979, the office has been charged with finding people who have perpetrated serious human rights abuses and crimes against humanity and are residing in the United States. Its mission is to prohibit such people from finding refuge in the United States. Initially, the OSI sought out World War II-era Nazi criminals, but since 2004 has sought other human rights violators as well.

Eli Rosenbaum joined the OSI in 1979 as a summer law clerk and first heard of Mittelbau-Dora shortly after returning for his final year of law school through a book he found on the camp.[11] He then came upon another book regarding the utilization of German missile engineers in the United States and began to feel a need to investigate.

Rosenbaum's job has been his passion for three decades. He began investigations on several fronts, but always kept Mittelbau-Dora in mind. It was too late to develop a case against Wernher von Braun, who had died in 1977, two years prior to the OSI's creation, but Arthur Rudolph was retired in California when Rosenbaum became a full-fledged prosecutor and investigator.[12]

Arthur Rudolph managed the Pershing Missile Program, a major weapons program, and the Saturn V program, which developed the first rocket to the moon. His background was not widely known when he arrived in the United States after the war, but by 1984, the OSI and Eli Rosenbaum had built a case against Rudolph, who had been a member of the Nazi Party from 1931, two years before Hitler took office.

Rudolph had been involved with space and rocketry in Germany from an early age and began working with von Braun. At Peenemünde, he was in charge of the development plants for the V-2 rockets and then became chief planning engineer at Peenemünde South. In Mittelbau-Dora, he was production manager and in charge of many others who had authority over the prisoners. In Mittelwerk, Rudolph voluntarily watched the slow strangulation by hanging from a movable crane of prisoners accused of sabotage, and he participated in forcing the prisoners to observe the gruesome spectacle. Rudolph stated that this was done "to show the penalty of making a plot for sabotaging the factory."[13] The OSI developed enough evidence that it became clear: a verdict would have denaturalized Rudolph. Instead, he chose to give up his U.S. citizenship and leave the country "voluntarily." He moved to Canada and attempted to reenter the United States by way of that country, but was unsuccessful. In May 1992, at the age of eighty-three, he was "excluded from Canada" by a Canadian Federal Court of Appeals. Thus, as an elderly man, he returned to Germany, where he died in 1996.

The OSI and Eli Rosenbaum were subjected to vitriol for their tireless prosecution of Rudolph, who had his own cheering section among space scientists and engineers, both American and German, in Huntsville, Alabama. Fortunately, there were many who also backed the excellent work of this government agency.

The Continuing Importance of the Gedenkstätte

Eli Rosenbaum never lost his interest in Mittelbau-Dora and has provided background information to many U.S. historians and writers, who have carried the story to the public. He still registers emotion when talking of Yves Béon or Johnny Nicholas and the sacrifice of the tens of thousands who died at the camp. Rosenbaum questions whether the Gedenkstätte will become a tourist destination. He believes strongly that the Gedenkstätte has a definite purpose: it should remain a place of serious reflection.[14]

The importance of reconciliation is not often openly stated, yet this place where horror and death are remembered is also a place where one can draw lessons for life. From those who think seriously about how life can be lived fully and inclusively come new ideas that are alive in the city of Nordhausen.

Pfarrer Peter Kube, who was active in the citizens' movement in the late 1980s, now uses his energy to make the city an open place where appreciation outweighs negativity. He has started a number of innovative programs that foster inclusivity. Such wonderful events include an open coffee hour through the church/city coffeehouse, the Eine Welt Café, whereby children serve adults coffee and cake in an open plaza and an international crowd comes to enjoy the little ones. Pfarrer Kube has also organized an annual bazaar where different international groups present for the public their best culinary offerings and crafts. There is both a point person and a place to meet for those with unusual backgrounds, different approaches to life, a place for meaningful innovation. Young people and older ones know there is a place and people who will listen to their ideas for projects and help them achieve their goals.

The Gedenkstätte Mittelbau-Dora both reflects and creates a transformation of meaning. It can promote a kind of reconciliation. Kind words to one another and a welcome instead of a distancing are exactly what create hope in Nordhausen and might just tie the city to the Gedenkstätte in ever more meaningful ways.

From the truth of the past, with a tolerance for some ambiguity, with willingness to remember and commemorate that which was a part of life, comes hope for the future. Twenty thousand dead because of Mittelbau-Dora and the eight thousand dead because of World War II Allied bombing raids are the cornerstones. Out of that pain, with the help of good people of very different political persuasions, comes a new day.

> We placed a memorial stone for you out of hard rock; it was really necessary, this stone; one could not forget you. You and the others. And also then we needed a place, that we could come as pilgrims if something was difficult for us, where we could meet with others and find again where we meet in thought.
>
> Tomorrow we will dedicate the stone. There will be people there and noise too, and many who would rather not look at your graves.
>
> And then we will talk. That will be hard, for that which we celebrate can never be expressed. We have always been shy about it, what we were to one another.
>
> Therefore, today we will be together this evening when it has become still, we will be together with you and with all the others who left us before and after you.
>
> And in the still hour that we devote to you, you will all be there as it was when we went our separate ways, and we will read the silent questions in your eyes.
>
> You will sit next to us: the blue eyes in which such astonishment shone, still look through the glass although the handbell has already rung.
>
> And you with your worn-out body and blond hair and the touch of irony on your lips, even then when the "judge" pronounced death.
>
> And you, little, insolent Berliner, you were always good-natured even when we were already in despair. Yes, they beat you, and you were so young.

And then you will come, you who always brought a piece of bread when we were tortured by hunger;—I had to clamp my teeth together, as before our eyes they strangled you, and we had to stand there and could do nothing for you but look on although it howled within us and today still bleeds.

And if we then talk, we will gather new strength, for we hear your voice and that admonishes.

If we dedicate the stone tomorrow, then we will be able to retain life, to find ourselves, and without words we will say: "We build a new memorial—not of stone—out of living people—a new Germany."[15]

Notes

Introduction

1. See the obituary to Clifford Geertz in the *American* (December 2007): 786–89.
2. Wagner, *Ellrich, 1944/45,* 11.
3. See Grygar, *Menschen, Ich Hatte Euch Lieb,* 323. All translations are the authors' except in previously published works.

Chapter 1. Conceptualizing Horror

1. The most extensive and reliable source for the history and structure of Mittelbau-Dora is undoubtedly Wagner's *Produktion des Todes.*
2. Wiesel, *From the Kingdom of Memories,*194.
3. See Endlich and Lutz, *Gedenken und Lernen an Historischen Orten.*
4. Gellately, *Backing Hitler,* 12–13.
5. Drobisch and Wieland, *System der NS-Konzentrationslager, 1933–1945,* 13.
6. Kershaw, *Hitler, 1889–1936,* 456, 460.
7. Sofsky, *Order of Terror,* 28.
8. Kühnrich, *Der KZ-Staat,* 42.
9. Herzog and Strebel, "Das Frauenkonzentrationslager Ravensbrück," 13–14.
10. Bartel et al., *Buchenwald,* 23.
11. Weinmann, *Das Nationalsozialistische Lagersystem,* 715. More recently, Megargee, *Encyclopedia of Camps and Ghettos,* has made the same point (xxxiii).
12. Megargee, *Encyclopedia of Camps and Ghettos,* xxxii.
13. These titles were changed and enhanced through the years of the Third Reich as Himmler consolidated police and political power.
14. Sofsky, *Order of Terror,* 29.
15. Weinmann, *Das Nationalsozialistische Lagersystem,* xci.
16. Whitehead, *Violence,* introduction.

17. Sofsky, *Order of Terror*, 131.

18. Bettelheim, *The Informed Heart*, 180.

19. Bruno Bettelheim's idea of infantalization among inmates was harshly debated. See Sutton, *Bettelheim*, 249.

20. Cohen, *Human Behavior in the Concentration Camp*, 177.

21. Buchenwald political prisoners did save hundreds of children in the camp and delayed the evacuation of Jews, thus saving hundreds of adults as well (testimonies at the Buchenwald memorial, commemoration of the sixty-fifth anniversary of the liberation of the camp, Weimar, Germany, May 11, 2010).

22. Lundholm, *Das Höllentor*, 194.

23. Although Bettelheim does not transition in his writing to the camps themselves at this juncture, he is probably writing here of the prisoners' experiences after arriving.

24. Bettelheim, *The Informed Heart*, 123–24.

25. Bettelheim, "Individual and Mass Behavior in Extreme Situations," 424.

26. Bettelheim, *The Informed Heart*, 131–34.

27. Jana Kopelentova Rehak in her doctoral dissertation, "Czech Political Prisoners: Remembering, Relatedness, Reconciliation," refers to Pamela Reynolds's work and her statement that "children do have bargaining power in families, and some manage to secure adult attention and care despite disruptions in relationships, changes in the composition of household units, and high mobility among family members" (167). See also Reynolds, "Ground of All Making."

28. See works by Veena Das, Ranajit Guha, Arthur Kleinman, Margaret Lock, Valentine Daniel, and Gyanendra Pandey, among others.

29. See Kertesz, *Fateless*.

30. Kuntz et al., "Albert Kuntz," 67.

31. Ibid., 71.

32. Kertesz, *Fateless*.

33. Cohen, *Human Behavior in the Concentration Camp*, 115–210.

34. See Pandey's excellent work on fragmentation.

35. Kertesz, *Fateless*, 91.

36. Weinmann, *Das Nationalsozialistische Lagersystem*, xcix.

37. Ibid., cii.

38. Burleigh, *The Third Reich*, 631.

39. Kaienberg, *Vernichtung durch Arbeit*.

40. See Allen, *Business of Genocide*; and Sofsky, *Order of Terror*, 167–71. Wagner's use of the term *impressed labor* (*Zwangsarbeit*) is based on the argument made earlier by Benjamin Ferencz in his book *Less than Slaves*. Ferencz argues that slaves were meant to be kept in sufficient health to continue working and multiplying, whereas Nazi prisoners were expendable. The effect of this use of "impressed labor," however, seems to these authors to mitigate the horror of the circumstances and implies that volition was still present in the labor conditions. This was true only intermittently for some prisoners, who were at any time subject to harsher and more dire circumstances.

41. Weinmann, *Das Nationalsozialistische Lagersystem*, xxx.

42. Archiwum Państwowe w Kalisz, Kalisz, Poland, January 14, 1942, Der Ortsbürg-

ermeister der Ortspolizeibehörde 149 1/1 Benutzung von Verkehrsmitteln durch Polen, Akta in Kalisz, Sig. 1 4311.

43. http//www.history.ucsb.edu/faculty/marcuse/projects/currency.htm/tables.

44. Diestel and Jakusch, *Concentration Camp Dachau, 1933–1945,* 139.

45. Thus, the movie *Schindler's List* reflected not an unusual case of private enterprise using slave labor but a normal use of available human resources for the time and place.

46. Kühnrich, *Der KZ-Staat,* 77.

47. Weinmann, *Das Nationalsozialistische Lagersystem,* lxxiii.

48. Bütow and Bindernagel, *Ein KZ in der Nachbarschaft,* 53.

49. Fest, *Speer: The Final Verdict,* 132: *Handbook of Organization Todt,* 34.

50. Bundesarchiv/ Militärarchiv, Freiburg, Germany, Archivmaterial RH 8/v 1210, 105–6.

Chapter 2. The Camp Mittelbau-Dora

1. Wagner, *Produktion des Todes,* 146–47.

2. Dieckmann and Hochmuth, *KZ Dora-Mittelbau.*

3. Neufeld, *Rocket and Reich,* 135–36.

4. Ibid., 41. See also Pachaly and Pelny, *KZ Mittelbau-Dora,* 9–10.

5. Neufeld, "Peenemünde, die Raketen, und der NS Staat," 37.

6. Ibid., 46–48.

7. Allen, *Business of Genocide,* 208–14, quote on 213.

8. There is a difference in nomenclature used in the literature on Peenemünde, Mittelbau-Dora, and other camps in which prisoners performed work for the Reich. See also chap. 1, n. 40.

9. Neufeld, *Von Braun,* 143.

10. Wagner, *Produktion des Todes,* 367, 192.

11. There are many memoirs that review this initiation into the camps, including Kertesz, *Fateless.*

12. Neufeld, *Rocket and Reich,* 108.

13. Ibid., 148.

14. Weinmann, *Das Nationalsozialistische Lagersystem,* 575.

15. Neufeld, *Rocket and Reich,* 163–64.

16. Ibid., 193.

17. Ericksen and Hoppe, *Peenemünde,* 224.

18. Wegener, *Peenemünde Wind Tunnels,* 61.

19. Pachaly and Pelny, *KZ Mittelbau-Dora,* 7.

20. Bartel, *Gutachten,* 9.

21. Schafft and Zeidler, *Die KZ-Mahn- und Gedenkstätten in Deutschland,* 164.

22. Wagner, *Produktion des Todes,* 498.

23. Ibid., 185–86.

24. Speer, *Inside the Third Reich,* 370–71.

25. Dieckmann and Hochmuth, *KZ Dora-Mittelbau,* 19.

26. Hunt, *Secret Agenda,* 57–77.

27. Litomisky, "Memories of Prisoner Number 113359," 31–32.

28. In his memoir, Litomisky does not indicate if he was labeled a Jew by the regime. This effort to get himself "relabeled" as a political prisoner would indicate that his earlier designation was even more damaging, thus perhaps that of "Jew."

29. Litomisky, *Brieven uit de Hel*.

30. Schafft and Zeidler, *Die KZ-Mahn- und Gedenkstätten in Deutschland*, 168.

31. Wagner, *Produktion des Todes*, 202.

32. Neufeld, *Rocket and Reich*, 230.

33. The Geneva Conventions included the prohibition of prisoner labor in weapon production following World War II.

34. Ibid.

35. Ibid., 211, 225–26.

36. See the National Air and Space Museum, Washington, D.C., Exhibit of Hitler's Terror Weapons, 1996, cited in Schafft and Zeidler, *KZ-Mahn- und Gedenkstätten in Deutschland*, 167.

37. Wagner, *Produktion des Todes*, 216.

38. Ibid., 364.

39. Wagner, *Konzentrationslager Mittelbau-Dora*, 92–97. Wagner doubts the degree of organization and the international character of the resistance that are asserted in books and documents printed in the German Democratic Republic. (Discussions with authors)

40. Discussions with Leo Kuntz, 2008, 2009.

41. Pachaly and Pelny, *KZ Mittelbau-Dora*, 29–30.

42. Wagner, *Produktion des Todes*, 208–15.

43. Arbeitsgemeinschaft Spurensuche in der Südharzregion, *Der Bau der Helmetalbahn. Ein Bericht von der Eisenbahngeschichte den KZ Aussenlagern der SS Baubrigaden, der Zwangsarbeit in Südharz in den Jahren 1944–45 und den Evakuierungsmärchen* (brochure, n.d.).

44. Weinmann, *Das Nationalsozialistisches Lagersystem*, 568–69.

45. Wagner, *Ellrich, 1944/45*, 56.

46. Van de Casteele, *Ellrich*, 346.

47. Ferencz, *Less than Slaves*.

48. Van de Casteele, *Ellrich*, 42–43.

49. Fiedermann, Hess, and Jaeger, *Das Konzentrationslager Mittelbau-Dora*, 65.

50. Wagner, *Produktion des Todes*, 352–57.

51. Bornemann, *Aktiver und passiver Widerstand*, 75.

52. Wagner, *Produktion des Todes*, 206–7.

53. Ibid., 218.

54. Wernher von Braun traveled by car.

55. Hunt, *Secret Agenda*.

56. Pelny, *Todesmarsch*. See also Neander, *Die Letzten von Dora*, 1993.

57. Pachaly and Pelny, *KZ Mittelbau-Dora*, 201–18.

58. Abzug, *Inside the Vicious Heart*.

59. Wagner, *Produktion des Todes*, 23.

60. Gellert, *Holocaust, Israel, and the Jews*, films 224 and 225, 48.

Chapter 3. An End and a Beginning

1. MacIsaac, *Strategic Bombing in World War II*, 7.
2. Grosscup, *Strategic Terror*, 5–16.
3. Downes, *Targeting Civilians in War*, 4.
4. Knell, *To Destroy a City*, 17, 175–93, quote on 177.
5. Grosscup, *Strategic Terror*, 64.
6. Knell, *To Destroy a City*, 189.
7. Biddle, *Rhetoric and Reality*, 182.
8. Knell, *To Destroy a City*, 216.
9. Ibid., 243. See also Grosscup, *Strategic Terror*, 66.
10. Beecham and Huston, *Strategic Air War*, 10–11.
11. Grosscup, *Strategic Terror*, 66.
12. Ketternacker, "Die Behandlung der Kriegsverbrecher als anglo-amerikanisches Rechtsproblem." See also Grayling, *Among the Dead Cities*.
13. Biddle, *Rhetoric and Reality*, 256. Churchill's figures came from Public Records Office, London, compiled most likely by Charles Portal for the Chief of Staff Committee, November 3, 1942.
14. Groehler, *Geschichte des Luftkrieges, 1910 bis 1970*, 456–57 (author's translation). Why did Groehler leave Nordhausen off this list? Perhaps because the Soviet Union had no desire to expose its role in taking German technicians, scientists, and machinery back to its country to enhance its own space program.
15. Sebald, *On the Natural History of Destruction*. See also Olaf Groehler, *Geschichte des Luftkrieges, 1910 bis 1970*, in which the author states the same number of large cities hit by bombing raids and reports 74 percent of the city of Nordhausen destroyed (508–9).
16. Stadtarchiv Nordhausen (hereafter cited as SN), "Der Erbe," S270, 32.
17. Schröter, *Die Zerstörung Nordhausens*.
18. Kuhlbrodt, *Nordhausen unter dem Sternenbanner*, 6.
19. Personal interviews by the authors, June 2008.
20. Kuhlbrodt, *Nordhausen unter dem Sternenbanner*, 13.
21. Ibid., 10.
22. Wagner, *Produktion des Todes*, 506–7.
23. Ibid.
24. Margry, "Nordhausen."
25. Schwarz, *Kinder die nicht zählen*, cited in Schafft, *From Racism to Genocide*, 137.
26. Chamberlin and Feldman, *Liberation of the Nazi Concentration Camps*, 103.
27. SN, S270, "Der Erbe," 32. See also Winter, *Öffentliche Erinnerungen*, 21–22.
28. Neander, *Die Letzten von Dora*, 6. See also Mirbach, "Damit du es später deinem Sohn einmal erzählen kannst."
29. Schafft and Zeidler, *Die KZ-Mahn- und Gedenkstätten in Deutschland*, 143–48.
30. Ibid., 144.
31. Mick, *With the 102nd Infantry Division*, 211, 216.
32. Zentner, *Der Zweite Weltkrieg*, 552; other eyewitness accounts; Museum Gardelegen Gedenkstätte.
33. This was most likely a faulty assumption, as only Auschwitz had tattooed numbers

onto inmates and not only Jewish ones. In reality, there was no way of knowing from the charred bodies how many were self-identified as Jewish.

34. Mick, *With the 102nd Infantry Division,* 126.

35. Mirbach, *"Damit du es später deinem Sohn einmal erzählen kannst,"* 189–90.

36. National Archives and Records Administration (hereafter cited as NARA), Record Group (hereafter cited as RG) 407, Records of the Adjutant General's Office 1917–, WWII Operations Reports, 1941–45, 104th Infantry Division, 3104-3-2 to 3104-3-2, Entry 427, April 9–14, 1945.

37. Hoegh and Doyle, *Timberwolf Tracks,* 328.

38. Third Armored Division, *Spearhead in the West,* 14.

39. NARA, RG 407, Records of the Adjutant General's Office, 1917–, WWII Operations Reports, 1941–48, 104th Infantry Division, 3104-0.3 to 3104-0.7, Entry 427.

40. NARA, RG 407, Records of the Adjutant General's Office, 1917–, WWII Operations Reports, 1941–48, 3rd Armored Division, 602-2.4 to 603-2.13, Entry 427.

41. Third Armored Division, *Spearhead in the West,* 148.

42. NARA, RG 407, Records of the Adjutant General's Office, 1917–, WWII Operations Reports, 1941–48, 3rd Armored Division, 602-2.4 to 603-2.13, Entry 427; Third Armored Division, *Spearhead in the West,* 148.

43. Kuhlbrodt, *Nordhausen unter dem Sternenbanner,* 3.

44. Herbert, *History of Foreign Labor in Germany,* 156.

45. Fritz Saukel was the district political officer and authorized leader of the labor force (*Gauleiter and Generalbevollmächtiger für den Arbeitseinstaz*) (Weiss, *Biographisches Lexikon zum Dritten Reich,* 394).

46. Schröter, *Die Zerstörung Nordhausens,* 13.

47. The renting out of prisoners was a profit center for the SS, but one that has been poorly explored. It is important in that it is an indicator of the degree to which bystanders were aware of and implicated in the KZ system.

48. Both Kurt Pelny and Jens-Christian Wagner, past and current directors of Mittelbau-Dora Gedenkstätte, stated in interviews that achieving cooperation from people in the area to share their experiences with prisoners was most difficult. This was in a time period from the mid-1960s until the end of the first decade of the 2000s.

49. Probert-Wright, *An der Hand meiner Schwester;* report by Nordhausen resident Christa Köhler, 2002, about hiding in tunnels around Nordhausen with prisoners in their midst.

50. Gellert, *Holocaust, Israel, and Jews,* 48.

51. Perhaps the burial of the dead by townspeople was an order from Dwight David Eisenhower, but archivists at the National Archives have not been able to find a record of such an order. One archivist told Gretchen Schafft that she had concluded it was a verbal order that was passed through the troops.

52. Chamberlin and Feldman, *Liberation of the Nazi Concentration Camps,* 78.

53. Kuhlbrodt, *Nordhausen unter dem Sternenbanner,* 43.

54. Kuhlbrodt, *Schicksalsjahr, 1945.*

55. Kuhlbrodt, *Nordhausen unter dem Sternenbanner,* 17–18.

56. Ibid.; personal conversation by Schafft with Nordhausen informant, 1993.

Chapter 4. *The Change of Command*

1. SN, S270, vol. 1.
2. Schröter, *Die Zerstörung Nordhausens,* 60.
3. SN, S270, vol. 1.
4. Burleigh, *The Third Reich,* 799.
5. NARA, RG 407, Records of the Adjutant General's Office 1917, WWII Operations Reports, 1941–45, 104th Infantry Division, Entry 427, April 9–14, 1945.
6. http://www.senate.gov//artandhistory/history/common/generic/VP_Harry_Truman.htm.
7. Burleigh, *The Third Reich,* 794–812.
8. Mee, *Meeting at Potsdam,*76; NARA, SHAEF, RG 331, Entry 23, May 1, 1945.
9. Benz, *Europa nach dem Zweiten Weltkrieg,* 22.
10. Knell, *To Destroy a City,* 266.
11. SN, S130.
12. Judt, "The Past Is Another Country," 297.
13. NARA, SHAEF, RG 331, Correspondence File, "Directives for Military Government prior to Defeat or Surrender," Entry 1, November 5, 1944.
14. NARA, RG 407, Records of the Adjutant General's Office, Entry 427, April 14, 1945.
15. NARA, RG 407, Records of the Adjutant General's Office 1917, WWII Operations Reports, 1941–45, 104th Infantry Division, Entry 427, April 9–14, 1945.
16. SN, S130, Bd 14, 194.
17. *Nordhäuser Allgemeine,* July 1, 1980.
18. NARA, RG 331, Office of the Chief of Staff, G-3 Division, Subject File 1942–1945, *Handbook Concerning Policy and Procedure for the Military Occupation of Germany,* Entry 23, NM8.
19. See Hoegh and Doyle, *Timberwolf Tracks.*
20. SN, S149, BL2.
21. SN, S411, BL10.
22. NARA, Film Archive 111, ADC 3951 and 3963.
23. Kuhlbrodt, *Schicksalsjahr, 1945,* 63.
24. Schafft's discussion with an unnamed Nordhausen citizen in 1995.
25. NARA, SHAEF, RG 331, Geographic Correspondence File, 1943–1945, 250 Germany to 350 Germany, Memo Subject: Non-Fraternization by Germans, Entry 2, May 15, 1945.
26. Kuhlbrodt, *Nordhausen unter dem Sternenbanner,* 22–23.
27. This vignette is based on separate interviews with Wolfgang Nossen and Elfriede Kowalski in May 2008.
28. NARA, SHAEF, RG 331, General Staff, G-5 Division, Entry NM132.
29. Schafft, *From Racism to Genocide,* 177.
30. NARA, SHAEF, RG 331, Entry 15, Report on Evacuees from Eastern Europe.
31. Schafft, *From Racism to Genocide,* 180.
32. NARA, SHAEF, RG 331, Decimal Files 383 6/11 through 383.7/, vol. 2, Entry 1.

33. NARA, SHAEF, RG 331, Subject: The Security Control of Displaced Persons and Prisoners of War in Germany, Entry 1, January 1, 1945.

34. NARA, SHAEF, RG 331, Entry 1.

35. NARA, SHAEF, RG 331, Secretary of the Chief of Staff, August 1943–July 1945, 270/66 to 2711/7.3, Entry 1, April 21, 1945.

36. Parsons, "Eisenhower Bids Congress," 3.

37. NARA, Film 228, *Camp Dora—Nordhausen, Germany,* U.S. Army Signal Corps, May 16, 1945 (111ADC 4609) .

38. NARA, SHAEF, RG 331, Memo "Control of Visitors to Forward Formations," Entry 1, May 14, 1945.

39. NARA, SHAEF, RG 331, Central Staff G-2 Division Intelligence Target ("T") Subdivision Decimal File, 1944–45, Main Headquarters, Scientific Advisory Section, G-2, March 8, 1945.

40. NARA, SHAEF, RG 332, Central Staff G-2 Division Intelligence Target ("T") Subdivision Decimal File, 1944–45, the OAFT Group No. 7, Subject: Investigation at Mühlhausen/Thuringia, To: 12th AG, Economic Brandh, FPO, 655, Entry NM13, April 11, 1945.

41. These Combined Intelligence Objectives Subcommittee reports are available in the NARA and are illustrative of the intensive work going on in the midst of war that did not have to do directly with military objectives.

42. Hunt, *Secret Agenda,* 7.

43. NARA, SHAEF, RG 331, Correspondence, Entry 18A.

44. Gedenkstätte Mittelbau-Dora Archives, GDDR 1d., 136.

45. Neufeld, *Rocket and Reich,* 267.

46. Neufeld, *Von Braun,* 195–202.

47. Hunt, *Secret Agenda,* 19–20.

48. SN, S130.

49. NARA, SHAEF, RG 331, G-5 Division; note on a meeting at Berlin on Friday, June 29, among Marshall Zhukov, General Clay, and General Weeks, Entry 23.

Chapter 5. Shaping the New Land and Its Memories

1. Fulbrook, *People's State,* 27.

2. Loth, *Stalin's Unwanted Child,* 29–34.

3. Spiker, *East German Leadership and the Division of Germany.*

4. Hellberg and Schmalz, *Der 17 Juni 1953 in Nordhausen,* 5.

5. Brunner, "Herrschaftssystem. Partei und Staat," 55–60.

6. SN, S263, 1.

7. SN, S2333.

8. Lauerwald, *Kämpfer gegen den Faschismus,* 22.

9. SN, S263, 4.

10. Ibid.

11. SN, S224.

12. SN, S18.

13. SN, S161, 7.

14. Potsdam Declaration, August 2, 1945, in Mee, *Meeting at Potsdam,* 258–70.

15. Ritscher, *Spezlager nr. 2 Buchenwald,* 30, 61. No exact number of deaths at Spezial Lager 2 exist.

16. Ibid.

17. Rathsfeld and Rathsfeld, *Die Graupen Strasse.*

18. SN, S263.

19. Gedenkstätte Mittelbau-Dora Archives, GDDR Pl, Bd 127.

20. Naimark, *Russians in Germany,* 141–204. Naimark presents a thorough analysis of the entire questions of formal and informal reparations to the Soviet Union from the GDR.

21. Phillips, *Soviet Policy toward East Germany Reconsidered,* 227–32.

22. SN, S263.

23. Hellberg and Schmalz, *Der 17 Juni 1953 in Nordhausen,* 20–21.

24. SN, S263.

25. Naimark, *Russians in Germany,* 145.

26. Ibid., 15.

27. Judt, "The Past Is Another Country," 294.

28. Conversation with Hans Grönke, archivist, at the Stadtarchiv Nordhausen, May 4, 2009.

29. Conversations with and undocumented reports of four Nordhausen women, 1998–2008.

30. Schwager, "Erinerungen an den 30. Januar."

31. Ibid.

32. Wagner, "Konzentrationslager Mittelbau-Dora," 153–54.

33. Stories from Nordhausen citizens, 2008–2009.

34. Interviews with elderly Nordhausen citizens, summer 2008.

35. SN, S263.

36. Lauerwald, *Kämpfer gegen den Faschismus,* 24.

37. SN, S270.

38. "Eine Stadt Baut Auf!" *Thüringer Volk,* February 26, 1949, SN, Z34.

39. Hellberg and Schmalz, *Der 17 Juni 1953 in Nordhausen,* 4.

40. Pelny, *Chronik,* 9.

41. SN, S1942, 24.

42. SN, S263.

43. Wagner, *Produktion des Todes,* 567–70.

44. Ibid.

45. Burleigh, *The Third Reich,* 802.

46. Wagner, *Produktion des Todes,* 670, 667.

47. Wagner, *Ellrich, 1944/45,* 170–75.

48. Ibid.

49. Eisfeld, *Die unmenschliche Fabrik,* 38–42.

50. Dieckmann and Hochmuth, *KZ Dora-Mittelbau,* 80–82.

51. Eisfeld, *Die unmenschliche Fabrik,* 38–42.

52. Wagner, *Ellrich, 1944/45,* 172–73.

53. See Hunt, *Secret Agenda.*

54. Naimark, *Russians in Germany,* 227.

Chapter 6. The Mahn- und Gedenkstätte in the GDR

1. Naimark, *Russians in Germany,* 351.

2. Phillips, *Soviet Policy toward East Germany Reconsidered,* 29.

3. There is little written about these visits shortly after the war, but pictures in the Mittelbau-Dora Gedenkstätte Archiv show these visits over the years.

4. SN, S1668.

5. Interviews with Irmgard Seidel, May 2008, and Irmgard Pelny, May 2009.

6. Hellberg and Schmalz, *Der 17 Juni 1953 in Nordhausen,* 20–40.

7. Phillips, *Soviet Policy toward East Germany Reconsidered,* 130.

8. Fisher, *Die Deutsche Demokratische Republik,* 121.

9. Neufeld, "Smash the Myth of the Fascist Rocket Baron."

10. Ibid.

11. *Gesetzblatt der DDR,* 381.

12. Gedenkstätte Mittelbau-Dora Archives, GDDR 1d, Bd 1.

13. Ibid.

14. Chronik, Gedenkstätte Mittelbau-Dora Archives, GDDR 1d, B6.

15. At the time, Makarenko's theories were seen as modern and democratic by many, but have become highly criticized as "Stalinistic" in the postcommunist era.

16. Čespiva, Geissler, and Pelny, *Geheim Waffen im Kohnstein.*

17. In April 2010, Irmgard Pelny, widow of Kurt Pelny, accepted a medal for their dedication to the Polish survivors over the years. It was presented at the ceremony commemorating the fallen of the Mittelbau-Dora concentration camp.

18. Allen, *Business of Genocide,* 274.

19. Burleigh, *The Third Reich,* 805.

20. Buscher, *War Crimes Trial Program,* 92.

21. See Völklein, *Geschäft mit dem Feind.*

22. Simpson, *Splendid Blond Beast,* 190.

23. *Zum "Dora-Prozess" vor dem Schwurgericht in Essen, geschrieben durch Lawrence Demps* (GMDA, JD2, Bd 12, 162).

24. Wamhof, "Aussagen ist gut."

25. Bornemann, *Aktiver und passiver Widerstand,* 86–91.

26. Wamhof, "Aussagen ist gut," 186.

27. Klee, *Das Personen-Lexikon zum Dritten Reich,* 105.

28. *Zum "Dora-Prozess" vor dem Schwurgericht in Essen, geschrieben durch Lawrence Demps* (GMDA, JD2, Bd 12).

29. Gedenkstätte Mittelbau-Dora Archives, GDDR 1d, Bd 12.

30. Stein, *Juden in Buchenwald.*

31. Wagner, "Überlebenskampf im Terror," 4–8.

32. Pelny, *Mittelbau-Dora,* 37–38. See also Bornemann, *Aktiver und passiver Widerstand.*

33. Beneś, *In Deutscher Gefangenschaft,* 76.

34. Leo Kuntz, unpublished manuscript, November 2006.

35. Beneś, *In Deutscher Gefangenschaft,* 79.

36. Béon, *Planet Dora,* 132.

37. Manfred Schröter, the first mayor of Nordhausen after reunification, was such a person of interest. His Stasi file included information about an observation at the Gedenkstätte.

38. Conversation with Christiane Grieb, December 20, 2009.

39. Conversations with Wolfgang and Christa Köhler, 1992–2004.

40. Conversation with Eli Rosenbaum, director of the U.S. Department of Justice, Office of Special Investigations.

Chapter 7. The Wall Comes Down

1. Leonhard, *Das kurze Leben der DDR,* 187–88.

2. Schumann, *100 Tage die die DDR erschütterten,* 35.

3. Conversation between Gretchen Schafft and Christa Köhler, 1991.

4. Conversation with Gretchen Schafft and Wolfgang Köhler, 2000.

5. Spindler, *Protestkulturen in Nordhausen im Herbst '89,* 18, 19. This is the only summation of events that took place in 1989 in Nordhausen and is used in the following pages extensively.

6. Ibid., 28.

7. Ibid., 37.

8. Ibid., 17.

9. "Der Umbruch in der DDR. Chronologie der revolutionären Ereignisse 1989/90," *Spiegel Spezial. 162 Tage Deutsche Geschichte,* no. 2 (1990): 146.

10. Spindler, *Protestkulturen in Nordhausen im Herbst '89,* 64.

11. See Kuhlbrodt, *Nordhausen unter dem Sternenbanner.*

12. Gretchen Schafft interview with Peter Kuhlbrodt, June 2008.

13. Many also laid claim to property that had been confiscated by the GDR government.

14. For the occupying forces, the question was less disposing of incriminating documentation than of retrieving documents that could be useful for future technology or for war crimes trials. Schoolbooks and other materials from the Nazi era had to be destroyed, however.

15. "Lässt man," 3.

16. Spindler, *Protestkulturen in Nordhausen im Herbst '89,* 51.

17. Conversation in 1992 in Nordhausen with a young woman.

18. "Lässt man."

19. Interviews with and observations by Gretchen Schafft and members of the Pelny family from 1991 to 2009.

20. "Die Stadt Nordhausen hat vom Lager und dem Mittelwerk gelebt," *Nordhäuser Tageblatt,* November 26, 1992.

21. Correspondence between Gretchen Schafft and Cornelia Klose, 1991, 1992.

22. Osang, *Das Jahr Eins,* 109.

23. In a 1996 collection of news articles compiled by the Gedenkstätte for interested persons was "Diskussion in der Gedenkstätte Dora. Zu den Perspektiven politischer Bildung," from the *Thüringer Allgemeine* of August 10, 1996, which stated, "Former prisoner Willi Frohwein [was there] as well as Rolf Spirak from the Thuringia Center for Political

Education. . . . Along with the work camp for young people, the school groups from Thuringia and Berlin expected the main theme of the event would be the possibilities and perspectives of political education in Concentration Camp Dora."

24. Schafft interview with Manfred Schröter and perusal of his personal documents, 2008.

25. Martin Adler was in close contact with the authors for several years before his death in 2005. They both visited him in Detroit, and Gretchen Schafft spoke to him on the telephone regularly, hearing his stories and experiencing his grief.

26. Martin Adler's father's name was Hershel Adler, but Martin spoke of him as Hermann.

27. Terry Katz's eulogy for her father, 2006.

28. Gilens, *Discovery and Despair.*

29. In the past few years, the terms *Ossie* and *Wessie* have entered into normal slang and are used regularly in discourse.

30. Wolf, *Sprache in der DDR.*

31. Elon, "In a Former Country."

32. Das and Kleinman, "Introduction," 1–30.

33. Javed, "Peasantry, Politics, and Historiography," 4–44.

34. Wegner, "In the Shadow of the Third Reich."

35. Schafft, conversation with Henry Bangemann, 1990.

36. Wegner, "In the Shadow of the Third Reich," 127.

37. Ibid.

38. Olick, "What Does It Mean to Normalize the Past?"

39. Wippermann, *Dämonisierung durch Vergleich.*

Chapter 8. The Modern Gedenkstätte

1. Brecht, "The Resistable Rise of Arturo Ui," written in 1941 in Helsinki where Brecht had taken refuge before he fled to the United States, later produced in German and English.

2. Olick, "What Does It Mean to Normalize the Past?" 259–88.

3. Habermas, "On the Public Use of History," 163–64.

4. Mommsen, "Search for the 'Lost History'?" 106.

5. Michael Neufeld has documented this history in his major publications for several decades.

6. Gottmann, "Stolzer Triumph oder zerknirschites Verschweigen der Leistung?"

7. Eventually, women in the GDR were provided with community laundries that handled individual households' wash on a regular basis, relieving working women of doing this major job on their own.

8. Mommsen, "Search for the 'Lost History'?" 104.

9. Meier, "Condemning and Comprehending," 27.

10. Schröter, "Absichten, Einsichten, Ansichten" (unpublished manuscript), 24.

11. Wagner, "Vorstellung als Kommissarischer Leiter der KZ-Gedenkstätte Mittelbau-Dora."

12. Interview conducted by Schafft and Zeidler with Jens-Christian Wagner, June 2, 2008.

13. Small towns in Germany often have clubs for people interested in local history. In Nordhausen in the early 2000s, there were at least two such groups.

14. Interview by Schafft and Zeidler with Wagner.

15. McCann, Smith, and Matthews, *Search for Johnny Nicholas.*

16. Schafft, "American Doctor Who Was Neither, but a Hero Nonetheless," 984.

17. Jugend für Dora, *Jugend für Dora,* 20; Schafft's conversations with several survivors living in the United States.

18. Bundeszentrale für politische Bildung, "DDR," http://www.bpb.de/publikationen/T21T07.0.0.DDR.html.

19. Interview by Schafft and Zeidler with Wagner.

20. Sparkasen-Kulturstiftung Hessen-Thüringen, *Ausgezeichnet!* 48.

Chapter 9. Major Themes and Conclusions

1. What better expression than the little book by Eggerath, written shortly after the war, *Nur Ein Mensch.*

2. See Koonz, "Between Memory and Oblivion."

3. Hermann, "Kurt's Story," 84.

4. Ibid., 92.

5. Ibid., 112, 114.

6. Hermann, "Es geschah vor sechzig Jahren."

7. Interview with Ilse Kirchhoff Hagen, May 2009.

8. Kuntz et al., "Albert Kuntz."

9. SN, S2156.

10. http://www.jewishvirtuallibrary.org/jsource/Holocaust/rosenbaum.html.

11. This book was *Dora* by Jean Michel, a survivor.

12. Schafft interview with Eli Rosenbaum, June 14, 2009. Rosenbaum mentioned this book was Ordway and Sharpe, *The Rocket Team.*

13. Selected public domain materials from the prisoner labor supply office at the Mittelwerk factory, March 13, 1953, provided by the U.S. Department of Justice.

14. Schafft interview with Rosenbaum.

15. Eggerath, *Nur Ein Mensch,* 8–9.

Bibliography

Abzug, Robert. *Inside the Vicious Heart*. New York: Oxford University Press, 1985.

Allen, Michael Thad. *The Business of Genocide: The SS, Slave Labor, and the Concentration Camps*. Chapel Hill: University of North Carolina Press, 2002.

Amnesty International. *German Democratic Republic*. London: Amnesty International Publications, 1977.

Antifaschistische Mahn- und Gedenkstätte Mittelbau-Dora. *SED Leadership of Nordhausen's Kommission zur "Erforschung der Geschichte der örtlichen Arbeiterbewegung."* Nordhausen: Rat der Stadt, n.d.

Bacque, James. *Crimes and Mercies: The Fate of German Civilians under Allied Occupation, 1944–1950*. Toronto: Little, Brown, 1997.

———. *Other Losses: An Investigation into the Mass Deaths of German Prisoners at the Hands of the French and Americans after World War II*. Toronto: Stoddart, 1989.

Baldwin, Peter, ed. *Reworking the Past: Hitler, the Holocaust, and the Historians' Debate*. Boston: Beacon, 1990.

Baranowski, Frank. *Rüstungsprojekte in der Region Nordhausen, Worbis und Heiligenstadt während der NS-Zeit*. Duderstadt: Verlag Mecke Druck, 1998.

Barnouw, Dagmar. *Germany, 1945: Views of War and Violence*. Bloomington: Indiana University Press, 1996.

———. *Visible Spaces: Hannah Arendt and the German-Jewish Experience*. Baltimore: Johns Hopkins University Press, 1990.

———. *The War in the Empty Air: Victims, Perpetrators, and Postwar Germans*. Bloomington: Indiana University Press, 2005.

Bartel, Walter. *Gutachten. Rolle und Bedeutung des Mittelwerkes einschliesslich des Konzentrationslagers Dora-Mittelbau und die Funktion der SS bei der A-4 Produktion*. Weimar-Buchenwald: MNG Buchenwald, 1983. (From the testimony of the Essen trial.)

Bartel, Walter, et al. *Buchenwald. Mahnung und Verpflichtung*. Berlin: Deutscher Verlag der Wissenschaften, 1983.

Beecham, Sir Michael, and Maj. Gen. John W. Huston. *The Strategic Air War against*

Germany, 1939–1945: Report of the British Bombing Survey Unit. London: Frank Cass, 1998.

"Beirater-Grenium für die Gedenkstätte." *Nordhäuser Tageblatt*, April 13, 1992.

Beneś, Jiff. *In Deutscher Gefangenschaft.* Prague: self-published, n.d.

Benz, Wolfgang. *Europa nach dem Zweiten Weltkrieg, 1945–1982.* Frankfurt am Main: Fischer Taschenbuch Verlag, 2002.

———. *Feindbild und Vorurteil. Beiträge über Ausgrenzung und Verfolgung.* Munich: Deutscher Taschenbuch Verlag, 1996.

Benz, Wolfgang, and Hermann Graul, eds. *Europa nach dem Zweiten Weltkrieg, 1945–1983.* Frankfurt: Fischer Taschenbuch Verlag, 1983.

Béon, Yves. *The Planet Dora: A Memoir of the Holocaust and the Birth of the Space Age.* Boulder: Westview Press, 1997.

Berger, Christel. *Gewissensfrage Antifaschismus. Analysen—Interpretationen—Interivewa.* Berlin: Dietz Verlag, 1990.

Bettelheim, Bruno. "Individual and Mass Behavior in Extreme Situations." *Journal of Abnormal Psychology* 38 (1943): 417–52.

———. *The Informed Heart.* Glencoe, Ill.: Free Press, 1960.

Biddle, Tami Davis. *Rhetoric and Reality in Air Warfare: The Evolution of British and American Ideas about Strategic Bombing, 1914–1945.* Princeton: Princeton University Press, 2002.

Bonwetsch, Bernd, Gennadij Bordjugov, and Norman Naimark. *Sowjetische Politik in der SBZ, 1945–1949. Dokumente zur Tätigkeit der Propagandaverwaltung (Informationsverwaltung) der SMAD under Sergei Tjul'phow.* Bonn: J. H. W. Dietz Nachfolger, 1998.

Bornemann, Manfred. *Aktiver und passiver Widerstand im KZ-Dora und im Mittelwerk. Eine Studie über den Widerstand im KZ Mittelbau-Dora.* Berlin: Westkreuz Verlag, 1994.

———. *Chronik des Lagers Ellrich, 1944/45. Ein vergessenes Konzentrationslager wird neu entdeckt.* Nordhausen: Landratsamt Nordhausen, 1987.

Botting, Douglas. *In the Ruins of the Reich.* London: George Allen and Unwin, 1985.

Brecht, Berthold. "The Resistible Rise of Arturo Ui." Translated by Ralph Mannheim. New York: Arcade, 1968.

Breger, Udo. *Der Raketenberg.* Ostheim: Verlag Peter Engstler, 1992.

British Bombing Survey Unit. *The Strategic Air War against Germany, 1939–1945.* Portland, Ore.: Frank Cass, 1998.

Brunner, Georg. "Herrschaftssystem. Partei und Staat." In *Ploetz Die Deutsche Demokratische Republik.* Würzburg: Verlag Ploetz, 1987.

Buck, Kurt. *Beiträge zur Geschichte der nationalsozialistischen Verfolgung in Norddeutschland.* Bremen: Temmen Edition, 1995.

Bundeszentrale für politische Bildung. "DDR." http:www.bpb.de/publikationen/ T21T07.0.DDR.html.

Burleigh, Michael. *The Third Reich.* New York: Hill and Wang, 2000.

Buscher, Frank M. *The U.S. War Crimes Trial Program in Germany, 1946–1955.* New York: Greenwood Press, 1989.

Bütow, Tobias, and Franka Bindernagel. *Ein KZ in der Nachbarschaft. Das Magdeburger*

Aussenlager der Brabag und der "Freundeskreis Himmler." Cologne: Böhlau Verlag, 2003.

Carr, Caleb. *The Lessons of Terror: A History of Warfare against Civilians.* New York: Random House, 2002.

Čespiva, Jan, Fritz Geissler, and Kurt Pelny. *Geheim Waffen im Kohnstein.* Erfurt: Das Volk, 1964.

Chamberlin, Brewster, and Marcia Feldman, eds. *The Liberation of the Nazi Concentration Camps: Eyewitness Accounts of the Liberators.* Washington, D.C.: United States Holocaust Council, 1987.

Cohen, Elie A. *Human Behavior in the Concentration Camp.* London: Free Association Books, 1988.

Confino, Alon. *Germany as a Culture of Remembrance: Promises and Limits of Writing History.* Chapel Hill: University of North Carolina Press, 2006.

Craine, Conrad C. *Bombs, Cities, and Civilians: American Air Power Strategy in World War II.* Lawrence: University Press of Kansas, 1993.

Das, Veena. *Life and Words: Violence and the Descent into the Ordinary.* Berkeley and Los Angeles: University of California Press, 2007.

Das, Veena, and Arthur Kleinman. Introduction to *Remaking a World: Violence, Social Suffering, and Recovery,* edited by Veena Das, Arthur Kleinman, Margaret Lock, Mamphela Ramphele, and Pamela Reynolds, 1–30. Berkeley and Los Angeles: University of California Press, 2001.

Dawidowicz, Lucy S. *The Holocaust and the Historians.* Cambridge: Harvard University Press, 1981.

Deák, István, Jan T. Gross, and Tony Judt, eds. *The Politics of Retribution in Europe: World War II and Its Aftermath.* Princeton: Princeton University Press, 2000.

Dieckmann, Götz, and Peter Hochmuth. *KZ Dora-Mittelbau. Producktionsstätte der V-Waffen—Kampffront gegen faschistischen Terror und Rüstungsproduktion.* Nordhausen: Rat der Stadt Nordhausen, n.d.

Diestel, Barbara, and Ruth Jakusch. *Concentration Camp Dachau, 1933–1945.* Brussels: Comité International de Dachau, 1978.

Downes, Alexander. *Targeting Civilians in War.* Ithaca: Cornell University Press, 2008.

Drobisch, Klaus, and Günther Wieland. *System der NS-Konzentrationslager, 1933–1939.* Berlin: Akademie Verlag, 1993.

Eggerath, Werner. *Nur Ein Mensch.* Weimar: Thüringer Volksverlag, 1947.

Eisfeld, Rainer. *Die unmenschliche Fabrik. V-2 Produktion und KZ-Mittelbau-Dora.* Erfurt: Thüringer Landeszentrale für politische Bildung, 1993.

Elon, Amos. "In a Former Country." *New York Review of Books,* April 23, 1992.

Endlich, Stefanie, and Thomas Lutz. *Gedenken und Lernen an Historischen Orten. Ein Wegweiser zu Gedenkstätten des Nationalsozialismus in Berlin.* Berlin: Landeszentrale für politische Bildungsarbeit, 1995.

Ericksen, Johannes, and Bernhard Hoppe, eds. *Peenemünde, Mythos und Geschichte der Rakete, 1923–1989.* Berlin: Nicolai, 2004.

Evans, Richard J. *In Hitler's Shadow: West German Historians and the Attempt to Escape from the Nazi Past.* New York: Pantheon Books, 1989.

Ferencz, Benjamin. *Less than Slaves: Jewish Forced Labor and the Quest for Compensation.* Bloomington: Indiana University Press in association with the United States Holocaust Museum, 2002.

Fest, Joachim. *Speer: The Final Verdict.* New York: Harcourt, 2001.

Fiedermann, Angela, Torsten Hess, and Markus Jaeger. *Das Konzentrationslager Mittelbau-Dora. Ein historischer Abriss.* Berlin: Westkreuz Verlag, 1993.

Fischer, Alexander. *Ploetz, die Deutsche Demokratische Republik. Daten, Fakten, Analysen.* Edited with the assistance of Nikolaus Katzer. Freiburg: Ploetz, 1988.

Frankl, Viktor E. *Man's Search for Meaning.* New York: Washington Square Press, 1959.

Fried, Morton, Marvin Harris, and Robert Murphy, eds. *War: The Anthropology of Armed Conflict and Aggression.* Garden City, N.Y.: American Museum of Natural History Press, 1968.

Fučik, Julius. *Notes from the Gallows.* New York: New Century, 1948.

Fulbrook, Mary. *The People's State: East German Society from Hitler to Honecker.* New Haven: Yale University Press, 2005.

Gay, Ruth. *Safe among the Germans: Liberated Jews after World War II.* New Haven: Yale University Press, 2002.

Gellateley, Robert. *Backing Hitler: Consent and Coercion in Nazi Germany.* New York: Oxford University Press, 2001.

Gellert, Charles Lawrence. *The Holocaust, Israel, and the Jews: Motion Pictures in the National Archives.* Washington, D.C.: National Archives and Records Administration, 1989.

Gesetzblatt der DDR. Vol. 1. Berlin: Büro des Ministerrats der DDR, 1968.

Gilens, Alvin. *Discovery and Despair: Dimensions of Dora. / Aufbruch und Verzweiflung. Dimensionen von Dora.* Berlin: Westkreuz Verlag, 1995.

Gillis, John R., ed. *Commemorations: The Politics of National Identity.* Princeton: Princeton University Press, 1994.

Göler, Daniel. *Postsozialistische Segregationstendenzen. Sozial- und bevölkerungsgeographische Aspekte von Wanderungen in Mittelstädten der Neuen Länder. Untersucht an den Beispielen Halberstadt und Nordhausen.* Bamberg: Geographie an der Universität Bamberg im Selbstverlag. 1999.

Gottmann, Günter. "Stolzer Triumph oder zerknirschites Verschweigen der Leistung?" *Tagesspiegel* (September 30, 1997).

Grayling, A. C. *Among the Dead Cities: The History and Moral Legacy of the WWII Bombing of Civilians in Germany and Japan.* New York: Walker, 2006.

Groehler, Olaf. *Bombenkrieg gegen Deutschland.* Berlin: Akademie Verlag, 1990.

———. *Geschichte des Luftkrieges, 1910 bis 1970.* Berlin: Militärverlag der Deutschen Demokratischen Republic, 1973.

———. *Geschichte des Luftkriegs, 1910 bis 1980.* Berlin: Militärverlag der Deutschen Demokratischen Republik, 1981.

———. *Kampf um die Luftherrschaft. Beiträge zur Luftkriegsgeschichte des Zweiten Weltkrieges.* Berlin: Militärverlag der Deutschen Demokratischen Republik, 1988.

Groehler, Olaf, and Mario Kessler. *Die SED-Politik, der Antifachismus und die Juden in der SBZ und der frühen DDR.* Berlin: Gesellschaftswissenschaftliches Forum, 1995.

Grosscup, Beau. *Strategic Terror: The Politics and Ethics of Aerial Bombardment.* London: Zed Books, 2006.

Grygen, Mojmir. *Menschen, Ich Hatte Euch Lieb. Das Leben Julius Fucik.* Berlin: Verlag Neues Leben, 1961.

Guha, Ranajit. *Elementary Aspects of Peasant Insurgency in Colonial India.* Durham: Duke University Press, 1999.

———, ed. *Subaltern Studies.* Vol. 1. Delhi: Oxford University Press, 1982.

Habermas, Jürgen. "On the Public Use of History: The Official Self-Understanding of the Federal Republic Is Breaking Up." In *Forever in the Shadow of Hitler? Original Documents of the "Historikerstreit,"* translated by James Knowlton and Truett Cates, 162–70. Atlantic Highlands, N.J.: Humanities Press, 1993.

Heinemann, Karl-Heinz, and Wilfried Schubarth, eds. *Der antifaschistische Staat entlässt seine Kinder. Jugend und Rechtsextremismus in Ostdeutschland.* Cologne: Papyrossa Verlag, 1992.

Hellber, Rainer, and Fritz Schmalz. *Der 17 Juni 1953 in Nordhausen. Die Ereignisse im Landkreis Nordhausen vor, während und nach den Unruhen.* Nordhausen: Petit Verlag and Agentur, 2007.

Henry, Frances. *Victims and Neighbors: A Small Town in Nazi Germany Remembered.* South Hadley, Mass.: Bergin and Garvey, 1984.

Herbert, Ulrich. *A History of Foreign Labor in Germany, 1880–1980.* Ann Arbor: University of Michigan Press, 1990.

———. *Hitler's Foreign Workers: Enforced Foreign Labor in Germany under the Third Reich.* Translated by William Templer. Cambridge: Cambridge University Press, 2006.

———. *Zweierlei Bewältigung. Vier Beiträge über den Umgang mit der NS-Vergangenheit in den beiden deutschen Staaten.* Hamburg: Ergebnisse, 1992.

Herbert, Ulrich, Karin Orth, and Christoph Dieckmann. *Die Nationalsozialistischen Konzentrationslager. Entwicklung und Struktur.* Göttingen: Wallstein, 1998.

Herbert, Ulrich, and Axel Schmidt. *Kriegsende in Europa. Von Beginn des deutschen Machtzerfalls bis zur Stabilisierung der Nachkriegsordnung, 1944–1948.* Essen: Klartext, 1998.

Herf, Jeffrey. *Divided Memory: The Nazi Past in the Two Germanies.* Cambridge: Harvard University Press, 1997.

Hermann, Kurt. "Es geschah vor sechzig Jahren. Eine Erinnerung an den April 1945." *Nordhäuser Nachrichten* 14 (March 1, 2005).

———. "Kurt's Story." In *Darling Mutti,* edited by Joan Marshall, 83–139. Johannesburg: Jacana Media, 2005.

Herzog, Monika, and Bernhard Strebel. "Das Frauenkonzentrationslager Ravensbrück." In *Frauen in Konzentrationslagern Bergen-Belsen Ravensbrück,* edited by Claus Füllberg-Strolberg et al., 13–28. Bremen: Temmen Edition, 1994.

Hess, Torsten, and Thomas A. Seidel. *Vernichtung durch Fortschritt.* Berlin: Westkreuz Verlag, 1994.

Hochmuth, Peter. *Der Illegale Widerstand der Häftlinge des KZ Mittelbau-Dora. Dokumentation.* Schkeuditz: GNN, 2000.

Hoegh, Leo A., and Howard J. Doyle. *Timberwolf Tracks: The History of the 104th Division, 1942–1945.* Washington, D.C.: Washington Infantry Journal Press, 1946.

Hunt, Linda. *Secret Agenda.* New York: St. Martin's Press, 1991.

Javed, Alam. "Peasantry, Politics, and Historiography." In *Reading Subaltern Studies: Cul-*

tural History, Contested Meaning, and the Globalization of South Asia, edited by David Ludden, 43–57. London: Anthern Press, 2007.

Judt, Tony. "The Past Is Another Country: Myth and Memory in Postwar Europe." In *The Politics of Retribution in Europe: World War II and Its Aftermath*, edited by István Deak, Jan T. Gross, and Tony Judt, 293–323. Princeton: Princeton University Press, 2000.

———. *Postwar: A History of Europe since 1945*. New York: Penguin Group, 2005.

———. "What Have We Learned, If Anything?" *New York Review of Books*, May 1, 2008, 17–20.

Jugend für Dora. *Jugend für Dora. Internationale Jugendvereinigung*. Duderstadt: Mecke Druck und Verlag, 2000.

Kaienberg, Hermann. *Vernichtung durch Arbeit. Der Fall Neuengamme*. Bonn: J. H. W. Dietz Verlag, 1990.

Kansteiner, Wolf. *In Pursuit of German Memory: History, Television, and Politics after Auschwitz*. Athens: Ohio University Press, 2006.

Kappelt, Olaf. *Die Entnazifizierung in der SBZ sowie die Rolle und der Einfluss ehemaliger Nationalsoziealisten in der DDR als ein soziologiches Phänomen*. Hamburg: Kovać, 1997.

Kaul, Friedrich Karl. *In Robe und Krawatte. Der Verteidiger hat das Wort*. Berlin: Verlag das Neue Berlin, 1981.

Kertesz, Imre. *Fateless*. Evanston: Northwestern University Press, 1992.

Ketternacker, Lothar. "Die Behandlung der Kriegsverbrecher als anglo-amerikanisches Rechtsproblem." In *Der Nationalsozialismus vor Gericht. Die Allierten Prozesse gegen Kriegsverbrecher und Soldaten, 1941–1952*, edited by Gerd R. Ueberschär, 17–31. Frankfurt am Main: Fischer Verlag, 1999.

Klee, Ernst. *Der Personal-Lexikon zum Dritten Reich*. Koblenz: Edition Kramer, 2001.

Knell, Hermann. *To Destroy a City: Strategic Bombing and Its Human Consequences in World War II*. Cambridge, Mass.: Da Capo Press, 2003.

Knowlton, James, and Truett Cates, trans. *Forever in the Shadow of Hitler? Original Documents of the "Historikerstreit."* Atlantic Highlands, N.J.: Humanities Press, 1993.

Kocka, Jürgen, ed. *Historische DDR-Forschung. Aufsätze und Studien*. Berlin: Akademie Verlag, 1993.

Koonz, Claudia. "Between Memory and Oblivion: Concentration Camps in German Memory." In *Commemorations: The Politics of National Identity*, edited by John R. Gillis, 258–80. Princeton: Princeton University Press, 1994.

Kramer, Helmut, Karsten Uhl, and Jens-Christian Wagner, eds. *Zwangsarbeit im Nationalsozialismus und die Rolle der Justiz. Täterschaft, Nachkriegsprozesse und die Auseinandersetzung um Entschädigungsleistungen*. Nordhausen: Landeszentrale für politische Bildung Thüringen, 2007.

Kranz, Tomasz, ed. *Die Verbrechen des Nationalsozialismus im Geschichtsbewusstsein und in der historischen Bildung in Deutschland und Polen*. Lublin: Państwowe Muzeum na Majdanku, 1998.

Kuhlbrodt, Peter. *"Mittelbau-Dora" bei Nordhausen, 1943–1945. Ein Überblick*. Nordhausen: Landratsamt Nordhausen, 1991.

———. *Nordhausen unter dem Sternenbanner. Die amerikanische Besetzung der Stadt Nordhausen*. Nordhausen: Archiv der Stadt Nordhausen, 1995.

——. *Schicksalsjahr, 1945. Inferno Nordhausen. Chronik, Dokumente, Erlebnisberichte.* Nordhausen: Archiv der Stadt Nordhausen, 1996.

Kuhn, Annette, and Kirsten Emiko McAllister, eds. *Locating Memory: Photographic Acts.* New York: Berghahn Books, 2006.

Kühnrich, Heinz. *Der KZ-Staat. Die faschistischen Konzentrationslager, 1933–1945.* Berlin: Dietz Verlag, 1983.

Kuntz, Leo, Leopoldine Kuntz, Götz Dieckmann, and Hannelore Dieckmann, eds. "Albert Kuntz: 'Liebste Ellen.' Briefe aus der Nazi-Haft." *UTOPIEkreativ* 171 (January 2005): 71–77.

——. *Liebste Ellen. Briefe aus der Nazi-Haft, 1933–1944.* Berlin: Dietz Berlin, 2005.

Kurowski, Franz. *Allierte Jagd auf deutsche Wissenschaftler.* Munich: Kristall bei Langen-Müller, 1982.

"Lässt man sich erneut auf weisse Flecken ein?" *Neues Deutschland,* September 12–13, 1992.

Lauerwald, Paul. *Kämpfer gegen den Faschismus—Vorbilder der Jugend. Leben und Kampf des Genossen Hans Himmler.* Vol. 2. Nordhausen: Kreisleitung der SED, 1979.

Lebow, Richard Ned, Wulf Kansteiner, and Claudio Fogu, eds. *The Politics of Memory in Postwar Europe.* Durham: Duke University Press, 2006.

Leo, Annette, and Peter Rolf-Spirek, eds. *Vielstimmiges Schweigen. Neue Studien zum DDR-Antifaschismus.* Berlin: Metropol Verlag, 2001.

Leonhard, Wolfgang. *Das kurze Leben der DDR. Berichte und Kommentare aus vier Jahrzehnten.* Stuttgart: Deutsche Verlags-Anstalt, 1990.

Levenson, Sanford. *Written in Stone: Public Monuments in Changing Societies.* Durham: Duke University Press, 1998.

Linenthal, Edward T. *Preserving Memory: The Struggle to Create America's Holocaust Museum.* New York: Penguin Books, 1995.

Litomisky, Otakar. *Brieven uit de Hel.* Vorselaar: Self-published, 1992.

——. "The Memories of Prisoner Number 113359." Translated by Gretchen Schafft. Unpublished, 1998.

Loth, Wilfried. *Stalin's Unwanted Child: The Soviet Union, the German Question, and the Founding of the GDR.* Translated by Robert F. Hogg. 1988. Reprint, New York: St. Martin's Press, 1998.

Lowenthal, David. *The Past Is a Foreign Country.* Cambridge: Cambridge University Press, 1985.

Lundholm, Anja. *Das Höllentor. Bericht einer Überlebenden.* Hamburg: Reinbek, 1988.

MacDonogh, Giles. *After the Reich: The Brutal History of the Allied Occupation.* New York: Basic Books, 2007.

MacIsaac, David. *Strategic Bombing in World War II: The Story of the United States Strategic Bombing Survey.* New York: Garland, 1976.

Marcuse, Harold. *Legacies of Dachau: The Uses and Abuses of a Concentration Camp, 1933–2001.* Cambridge: Cambridge University Press, 2001.

Marcuse, Harold, Frank Schimmelfennig, and Jochen Spielmann. *Steine des Anstosses. Nationalsozialismus und Zweiter Weltkrieg in Denkmalen, 1945–1985.* Hamburg: Museum für Hamburgische Geschichte, 1985.

Margry, Karol. "Nordhausen." *After the Battle* 101 (1998): 2–43.

Markusen, Eric, and David Kopf. *The Holocaust and Strategic Bombing: Genocide and Total War in the 20th Century.* Boulder: Westview Press, 1995.

Marshall, Joan, ed. *Darling Mutti.* Johannesburg: Jacama, 2005.

McCann, Hugh Wray, David C. Smith, and David Matthews. *The Search for Johnny Nicholas.* Reading, Pa.: Cox and Wyman, 1982.

Mee, Charles L., Jr. *Meeting at Potsdam.* New York: Franklin Square Press, 1975.

Megargee, Geoffrey, ed. *Encyclopedia of Camps and Ghettos, 1933–1945.* Bloomington: Indiana University Press, 2009.

Meier, Christian. "Condemning and Comprehending." In *Forever in the Shadow of Hitler? Original Documents of the "Historikerstreit,"* translated by James Knowlton and Truett Cates, 24–33. Atlantic Highlands, N.J.: Humanities Press, 1993.

Menschel, Sigrid. *Legitimation und Parteiherrschaft. Zum Paradox von Stabilität un Revolution in der DDR, 1945–1982.* Frankfurt am Main: Suhrkamp, 1989.

Michel, Jean. *Dora.* Marchette, France: Éditions J.-C. Lattés, 1975.

Mick, Maj. Allen H. *With the 102nd Infantry Division through Germany.* Nashville: Battery Press, 1980.

Milburn, Michael A., and Sheree D. Conrad. *The Politics of Denial.* Cambridge: MIT Press, 1996.

Mirbach, Willy. *"Damit du es spater deinem Sohn einmal erzählen kannst . . ." Der autobiographische Bericht eines Luftwaffensoldaten aus dem KZ Mittelbau (August 1944–1945).* Geldern: Verlag Gelden, 1997.

Mitscherlich, Alexander, and Margarete Mitscherlich. *Die Unfähigkeit zu Trauern.* Munich: Piper Verlag, 1967.

Mittlebrook, Martin, and Chris Everitt. *The Bomber Command War Diaries: An Operational Reference Book, 1939–1945.* London: Penguin Books, 1990.

———. *The Peenemünde Raid: 17–18 August 1943.* Barnsley, South Yorkshire: Pen and Sword Aviation, 2006.

Moeller, Robert G. *War Stories: The Search for a Usable Past in the Federal Republic of Germany.* Berkeley and Los Angeles: University of California Press, 2001.

Mommsen, Hans. "Search for the 'Lost History'? Observations on the Historical Self-Evidence of the Federal Republic." In *Forever in the Shadow of Hitler? Original Documents of the "Historikerstreit,"* translated by James Knowlton and Truett Cates, 101–13. Atlantic Highlands, N.J.: Humanities Press, 1993.

Morgan, Curtis. *James Byrnes, Lucius Clay, and American Policy in Germany.* Lampster, Ceredigion, Wales: Edwin Mellen Press, 2002.

Naimark, Norman. *The Russians in Germany: A History of the Soviet Zone of Occupation, 1945–1949.* Cambridge: Belknap Press of Harvard University Press, 1995.

Naimark, Norman, and Leonid Gibianskii, eds. *The Establishment of Communist Regimes in Eastern Europe, 1944–1949.* Boulder: Westview Press, 1997.

Neander, Joachim. *Die Letzten von Dora. Im Gebiet von Osterode. Zur Geschichte eines KZ-Evakuierungs-marsches im April 1945.* Berlin: Westkreuz-Verlag, 1994.

Neufeld, Michael. "Peenemünde, die Raketen, und der NS Staat." In *Peenemünde, Mythos und Geschichte der Rakete, 1923–1989,* edited by Johannes Ericksen and Bernhard Hoppe. Berlin: Nicolai, 2004.

———. *The Rocket and the Reich: Peenemünde and the Coming of the Ballistic Missile Era.* New York: Free Press, 1995.

———. "Smash the Myth of the Fascist Rocket Baron: East German Attacks on Wernher von Braun in the 1960's." In *Imagining Outer Space, 1900–2000, 6–9.* Copyright Smithsonian Institution, unpublished manuscript, [2008].

———. *Von Braun: Dreamer of Space, Engineer of War.* New York: Alfred A. Knopf, 2007.

Niethammer, Lutz, ed. *Der gesäuberte Antifaschismus. Die SED und die Roten Kapos von Buchenwald.* Berlin: Akademie Verlag, 1994.

Olick, Jeffrey K. "What Does It Mean to Normalize the Past? Official Memory in German Politics since 1989." In *States of Memory, Continuities, Conflicts, and Transformations in National Retrospection,* edited by Jeffrey K. Olick, 259–88. Durham: Duke University Press, 2003.

Ordway, Frederick, III, and Michael Sharpe. *The Rocket Team.* Cambridge: MIT Press, 1982.

Osang, Alexander. *Das Jahr Eins. Berichte aus der neuen Welt der Deutschen.* Berlin: Verlag Volk und Welt, 1992.

Overesch, Manfred. *Buchenwald und die DDR oder Die Suche nach Selbst-legitimation.* Göttingen: Vendenhoeck and Ruprecht, 1995.

Pachaly, Erhard, and Kurt Pelny. *KZ Mittelbau-Dora. Zum antifaschistischen Widerstandskampf im KZ Dora 1943 bis 1945.* Berlin: Dietz Verlag, 1990.

Pandey, Gyanendra. "In Defense of the Fragment: Writing about Hindu-Muslim Riots in India Today." *Representations,* no. 37 (Winter 1992): 27–55. Also found in *A Subaltern Studies Reader, 1986–1995,* edited by Ranajit Guha, 1–33. Minneapolis: University of Minnesota Press, 1997.

———. "Peasant Revolt and Indian Nationalism in Awadhi, 1919–1922." In vol. 1 of *Subaltern Studies,* edited by Ranajit Guha. Delhi: Oxford University Press, 1982.

Parsons, Geoffrey. "Eisenhower Bids Congress, Press View Nazi Prison Camp Horrors." *New York Herald Tribune.*

Pelny, Kurt. *Chronik der antifaschistischen Mahn- und Gedenkstätte Mittelbau-Dora.* Vol. 2. Berlin: DEWAG, 1983.

———. *Das ehemalige KZ "Mittelbau-Dora." Seine Aussenlager und Kommandos, die Todesmärsche und Transporte und die Bewahrung des Vermächtnisses der Helden des antifaschistischen Widerstandskampfes.* Nordhausen: Rat des Kreises Nordhausen, 1984.

———. *Mittelbau-Dora. Kurzgefasste Chronik eines faschistischen Konzentrationslagers.* Nordhausen: Mahn- und Gedenkstätte Mittelbau-Dora, 1981.

———. *Todesmarsch. Der Häftlinge des KZ Mittelbau-Dora und seiner Aussenlager im April 1945.* Nordhausen: Rat des Kreises Nordhausen, 1984.

Pence, Katherine, and Paul Betts, eds. *Socialist Modern: East German Everyday Culture and Politics.* Ann Arbor: University of Michigan Press, 2008.

Peterson, Michael B. *Missiles for the Fatherland: Peenemünde, National Socialism, and the V-2 Missile.* New York: Cambridge University Press, 2009.

Phillips, Ann L. *Soviet Policy toward East Germany Reconsidered: The Postwar Decade.* Westport, Conn.: Greenwood Press, 1986.

Probert-Wright, Bärbel. *An der Hand meiner Schwester. Zwei Mädchen im Kriegszerstörten Deutshcland.* Munich: Knaur Taschenbuch Verlag, 2006.

Puvogel, Ulrike, and Martin Stankowski. *Gedenkstätten für die Opfer des Nationalsozialismus. Eine Dokumentation.* Vol. 2. Bonn: Bundeszentrale für politische Bildung, 1996.

Rathsfeld, Werner, and Ursula Rathsfeld. *Die Graupen Strasse. Erlebtes und Erlittenes.* Bad Lauterberg im Harz: C. Kohlmann Druck und Verlag, 1993.

Rehak, Jana Kopelentova. "Czech Political Prisoners: Remembering, Relatedness, Reconciliation." Ph.D. diss., American University, 2005.

Reynolds, Pamela. "The Ground of All Making: State Violence, the Family, and Political Activists." In *Violence and Subjectivity,* edited by Veena Das, Arthur Kleinman, Mamphela Ramphele, and Pamela Reynolds, 141–70. Berkeley and Los Angeles: University of California Press, 2000.

Ritscher, Bodo. *Spezlager Nr. 2 Buchenwald.* Erfurt: Landeszentrale für politische Bildung Thüringen, 1993.

Rodenberger, Axel. *Der Tod von Dresden. Ein Bericht über das Sterben einer Stadt.* Dortmund: Landverlag GmbH, 1951.

Ross, Stewart Halsey. *Strategic Bombing by the United States in World War II: The Myths and the Facts.* Jefferson, N.C.: McFarland, 2003.

Samuel, Wolfgang W. E. *American Raiders: The Race to Capture the Luftwaffe's Secrets.* Jackson: University Press of Mississippi, 2004.

Schafft, Gretchen. "The American Doctor Who Was Neither, but a Hero Nonetheless." *National Medical Journal* 84, no. 11 (November 1992): 983–84.

———. "Civic Denial and the Memory of War." *Journal of the American Academy of Psychoanalysis* 26, no. 2 (1998): 255–72.

———. *From Racism to Genocide: Anthropology in the Third Reich.* Urbana: University of Illinois Press, 2004.

Schafft, Gretchen, and Gerhard Zeidler. *Die KZ-Mahn- und Gedenkstätten in Deutschland.* Berlin: Dietz Verlag, 1996.

Schröter, Manfred. *Die Verfolgung der Nordhäuser Juden, 1933 bis 1945.* Bad Lauterberg im Harz: C Kohlnann, 1992.

———. *Die Zerstörung Nordhausens und das Kriegsende im Kreis Grafschaft Hohenstein, 1945. Beiträge zur Heimatkunde aus Stadt und Kreis Nordhausen.* Nordhausen: Meyenburg-Museum, 1988.

Schumann, Frank, ed. *100 Tage die die DDR ershütterten.* Berlin: Verlag Neues Leben, 1990.

Schwagel, Peter. "Erinnerungen an den 30. Januar. Vergessen Wir es nicht so schnell." *Thüringer Volk,* February 26, 1949.

Schwarz, Gisela. *Kinder die nicht zählen. Ostarbeiterinnen und Ihre Kinder im Zweiten Weltkrieg.* Essen: Klartext Verlag, 1987.

Scott, James C. *Domination and the Arts of Resistance: Hidden Transcripts.* New Haven: Yale University Press, 1990.

Sebald, W. G. *On the Natural History of Destruction.* Translated by Anthea Bell. New York: Modern Library, 2004.

Seghers, Anna. *Transit.* Frankfurt am Main: Luchterhand Literaturverlag, 1978.

Semprun, Jorge. *The Long Voyage.* New York: Grove Press, 1990.

Siegelbaum, Lewis, and Andrei Sokolov. *Stalinism as a Way of Life.* Abridged ed. New Haven: Yale University Press, 2004.

Simpson, Christopher. *The Splendid Blond Beast: Money, Law, and Genocide in the Twentieth Century.* New York: Grove Press, 1993.

Sofsky, Wolfgang. *The Order of Terror: The Concentration Camp.* Princeton: Princeton University Press, 1993.

Spiker, Dirk. *The East German Leadership and the Division of Germany: Patriotism and Propaganda, 1945–1953.* Oxford: Oxford University Press, 2006.

Spindler, Anja. *Protestkulturen in Nordhausen im Herbst '89.* Erfurt: Landesbeauftragten des Freistaates Thüringen für die Unterlagen des Staatssicherheitsdienstes der ehemaligen DDR, 2007.

Stein, Harry. *Juden in Buchenwald, 1937–1942.* Weimar: Gedenkstätte Buchenwald, Sonderdruck der Landeszentrale für politische Bildung Thüringen, 1992.

Stern, Heinrich. *Geschichte der Juden in Nordhausen.* Nordhausen: Im Selbstverlag des Besassers, 1927.

Sutton, Nina. *Bettelheim: A Life and a Legacy.* Translated by David Sharp in collaboration with the author. Boulder: Westview Press, 1996.

Thiessen, Malte. *Eingebrandt in Gedächtnis. Hamburgs Gedenken an Luftkrieg und Kriegsende, 1943 bis 2005.* Munich: Dölling und Galitz Verlag, 2007.

Third Armored Division. *Spearhead in the West.* Frankfurt am Main: Henrich Druckerei und Verlag, 1945.

Tjul'panow, Sergei, et al. *Sowjetische Politik in der SBZ, 1945–1949. Dokumente zur Tätigkeit der Propagandaverwaltung (Informationsverwaltung) der SMAD.* Bonn: J. H. W. Dietz Nachf., 1998.

Trouillot, Michel-Rolph. *Silencing the Past: Power and the Production of History.* Boston: Beacon Press, 1995.

Van de Casteele, Edgard. *Ellrich. Leben und Tod in einem Konzentrationslager. Leven en Dood in een Concentratiecamp.* Berlin: Westkreuz-Verlag, 1997.

Völklein, Ulrich. *Geschäfte mit dem Feind. Die geheime Allianz des grossen Geldes während des Zweiten Weltkriegs auf beiden Seiten der Front.* Hamburg: Europa Verlag, 2002.

Wagner, Jens-Christian. *Ausgezeichnet!* Frankfurt am Main: Sparkasen-Kulturstiftung Hessen-Thüringen, 2008.

———. *Ellrich, 1944/45. Konzentrationslager und Zwangsarbeit in einer deutschen Kleinstadt.* Göttingen: Wallstein Verlag, 2009.

———. *Konzentrationslager Mittelbau-Dora, 1943–1945. Begleit Band zur ständigen Ausstellung in der KZ-Gedenkstätte Mittelbau-Dora.* Göttingen: Wallstein Verlag, 2002.

———. *Produktion des Todes. Das KZ Mittelbau-Dora.* Göttingen: Wallstein Verlag, 2001.

———. "Überlegenskampf im Terror. Möglichkeiten und Grenzen des Widerstandes im KZ Mittelbau-Dora." *Informationen 66* (Nordhausen: KZ Gedenkstätte Mittelbau-Dora) (n.d.): 4–8.

———. "Vorstellung als Kommisarischer Leiter der KZ-Gedenkstätte Mittelbau-Dora." Speech given on October 12, 2001.

Wamhof, Georg. "Aussagen sind gut, aber Auftreten als Zeuge nicht möglich. Die Rechtshilfe der DDR in KZ Mittelbau-Dora-Verfahren, 1962–1970." In *Beitrage zur*

Geschichte der nationalistische Verfolgung in Norddeutscshland, Bd 9. Bremen: Temmen Edition, 2005.

——. "Geschichtspolitik und NS-Strafverfahren. Der Essener Dora-Prozess (1967–1970) im deutsch-deutschen System konflikt." In *Zwangsarbeit im Nationalsozialismus und die Rolle der Justiz. Täterschaft, Nachkriegsprozesse und die Auseinandersetzung um Entschädigungsleistungen,* edited by Helmut Kramer, Karsten Uhl, and Jens-Christian Wagner, 186–208. Nordhausen: Landeszentrale für politische Bildung Thüringen, 2007.

Wegener, Peter P. *The Peenemünde Wind Tunnels: A Memoir.* New Haven: Yale University Press, 1996.

Wegner, Gregory. "In the Shadow of the Third Reich: The 'Jugendstunde' and the Legitimation of Anti-Fascist Heroes for East German Youth." *German Studies Review* 19, no. 1 (February 1996): 127–46.

Weinmann, Martin. *Das Nationalsozialistische Lagersystem.* Frankfurt am Main: Zweitausendeins, 1990.

Weiss, Hermann. *Biographisches Lexikon zum Dritten Reich.* Frankfurt am Main: Fischer Taschenbuch Verlag, 1999.

Whitehead, Neil, ed. *Violence.* Santa Fe: School of American Research, 2004.

Wiesel, Elie. *From the Kingdom of Memory.* New York: Schocken Books, 1990.

Winter, Martin Clemens. *Öffentliche Erinnerungen an den Luftkrieg in Nordhausen, 1945–2005.* Marburg: Tectum Verlag, 2010.

Wippermann, Wolfgang. *Dämonisierung durch Vergleich. DDR und Drittes Reich.* Berlin: Rotbuch Verlag, 2009.

Wolf, Birgit. *Sprache in der DDR. Ein Wörterbuch.* Berlin: Walter de Gruyter, 2000.

Young, Marilyn, and Yuki Tanaka, eds. *Bombing Civilians: A Twentieth-Century History.* New York: New Press, 2008.

Zentner, Christian. *Der Zweite Weltkrieg: Ein Lexikon.* Munich: W. Heyne, 1995.

Zorn, Monika, ed. *Hitlers zweimal getötete Opfer. Westdeutsche Endlösung des Antifaschismus auf dem Gebiet der DDR.* Freiburg: Ahrunan-Verlag, 1994.

Index

GRETCHEN SCHAFFT is Applied Anthropologist
in Residence at American University and the author of
From Racism to Genocide: Anthropology in the Third Reich.

GERHARD ZEIDLER is a former archivist at the
concentration camp memorial for Mittelbau-Dora.

The University of Illinois Press
is a founding member of the
Association of American University Presses.

———————————————————————

University of Illinois Press
1325 South Oak Street
Champaign, IL 61820-6903
www.press.uillinois.edu